Holt Literature & Language Arts

Introductory Course

UNIVERSAL ACCESS Interactive Reading

- **Word Analysis, Fluency, and Systematic Vocabulary Development**
- **Reading Comprehension**
- **Literary Response and Analysis**

HOLT, RINEHART AND WINSTON

A Harcourt Classroom Education Company

Austin · New York · Orlando · Atlanta · San Francisco · Boston · Dallas · Toronto · London

Credits

Editorial

Project Director: Kathleen Daniel
Editor: Amy Fleming
Managing Editor: Mike Topp
Manager of Editorial Services: Abigail Winograd
Senior Product Manager: Don Wulbrecht
Editorial Staff: Brenda Sanabria, Susan Kent Cakars, Steven Fechter,
Rob Giannetto, Kerry Johnson, Dan Unger
Project Administration: Elizabeth LaManna
Editorial Support: Renée Benitez, Louise Fernandez, Soojung Christine Han,
Bret Isaacs, Laurie Muir
Editorial Permissions: David Smith, Carrie Jones
Conceptual Framework and Writing: e2 Publishing Services, Inc.

Art, Design, and Production

Director: Athena Blackorby
Senior Design Director: Betty Mintz
Series Design: Proof Positive/Farrowlyne Associates, Inc.
Design and Electronic Files: Proof Positive/Farrowlyne Associates, Inc.
Photo Research: Proof Positive/Farrowlyne Associates, Inc.
Production Manager: Catherine Gessner

Requests for permission to make copies of any part of the work should be mailed to the following address: Permissions Department, Holt, Rinehart and Winston, 10801 N. MoPac Expressway, Building 3, Austin, Texas 78759-5415.

Printed in the United States of America
ISBN 0-03-065027-5

10 11 12 082 08 07 06 05

Contents

CHAPTER 1 Structures: Building Blocks of Meaning xx

CHAPTER 5   Biography and Autobiography:
                    Looking at Lives 178

Interactive Readings for Independence

CHAPTER 6 Looking at Texts: Uses of the Imagination 222

Getting Ready

Graphic Organizers

for *Holt Literature and Language Arts,* Chapter 6

CHAPTER 7 Rhyme and Reason 262

CHAPTER 8 You the Critic **292**

Mastering the California Standards in Reading*

Chapter 1   Structures: Building Blocks of Meaning
Standards Focus

Vocabulary Development 1.4   Monitor expository text for unknown words or words with novel meanings by using word, sentence, and paragraph clues to determine meaning.

Reading Comprehension (Focus on Informational Materials) 2.1   Identify the structural features of popular media (for example, newspapers, magazines, online information), and use the features to obtain information.

Literary Response and Analysis 3.3   Analyze the influence of setting on the problem and its resolution.

Chapter 2   Characters: The People You'll Meet
Standards Focus

Vocabulary Development 1.3   Recognize the origins and meanings of frequently used foreign words in English, and use these words accurately in speaking and writing.

Reading Comprehension (Focus on Informational Materials) 2.4   Clarify an understanding of texts by creating outlines, logical notes, summaries, or reports.

Literary Response and Analysis 3.2   Analyze the effect of the qualities of the character (for example, courage or cowardice, ambition or laziness) on the plot and the resolution of the conflict.

Chapter 3   The Heart of the Matter: Themes and Conclusions
Standards Focus

Vocabulary Development 1.2   Identify and interpret figurative language and words with multiple meanings.

Reading Comprehension (Focus on Informational Materials) 2.6   Determine the adequacy and appropriateness of the evidence for an author's conclusions.

Literary Response and Analysis 3.6   Identify and analyze features of themes conveyed through characters, actions, and images.

Chapter 4   Forms and Patterns: Stories and Explanations
Standards Focus

Vocabulary Development 1.2   Identify and interpret figurative language and words with multiple meanings.

Reading Comprehension (Focus on Informational Materials) 2.2   Analyze text that uses the compare-and-contrast organizational pattern.

Literary Response and Analysis 3.1   Identify the forms of fiction and describe the major characteristics of each form.

---

* Unless otherwise noted, the standards listed are grade-level standards.

Chapter 5 Biography and Autobiography: Looking at Lives
Standards Focus

Vocabulary Development 1.4 Monitor expository text for unknown words or words with novel meanings by using word, sentence, and paragraph clues to determine meaning.

Reading Comprehension (Focus on Informational Materials) 2.3 Connect and clarify main ideas by identifying their relationships to other sources and related topics.

Literary Response and Analysis 3.5 Identify the speaker, and recognize the difference between first- and third-person narration (for example, autobiography compared with biography).

Chapter 6 Looking at Texts: Uses of the Imagination
Standards Focus

Vocabulary Development 1.5 Understand and explain "shades of meaning" in related words (for example, *softly* and *quietly*).

Reading Comprehension (Focus on Informational Materials) 2.7 Make reasonable assertions about a text through accurate supporting citations.

Literary Response and Analysis 3.7 Explain the effects of common literary devices (for example, symbolism, imagery, metaphor) in a variety of fictional and nonfictional texts.

Chapter 7 Rhyme and Reason
Standards Focus

Vocabulary Development 1.2 Identify and interpret figurative language and words with multiple meanings.

Reading Comprehension 2.8 Note instances of unsupported inferences, fallacious reasoning, persuasion, and propaganda in text.

Literary Response and Analysis 3.4 Define how tone or meaning is conveyed in poetry through word choice, figurative language, sentence structure, line length, punctuation, rhythm, repetition, and rhyme.

Chapter 8 You the Critic
Standards Focus

Vocabulary Development 1.4 (Grade 4 Review) Know common affixes, and use this knowledge to analyze the meaning of words.

Reading Comprehension (Focus on Informational Materials) 2.5 Follow multiple-step instructions for preparing applications (for example, for a public library card, bank savings account, sports club, league membership).

Literary Response and Analysis 3.8 Critique the credibility of characterization and the degree to which plot is contrived or realistic (for example, compare use of fact and fantasy in historical fiction).

To the Student

A Book for You

A book is like a garden carried in the pocket.
—Chinese Proverb

Picture this: a book chock full of intriguing stories that you want to read and informational articles that are really interesting. Make it a book that actually tells you to write in it, circling, underlining, adding your own questions, jotting down responses. Fill it with graphic organizers that encourage you to think in a different way. Make it a size that's easy to carry around. That's *Interactive Reading*—a book created especially for you.

A Book Designed for Success

Reading is a creative activity. You have to visualize the characters,
you have to hear what their voices sound like.
—Madeleine L'Engle

Interactive Reading is designed to accompany *Holt Literature and Language Arts.* Like *Holt Literature and Language Arts,* it's designed to help you interact with the literature and master the California language arts content standards.

Each chapter has three parts:
- Getting Ready
- Graphic Organizers for use with the selections in *Holt Literature and Language Arts*
- Interactive Readings for Independence

Getting Ready

Actors, athletes, dancers, and musicians all prepare before they perform. Getting Ready helps you prepare to read each chapter in *Holt Literature and Language Arts.*

To help you prepare, Getting Ready provides—
- an overview of what to expect in the chapter
- a strategy that will help you read the selections successfully and master the standards

- a Practice Read that is easy and fun to read
- questions and comments to help you interact with the Practice Read and apply the strategy
- a graphic organizer or chart for applying the strategy

Graphic Organizers for *Holt Literature and Language Arts*

Reading effectively involves interacting with the text. Graphic organizers give you a visual and fun way to organize, interpret, and understand the selections in *Holt Literature and Language Arts.*

To help you organize, interpret, and understand the selections, the graphic organizers provide—

- support for reading each literary and informational selection
- support for mastering the standards
- a creative way for you to think about and interact with the selections

Interactive Readings for Independence

Each chapter ends with new selections for you to read as you build toward independence. These selections provide new opportunities for you to apply your skills and strategies and interact with the text.

In this section, you will find—

- new literary and informational selections
- information for author study
- questions and comments to guide your reading and help you interact with the text
- projects that help you explore ideas and extend your knowledge

A Book for Your Thoughts and Ideas

....

Reading helps you think about things, it helps you imagine what it feels like to be somebody else . . . even somebody you don't like!
—*Paula Fox*

....

Reading is about you. It is about your own thoughts and feelings. It is about making connections between what you read and your own life and experience. The more you give of yourself to your reading, the more you will get out of it.

A Walk Through the Book

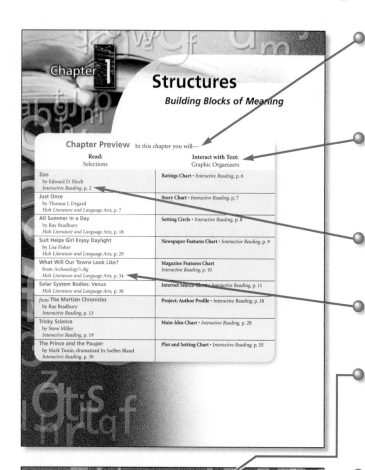

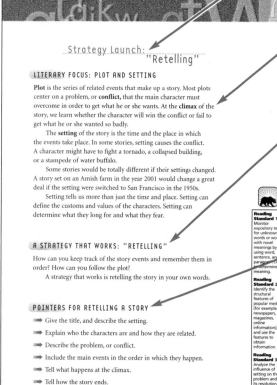

Chapter Preview
Knowing what to expect helps you be more successful. The Chapter Preview provides an overview of what's in each *Interactive Reading* chapter.

Read and Interact
In each chapter you will read both literary and informational texts and use graphic organizers as one way of interacting with the selections.

Highlighted Selections
The highlighted selections appear only in *Interactive Reading*.

Other Selections
The unhighlighted selections appear only in *Holt Literature and Language Arts*.

Strategy Launch
This page is designed to give you an advantage. Like strategies used in sports and business, reading strategies help you reach your goal—mastery of the standards.

Literary Focus
This feature introduces a literary focus for the chapter. The focus ties into a California reading standard.

A Strategy That Works
This feature introduces a reading strategy that will be used throughout the chapter. Each strategy helps you make sense of the text and understand the literary focus. It guides you in exploring and interpreting the text in a creative way while mastering the standard.

Pointers
See at a glance how to use the strategy. Pointers make each strategy easy to follow and use.

Reading Standards
Here are the California reading standards that are covered in this chapter. Each part of the chapter is designed to help you master these standards.

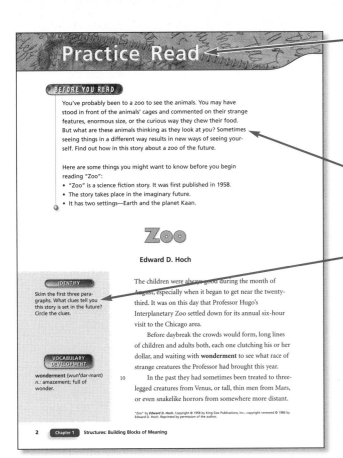

Practice Read

A Practice Read is an easy-to-read selection that gives you practice in applying the strategy and interacting with the text. Using the Practice Read helps you warm up before reading the selections in *Holt Literature and Language Arts.*

Before You Read

This feature tells you what the selection is about and gives you background information.

Side-Column Notes

Each selection is accompanied by notes in the side columns. They guide your interaction with the selection and show you how to apply the reading strategy. Many notes ask you to circle or underline in the text itself. Others provide lines on which you can write your responses to questions.

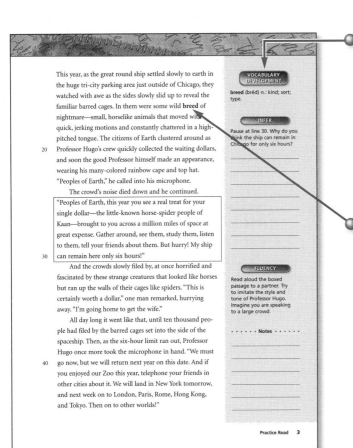

Types of Notes

The different types of notes throughout the selection help you—

- apply the reading strategy
- use reading skills to comprehend and interpret
- focus on a literary element
- build vocabulary
- develop word knowledge
- decode unfamiliar words

Vocabulary Development

Vocabulary words for you to learn and own are set in boldface in the selection, letting you see words in context. Vocabulary words are defined for you right there in the side column.

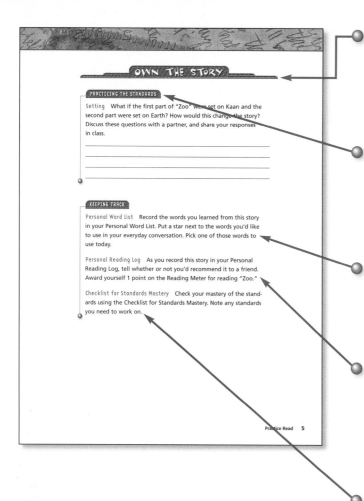

Own the Story, Text, or Poem
The meaning you take from a selection is based on the thought and reflection you put into it. Make each selection your own. Mark it up with your own comments and questions.

Practicing the Standards
You have a major goal in front of you: to master the California standards. This feature appears at the end of each selection to help you practice the skill in the standard.

Personal Word List
At the back of the book, you will find a Personal Word List for recording words you have learned and words you especially like.

Personal Reading Log
The more you read, the better you will read. Keep track of how much you read in your Personal Reading Log at the end of the book. By the year's end the Reading Meter will show the approximate number of words you have read in the book.

Checklist for Standards Mastery
With each selection you read and each standard you master, you come closer and closer to reaching your goal. Keep track of your progress with the Checklist for Standards Mastery at the end of the book.

Reading Strategy Graphic Organizer
At the end of every Practice Read is a graphic organizer that guides you in applying the reading strategy to the selection.

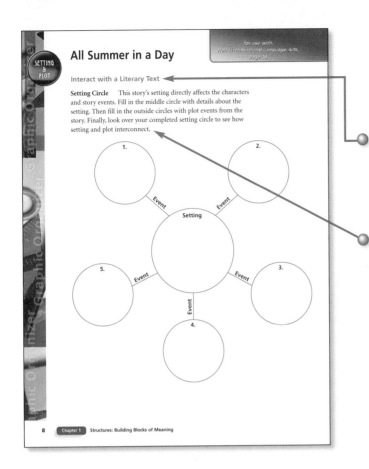

All Summer in a Day

for use with Holt Literature and Language Arts, page 18

Interact with a Literary Text

Setting Circle This story's setting directly affects the characters and story events. Fill in the middle circle with details about the setting. Then fill in the outside circles with plot events from the story. Finally, look over your completed setting circle to see how setting and plot interconnect.

8　Chapter 1　Structures: Building Blocks of Meaning

Holt Literature and Language Arts

Now that you have prepared and practiced, it's time to turn to the selections in *Holt Literature and Language Arts.*

Interact with a Literary Text

For every literary selection in *Holt Literature and Language Arts,* there is a graphic organizer to help you read the text with increased understanding.

Reading Standard

Each graphic organizer reinforces the literary focus and moves you closer toward mastering a California reading standard.

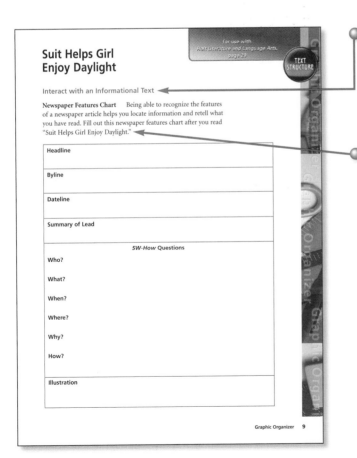

Suit Helps Girl Enjoy Daylight

for use with Holt Literature and Language Arts, page 29

Interact with an Informational Text

Newspaper Features Chart Being able to recognize the features of a newspaper article helps you locate information and retell what you have read. Fill out this newspaper features chart after you read "Suit Helps Girl Enjoy Daylight."

Headline
Byline
Dateline
Summary of Lead
5W-How Questions
Who?
What?
When?
Where?
Why?
How?
Illustration

Graphic Organizer　9

Interact with an Informational Text

For every informational selection in *Holt Literature and Language Arts,* there is a graphic organizer to help you read the text with increased understanding.

Reading Standard

Each graphic organizer reinforces the informational focus and moves you closer toward mastering a California reading standard.

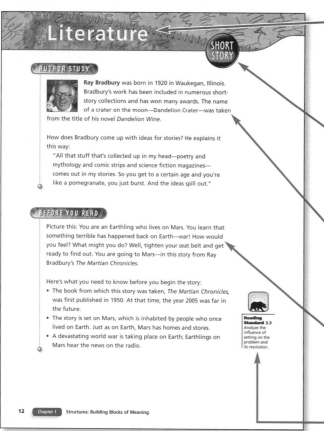

Interactive Selections

After you read the selections in a chapter of *Holt Literature and Language Arts,* build toward independence by reading the selections at the end of each *Interactive Reading* chapter.

Types of Literature

Effective readers are skilled at reading many different types of text. Each text type is identified so that you can keep track of your mastery.

Author Study

Some interactive selections give you an opportunity to read more by an author you have studied in *Holt Literature and Language Arts.*

Before You Read

This feature tells you what the selection is about and gives you background information.

Reading Standard

The California reading standard you will concentrate on with each interactive selection is identified here in the side column.

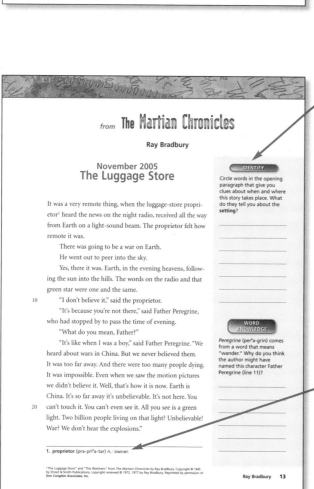

Side-Column Notes

Each selection is accompanied by notes in the side columns. They guide your interaction with the selection and show you how to apply the reading strategy. Many notes ask you to circle or underline the text itself. The different types of notes are designed to help you

- apply the reading strategy
- use reading skills to comprehend and interpret
- focus on a literary element
- build vocabulary
- develop word knowledge
- decode unfamiliar words
- understand text structures
- build fluency

Footnotes

Difficult or unusual terms are defined in footnotes.

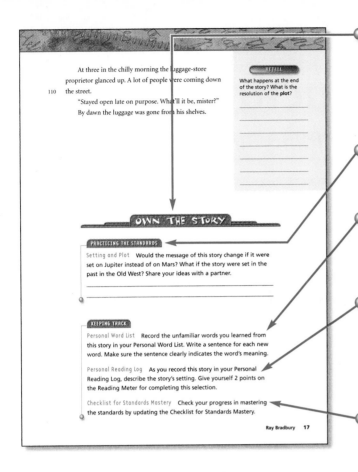

Own the Story, Text, or Poem
The meaning you take from a selection is based on the thought and reflection you put into it. Make each selection your own. Mark it up with your own comments and questions.

Practicing the Standards
This feature appears at the end of each selection to help you check your mastery.

Personal Word List
Record words you have learned and words you especially like in your Personal Word List at the end of the book.

Personal Reading Log
Keep track of how much you read in your Personal Reading Log at the end of the book. By the year's end the Reading Meter will show the approximate number of words you have read in this book.

Checklist for Standards Mastery
With each selection you read and each standard you master, you come closer and closer to reaching your goal. Keep track of your progress with the Checklist for Standards Mastery at the end of the book.

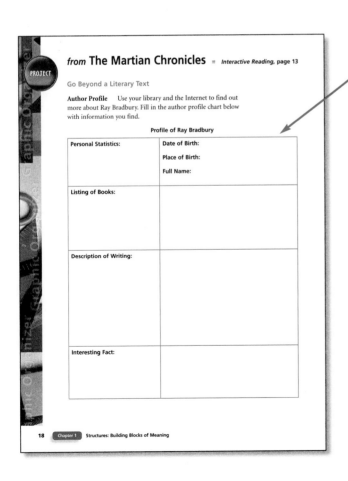

Project Graphic Organizer
Don't just stop after you read the selection. The project graphic organizer helps you go beyond the selection and extend your knowledge and understanding.

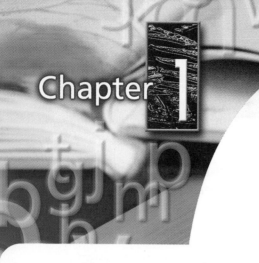

Chapter 1

Structures
Building Blocks of Meaning

Chapter Preview In this chapter you will—

Strategy Launch: "Retelling"

LITERARY FOCUS: PLOT AND SETTING

Plot is the series of related events that make up a story. Most plots center on a problem, or **conflict,** that the main character must overcome in order to get what he or she wants. At the **climax** of the story, we learn whether the character will win the conflict or fail to get what he or she wanted so badly.

The **setting** of the story is the time and the place in which the events take place. In some stories, setting causes the conflict. A character might have to fight a tornado, a collapsed building, or a stampede of water buffalo.

Some stories would be totally different if their settings changed. A story set on an Amish farm in the year 2001 would change a great deal if the setting were switched to San Francisco in the 1950s.

Setting tells us more than just the time and place. Setting can define the customs and values of the characters. Setting can determine what they long for and what they fear.

A STRATEGY THAT WORKS: "RETELLING"

How can you keep track of the story events and remember them in order? How can you follow the plot?

A strategy that works is retelling the story in your own words.

POINTERS FOR RETELLING A STORY

))➡ Give the title, and describe the setting.

))➡ Explain who the characters are and how they are related.

))➡ Describe the problem, or conflict.

))➡ Include the main events in the order in which they happen.

))➡ Tell what happens at the climax.

))➡ Tell how the story ends.

Reading Standard 1.4 Monitor expository text for unknown words or words with novel meanings by using word, sentence, and paragraph clues to determine meaning.

Reading Standard 2.1 Identify the structural features of popular media (for example, newspapers, magazines, online information), and use the features to obtain information.

Reading Standard 3.3 Analyze the influence of setting on the problem and its resolution.

Practice Read

BEFORE YOU READ

You've probably been to a zoo to see the animals. You may have stood in front of the animals' cages and commented on their strange features, enormous size, or the curious way they chew their food. But what are these animals thinking as they look at *you*? Sometimes seeing things in a different way results in new ways of seeing yourself. Find out how in this story about a zoo of the future.

Here are some things you might want to know before you begin reading "Zoo":
- "Zoo" is a science fiction story. It was first published in 1958.
- The story takes place in the imaginary future.
- It has two settings—Earth and the planet Kaan.

Zoo

Edward D. Hoch

IDENTIFY

Skim the first three paragraphs. What clues tell you this story is set in the future? Circle the clues.

VOCABULARY DEVELOPMENT

wonderment (wun′dər·mənt) *n.:* amazement; full of wonder.

The children were always good during the month of August, especially when it began to get near the twenty-third. It was on this day that Professor Hugo's Interplanetary Zoo settled down for its annual six-hour visit to the Chicago area.

Before daybreak the crowds would form, long lines of children and adults both, each one clutching his or her dollar, and waiting with **wonderment** to see what race of strange creatures the Professor had brought this year.

10   In the past they had sometimes been treated to three-legged creatures from Venus, or tall, thin men from Mars, or even snakelike horrors from somewhere more distant.

This year, as the great round ship settled slowly to earth in the huge tri-city parking area just outside of Chicago, they watched with awe as the sides slowly slid up to reveal the familiar barred cages. In them were some wild **breed** of nightmare—small, horselike animals that moved with quick, jerking motions and constantly chattered in a high-pitched tongue. The citizens of Earth clustered around as

20 Professor Hugo's crew quickly collected the waiting dollars, and soon the good Professor himself made an appearance, wearing his many-colored rainbow cape and top hat. "Peoples of Earth," he called into his microphone.

The crowd's noise died down and he continued.

"Peoples of Earth, this year you see a real treat for your single dollar—the little-known horse-spider people of Kaan—brought to you across a million miles of space at great expense. Gather around, see them, study them, listen to them, tell your friends about them. But hurry! My ship

30 can remain here only six hours!"

And the crowds slowly filed by, at once horrified and fascinated by these strange creatures that looked like horses but ran up the walls of their cages like spiders. "This is certainly worth a dollar," one man remarked, hurrying away. "I'm going home to get the wife."

All day long it went like that, until ten thousand people had filed by the barred cages set into the side of the spaceship. Then, as the six-hour limit ran out, Professor Hugo once more took the microphone in hand. "We must

40 go now, but we will return next year on this date. And if you enjoyed our Zoo this year, telephone your friends in other cities about it. We will land in New York tomorrow, and next week on to London, Paris, Rome, Hong Kong, and Tokyo. Then on to other worlds!"

VOCABULARY DEVELOPMENT

breed (brēd) *n.:* kind; sort; type.

INFER

Pause at line 30. Why do you think the ship can remain in Chicago for only six hours?

_____

_____

_____

_____

_____

_____

_____

FLUENCY

Read aloud the boxed passage to a partner. Try to imitate the style and tone of Professor Hugo. Imagine you are speaking to a large crowd.

· · · · · · Notes · · · · · ·

_____

_____

_____

_____

parting (pär′tin) *adj.:* last;
departing.

mate (māt) *n.:* life partner;
husband or wife.

offspring (ôf′sprin) *n.:* child.

RETELL

Retell the main events of the
story. Be sure to explain the
twist at the end.

_____

_____

_____

_____

_____

_____

_____

_____

_____

_____

_____

_____

_____

_____

_____

_____

_____

He waved farewell to them, and as the ship rose from
the ground, the Earth peoples agreed that this had been the
very best Zoo yet. . . .

Some two months and three planets later, the silver
ship of Professor Hugo settled at last onto the familiar
50 jagged rocks of Kaan, and the odd horse-spider creatures
filed quickly out of their cages. Professor Hugo was there
to say a few **parting** words, and then they scurried away
in a hundred different directions, seeking their homes
among the rocks.

In one house, the she-creature was happy to see the
return of her **mate** and **offspring.** She babbled a greeting
in the strange tongue and hurried to embrace them. "It
was a long time you were gone! Was it good?"

And the he-creature nodded. "The little one enjoyed
60 it especially. We visited eight worlds and saw many things."

The little one ran up the wall of the cave. "On the
place called Earth it was the best. The creatures there wear
garments over their skins, and they walk on two legs."

"But isn't it dangerous?" asked the she-creature.

"No," her mate answered. "There are bars to protect
us from them. We remain right in the ship. Next time you
must come with us. It is well worth the nineteen commocs
it costs."

And the little one nodded. "It was the very best Zoo
70 ever. . . ."

OWN THE STORY

Setting   What if the first part of "Zoo" were set on Kaan and the second part were set on Earth? How would this change the story? Discuss these questions with a partner, and share your responses in class.

_____

_____

_____

_____

KEEPING TRACK

Personal Word List   Record the words you learned from this story in your Personal Word List. Put a star next to the words you'd like to use in your everyday conversation. Pick one of those words to use today.

Personal Reading Log   As you record this story in your Personal Reading Log, tell whether or not you'd recommend it to a friend. Award yourself 1 point on the Reading Meter for reading "Zoo."

Checklist for Standards Mastery   Check your mastery of the standards using the Checklist for Standards Mastery. Note any standards you need to work on.

Zoo ▪ *Interactive Reading,* page 2

Interact with a Literary Text

Ratings Chart Work with a partner. Take turns retelling "Zoo." Pay special attention to the setting of the story. Then complete the ratings chart below to evaluate your partner's retelling. A **0** on the scale means the retelling didn't address the point at all; a **3** means that the retelling answered the question completely.

Reteller _____   **Listener** _____

Does this retelling	NO			YES
1. have an introduction that includes the title and author?	0	1	2	3
2. include the names of the main characters and tell how they are related?	0	1	2	3
3. identify the main situation?	0	1	2	3
4. describe the story's settings?	0	1	2	3
5. present the events in the order in which they happened?	0	1	2	3
6. explain how the problem is resolved?	0	1	2	3
7. seem well organized?	0	1	2	3
8. connect the story to other stories?	0	1	2	3
Total Score			_____	

Comments from the listener about the retelling:

_____

_____

Suggestion for the next retelling:

_____

_____

Just Once

Interact with a Literary Text

Story Chart   Fill out the story chart below as you review "Just Once." You should be able to identify six major story events.

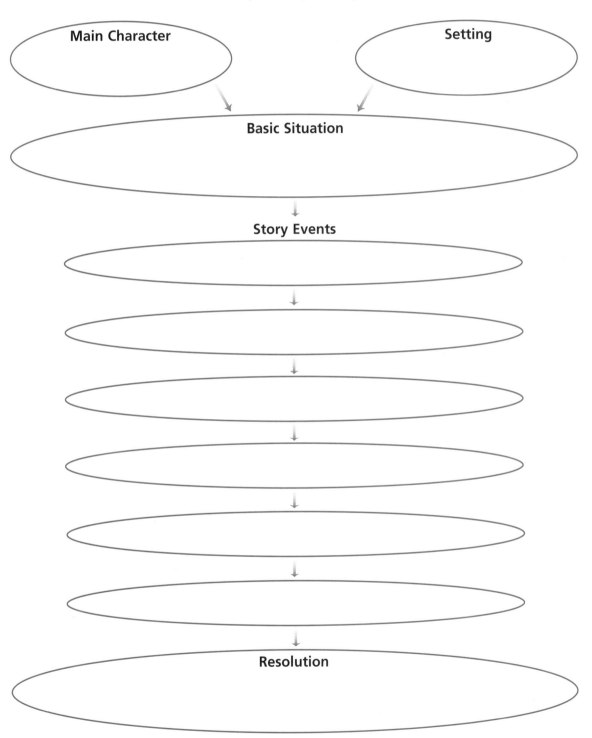

Main Character

Setting

Basic Situation

Story Events

Resolution

All Summer in a Day

Interact with a Literary Text

Setting Circle   This story's setting directly affects the characters and story events. Fill in the middle circle with details about the setting. Then fill in the outside circles with plot events from the story. Finally, look over your completed setting circle to see how setting and plot interconnect.

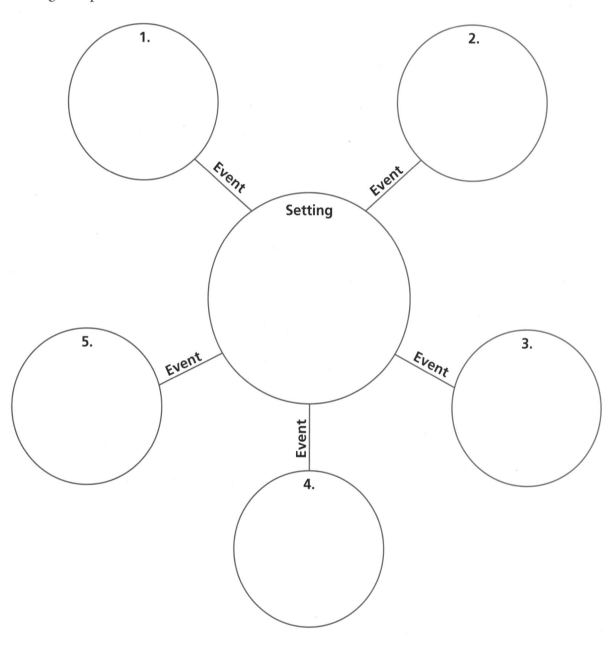

Suit Helps Girl Enjoy Daylight

Interact with an Informational Text

Newspaper Features Chart   Being able to recognize the features of a newspaper article helps you locate information and retell what you have read. Fill out this newspaper features chart after you read "Suit Helps Girl Enjoy Daylight."

Headline	thetlesuite help the enjoy daylight
Byline	Lise fisher ighhs me out
Dateline	Keystones Heights out it
Summary of Lead	Lise first day out side
5W-How Questions	
Who?	
What?	
When?	On a Saturday
Where?	Keystone Height
Why?	Be Protected from the sun
How?	D suit Protected her
Illustration	

What Will Our Towns Look Like?

for use with
Holt Literature and Language Arts,
page 34

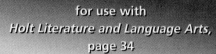

Interact with an Informational Text

Magazine Features Chart   You can use the features of a magazine article to find different kinds of information. Fill out this magazine features chart after you read "What Will Our Towns Look Like?"

Magazine: _____

Article Title:

_____

_____

Article Subtitle:

_____

_____

Headings (What Are They?):

_____

_____

_____

_____

Illustration & Caption (What Is It About?):

_____

_____

_____

_____

_____

Main Idea of Article:

_____

_____

_____

_____

_____

_____

Solar System Bodies: Venus

Interact with an Informational Text

Internet Search Chart   If you're using the Internet as a research tool, it's a good idea to know standard Web site features. Fill out this Internet search chart after you read "Solar System Bodies: Venus."

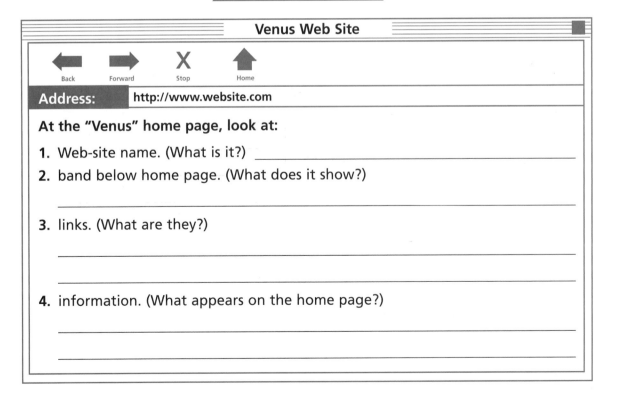

To get to the "Venus" Web site, use a . . .

1. URL. What do you do with the URL (uniform resource locator)?

   _____

2. search engine. How do you use a search engine?

   _____

   _____

Venus Web Site

Back   Forward   Stop   Home

Address: http://www.website.com

At the "Venus" home page, look at:

1. Web-site name. (What is it?) _____

2. band below home page. (What does it show?)

   _____

3. links. (What are they?)

   _____

   _____

4. information. (What appears on the home page?)

   _____

   _____

Literature

AUTHOR STUDY

Ray Bradbury was born in 1920 in Waukegan, Illinois. Bradbury's work has been included in numerous short-story collections and has won many awards. The name of a crater on the moon—Dandelion Crater—was taken from the title of his novel *Dandelion Wine*.

How does Bradbury come up with ideas for stories? He explains it this way:

> "All that stuff that's collected up in my head—poetry and mythology and comic strips and science fiction magazines— comes out in my stories. So you get to a certain age and you're like a pomegranate, you just burst. And the ideas spill out."

BEFORE YOU READ

Picture this: You are an Earthling who lives on Mars. You learn that something terrible has happened back on Earth—war! How would you feel? What might you do? Well, tighten your seat belt and get ready to find out. You are going to Mars—in this story from Ray Bradbury's *The Martian Chronicles.*

Here's what you need to know before you begin the story:

• The book from which this story was taken, *The Martian Chronicles,* was first published in 1950. At that time, the year 2005 was far in the future.

• The story is set on Mars, which is inhabited by people who once lived on Earth. Just as on Earth, Mars has homes and stores.

• A devastating world war is taking place on Earth; Earthlings on Mars hear the news on the radio.

Reading Standard 3.3
Analyze the influence of setting on the problem and its resolution.

from The Martian Chronicles

Ray Bradbury

November 2005
The Luggage Store

It was a very remote thing, when the luggage-store proprietor[1] heard the news on the night radio, received all the way
from Earth on a light-sound beam. The proprietor felt how
remote it was.

There was going to be a war on Earth.

He went out to peer into the sky.

Yes, there it was. Earth, in the evening heavens, following the sun into the hills. The words on the radio and that
green star were one and the same.

10 "I don't believe it," said the proprietor.

"It's because you're not there," said Father Peregrine,
who had stopped by to pass the time of evening.

"What do you mean, Father?"

"It's like when I was a boy," said Father Peregrine. "We
heard about wars in China. But we never believed them.
It was too far away. And there were too many people dying.
It was impossible. Even when we saw the motion pictures
we didn't believe it. Well, that's how it is now. Earth is
China. It's so far away it's unbelievable. It's not here. You
20 can't touch it. You can't even see it. All you see is a green
light. Two billion people living on that light? Unbelievable!
War? We don't hear the explosions."

---

1. **proprietor** (prə·prī′ə·tər) *n.*: owner.

Ray Bradbury **13**

IDENTIFY

Circle words in the opening
paragraph that give you
clues about when and where
this story takes place. What
do they tell you about the
setting?

_____

_____

_____

_____

_____

_____

WORD KNOWLEDGE

Peregrine (per′ə·grin) comes
from a word that means
"wander." Why do you think
the author might have
named this character Father
Peregrine (line 11)?

_____

_____

_____

_____

_____

Pause at line 45. What reasons does the proprietor give
for his opinion of people's
reaction to war?

_____

_____

_____

_____

_____

_____

_____

_____

_____

_____

INTERPRET

How does the **setting**
contribute to the characters'
emotions and conflicts?

_____

_____

_____

_____

_____

_____

_____

_____

_____

"We will," said the proprietor. "I keep thinking about all those people that were going to come to Mars this week. What was it? A hundred thousand or so coming up in the next month or so. What about *them* if the war starts?"

"I imagine they'll turn back. They'll be needed on Earth."

"Well," said the proprietor, "I'd better get my luggage
30 dusted off. I got a feeling there'll be a rush sale here any time."

"Do you think everyone now on Mars will go back to Earth if this *is* the Big War we've all been expecting for years?"

"It's a funny thing, Father, but yes, I think we'll *all* go back. I know, we came up here to get away from things— politics, the atom bomb, war, pressure groups, prejudice, laws—I know. But it's still home there. You wait and see. When the first bomb drops on America the people up
40 here'll start thinking. They haven't been here long enough. A couple years is all. If they'd been here forty years, it'd be different, but they got relatives down there, and their home towns. Me, I can't believe in Earth any more; I can't imagine it much. But I'm old. I don't count. I might stay on here."

"I doubt it."

"Yes, I guess you're right."

They stood on the porch watching the stars. Finally Father Peregrine pulled some money from his pocket and
50 handed it to the proprietor. "Come to think of it, you'd better give me a new valise.² My old one's in pretty bad condition. . . ."

---

2. **valise** (və·lēs′) *n.:* suitcase.

November 2005
The Watchers

IDENTIFY

Describe the **setting** at this point in the story. Circle clues that lead to your response.

_____

_____

_____

_____

They all came out and looked at the sky that night. They left their suppers or their washing up or their dressing for the show and they came out upon their now-not-quite-as-new porches and watched the green star of Earth there. It was a move without **conscious** effort; they all did it, to help them understand the news they had heard on the radio a moment before. There was Earth and there the

60 coming war, and there hundreds of thousands of mothers or grandmothers or fathers or brothers or aunts or uncles or cousins. They stood on the porches and tried to believe in the existence of Earth, much as they had once tried to believe in the existence of Mars; it was a problem reversed. To all intents and purposes, Earth now was dead; they had been away from it for three or four years. Space was an **anesthetic;** seventy million miles of space numbed you, put memory to sleep, **depopulated** Earth, erased the past, and allowed these people here to go on with their work. But

70 now, tonight, the dead were risen, Earth was reinhabited, memory awoke, a million names were spoken: What was so-and-so doing tonight on Earth? What about this one and that one? The people on the porches glanced sideways at each other's faces.

At nine o'clock Earth seemed to explode, catch fire, and burn.

The people on the porches put up their hands as if to beat the fire out.

They waited.

VOCABULARY
DEVELOPMENT

conscious (kən′shəs) *adj.:* having feeling; aware.

anesthetic (an′es·*th*et′ik) *n.:* drug causing numbness.

depopulated (dē·päp′yə·lā·tid) *v.:* reduced the number of people.

CONNECT

When Bradbury wrote this story, people all over the world were concerned about the threat of nuclear war. What might Bradbury's message be to the readers of this story?

_____

_____

_____

_____

_____

_____

Ray Bradbury 15

80   By midnight the fire was **extinguished.** Earth was still there. There was a sigh, like an autumn wind, from the porches.

"We haven't heard from Harry for a long time."

"He's all right."

"We should send a message to Mother."

"She's all right."

"*Is* she?"

"Now, don't worry."

"Will she be all right, do you think?"

90   "Of course, of course; now come to bed."

But nobody moved. Late dinners were carried out onto the night lawns and set upon collapsible tables, and they picked at these slowly until two o'clock and the light-radio message flashed from Earth. They could read the great Morse-code flashes which flickered like a distant firefly:

> AUSTRALIAN CONTINENT **ATOMIZED** IN PREMATURE EXPLO-
> SION OF ATOMIC STOCKPILE. LOS ANGELES, LONDON BOMBED.
> WAR. COME HOME. COME HOME. COME HOME.

     They stood up from their tables.

100   COME HOME. COME HOME. COME HOME.

"Have you heard from your brother Ted this year?"

"You know. With mail rates five bucks a letter to Earth, I don't write much."

COME HOME.

"I've been wondering about Jane; you remember Jane, my kid sister?"

COME HOME.

At three in the chilly morning the luggage-store proprietor glanced up. A lot of people were coming down the street.

110 the street.

"Stayed open late on purpose. What'll it be, mister?"

By dawn the luggage was gone from his shelves.

RETELL

What happens at the end of the story? What is the resolution of the **plot**?

_____

_____

_____

_____

_____

_____

OWN THE STORY

PRACTICING THE STANDARDS

Setting and Plot   Would the message of this story change if it were set on Jupiter instead of on Mars? What if the story were set in the past in the Old West? Share your ideas with a partner.

_____

_____

KEEPING TRACK

Personal Word List   Record the unfamiliar words you learned from this story in your Personal Word List. Write a sentence for each new word. Make sure the sentence clearly indicates the word's meaning.

Personal Reading Log   As you record this story in your Personal Reading Log, describe the story's setting. Give yourself 2 points on the Reading Meter for completing this selection.

Checklist for Standards Mastery   Check your progress in mastering the standards by updating the Checklist for Standards Mastery.

from **The Martian Chronicles** ▪ *Interactive Reading,* page 13

Go Beyond a Literary Text

Author Profile　Use your library and the Internet to find out more about Ray Bradbury. Fill in the author profile chart below with information you find.

Profile of Ray Bradbury

Personal Statistics:	Date of Birth:
	Place of Birth:
	Full Name:
Listing of Books:	
Description of Writing:	
Interesting Fact:	

Information

Reading
Standard 2.1
Identify the
structural
features of
popular media
(for example,
newspapers,
magazines,
online
information),
and use the
features to
obtain
information.

BEFORE YOU READ

Is there life on Mars? Is there a monster living in Loch Ness? Is Big Foot real? How do you know if something is a fact or a trick? Get ready to read "Tricky Science," which is all about famous scientific pranks of the past.

from *Muse* magazine, September 2000

Tricky Science

Steve Miller

Do you believe in alien **abductions** or that a spaceship crashed in the desert near Roswell, New Mexico, in 1947? Do you believe a meteor the size of Manhattan smashed into the earth, killing the dinosaurs, or that people have walked on the moon? Which is more believable: that there is a monster swimming around in Loch Ness or that there's a black hole at the center of our galaxy sucking up everything passing nearby?

10　How do you decide what to believe? Do you believe something because it sounds right, or because there's nothing obviously wrong with it, or because it was published in the newspaper? Perhaps you believe science stories if scientists believe them. That's a good answer. But is this method foolproof?

It's actually pretty easy to pull off a scientific **hoax.** Most people are used to believing what they hear, especially if it has to do with science. Scientists like to think that even if they are fooled at first, someone usually comes along and

TEXT STRUCTURE

Preview the subheadings. What three subjects might this article be about?

_____

_____

_____

VOCABULARY DEVELOPMENT

abductions (ab·duk′shənz) *n. pl.*: kidnappings.

hoax (hōks) *n.*: trick or fraud.

DECODING TIP

Circle the word *foolproof* (line 14). Draw a line that breaks the word in two. What does the word mean?

_____

_____

Underline the remarks enclosed in parentheses on this page and the next. Why do you suppose the writer uses these parentheses?

_____

_____

_____

_____

_____

_____

· · · · · · **Notes** · · · · · ·

_____

_____

_____

_____

_____

_____

_____

_____

_____

_____

_____

_____

_____

20 figures out the truth. Obviously that's happened with all the hoaxes we know about. But what about the *really* great hoaxes? They still haven't been uncovered! Deciding what's true and what's false isn't easy.

At Home on the Moon

On 25 August 1835, the *New York Sun* ran a story about some extraordinary discoveries made by the famous astronomer Sir John Herschel. The paper claimed Herschel had just assembled the world's largest telescope in South Africa, with a lens 24 feet in diameter. (The largest lens ever made is only 40 inches.) When he aimed it at the moon, he
30 spied some truly amazing things. Over the next week, the newspaper told the story of his observations. (Herschel

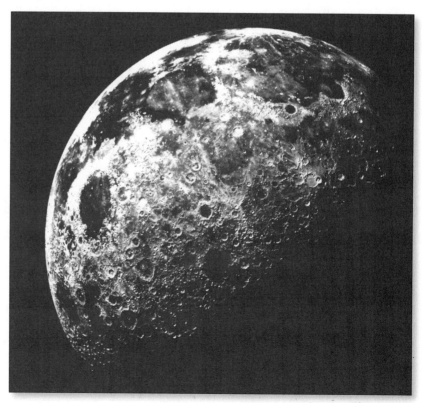

The moon.

really *was* in South Africa at the time, so no one could check with him.)

What did he see? A landscape of forests and plains, broad rivers, and beautiful white beaches. Masses of gold were draped over rock ledges. There was a crystal river of quartz five miles wide and 340 miles long. Oh, the planet was inhabited, too. Grazing on the plains were **herds** of bison with flaps over their eyes to protect them from the sun. (Sort of like the bill of a baseball cap, even though baseball hadn't been invented yet.) There were blue antelopes with a single horn (can't forget the unicorn), and a kind of huge beaver that had no tail and walked on its hind legs. But these were no ordinary beavers. They carried their babies in their arms like people, built huts to live in, and used fire to heat their homes. Most amazing of all, there were creatures that looked human, but had large bat-like wings. The expressions on their faces were human (that's some telescope) and they built beautiful temples of **sapphire.**

You're probably thinking this is an obvious fraud. But 165 years ago, people didn't know that much about the moon and they had a lot of respect for authority. And since Herschel was the most famous astronomer in the world with the world's best telescope, of course he saw things no one else had ever seen. After all, what would you think if it was a report from NASA about life on Mars? (OK, maybe you wouldn't believe the part about the bison with a baseball cap—but how about a football helmet?)

It turned out that a reporter named Richard Locke spun the whole thing as a joke. He claimed to have been surprised that anyone believed it. But since he was selling so many papers, he kept going for awhile. When Sir John

40

50

60

Read the boxed paragraph to a small group of classmates. Can they identify the author's remarks by the tone of your voice? Re-read the paragraph, and try to improve your speed and the smoothness of your delivery.

VOCABULARY DEVELOPMENT

herds (hʉrdz) *n.:* groups of cattle, sheep, or other animals.

sapphire (saf'ĭr) *n.:* deep-blue variety of corundum, a precious stone.

IDENTIFY

What is a unicorn (line 42)? Can you guess from the context?

_____

_____

_____

_____

_____

_____

_____

_____

_____

Why do you think this section of the article appears in a tinted box?

_____

_____

_____

_____

_____

_____

_____

_____

_____

_____

_____

WORD KNOWLEDGE

Circle the word *hotheaded* (line 71). This passage says that the hotheaded borer's head was so hot it could drill through ice. *Hotheaded,* however, has another meaning. What do we mean when we say a person is hotheaded?

_____

_____

_____

_____

Herschel heard about it, he had a good laugh, but said he was afraid his real report was going to be much less interesting. But many of the people who fell for the joke didn't think it was so funny.

WHEN IN DOUBT, CHECK THE DATE

Occasionally—most often in April—a hoax is just for fun. In
70 *1995,* Discover *magazine reported the discovery of a truly unusual creature in Antarctica. The hotheaded naked ice borer looks like a naked mole-rat with a big bulb on its head. Since it burns calories fast, it's very warm, and it uses its hot head to bore tunnels through the ice.*

The most amazing thing about the hothead is its hunting technique. Whole families of the warm, ugly creatures gather beneath a penguin, melting the ice with their heads until the snow collapses and the bird is trapped below. Then the hotheads devour it. The creatures were discovered by Aprille
80 *Pazzo (pazzo is "fool" in Italian).*

Other April Fool's jokes in Discover *have included a Neanderthal tuba made from a hollowed-out mastodon tusk, a huge bellows to blow pollution away from Los Angeles (hey, it might work), and the discovery of the bigon, an elementary particle as big as a bowling ball.*

Nessie, Is That You?

Hundreds of people claim to have seen Nessie, the Loch Ness monster. Some have even claimed to have taken pictures of it. The most famous photograph of all was shot in 1934 by R. Kenneth Wilson, a respected surgeon from London. The photo shows a head and long neck sticking out of the water. Ripples at the base of the neck suggest the creature is swimming.

For decades, people argued about this picture. Did it show a dinosaur, a log that looked like a neck and head, or a duck in the distance? (Try drawing something that looks like a dinosaur, a log, *and* a duck. It's pretty hard to do!) Then in 1993, a man named Christian Spurling confessed that the photograph was a hoax. He had helped his stepfather, Marmaduke Weatherell, build a model neck and head

Is this the Loch Ness monster?

INTERPRET

What does "Nessie" in the heading refer to?

TEXT STRUCTURE

How does the photo of the Loch Ness monster help you understand the hoax?

VOCABULARY DEVELOPMENT

traces (trā'səz) *n.:* marks left by a past person, thing, or event.

· · · · · · **Notes** · · · · · ·

_____

_____

_____

_____

_____

_____

_____

_____

_____

_____

_____

_____

_____

_____

_____

_____

_____

_____

_____

_____

_____

_____

on top of a toy windup submarine. The photograph was taken as the sub puttered around underwater. Eventually the model sank. (It probably became a toy for a baby monster.)

Weatherell took the photo to get revenge. He was upset because he had been fired from his job as monster hunter—and it probably wasn't easy to find a new job of the same sort. Someone had actually paid him money the year before to look for evidence of a creature in the lake.

110 And guess what? He found it! There were footprints of a large animal, proof of Nessie's existence. He made casts of the footprints, and then someone noticed that the monster prints were remarkably similar to hippopotamus prints. That, in itself, was strange, since hippos are somewhat rare in Scotland. Someone else uncovered a stuffed hippopotamus foot with **traces** of mud—also not too common. (It isn't clear, though, whether Weatherell made the prints himself or whether he fell for someone else's trick.) The blunder cost him his job. Out of disgust and anger he came

120 up with the idea of the faked photo and got Dr. Wilson to help him.

Does this prove that the Loch Ness monster doesn't exist? No, but it does remove one of the strongest pieces of evidence. Still, there are a few people who believe the photograph is genuine and the *real* hoax is the story of the toy submarine. This shows that some people will continue to believe in some hoaxes no matter what.

At Home in the Forest

130 The last Stone Age people were discovered in 1971 by a Philippine government official named Manuel Elizalde— maybe. Called the Tasaday, these people lived in a cave deep in the rain forest. They didn't farm or herd animals. Instead they lived on wild yams, grubs, berries, and frogs. They had no contact with other people, even those living just a few miles away, for thousands of years. The 26 Tasaday had no tools except stone axes and no clothing other than forest leaves. No one expected to find people this isolated in the second half of the 20th century.

140 Their story caught the world's imagination. Because of his position in the Philippine government, Elizalde was able to control contact with the Tasaday, and all information about them came from him. Very few scientists were allowed to study the tribe—Elizalde said he wanted to protect them from the outside world. A lot of people agreed with him and figured that scientists would rob the Tasaday of their innocence.

INTERPRET

What do you think is meant by "Stone Age people"? Read the rest of the paragraph to see if you find a clue.

Manuel Elizalde.

What allowed the Tasaday hoax to continue for fifteen years?

_____

_____

_____

_____

_____

_____

_____

_____

INTERPRET

According to the article, why were so many people fooled by these scientific hoaxes?

_____

_____

_____

_____

_____

_____

_____

_____

_____

_____

_____

_____

Photograph of the Tasaday, distributed by Elizalde.

This situation continued for 15 years until the Philippine government fell. As soon as they could, journalists went to the jungle to visit the Tasaday. They found

150   them living in regular houses, wearing Western clothes, and tending gardens just like those of other rural people in the southern Philippines. They told reporters and scientists that the whole thing was a hoax, and that they had gone along with it because Elizalde had paid them to.

So why did Elizalde make it all up? Probably just to get attention. And why did people believe it? In part because Elizalde, like Herschel, was supposed to be an authority, and in part because they couldn't check the story themselves. Also, probably just because it's fun to believe that

160   there are still undiscovered places in the world.

PRACTICING THE STANDARDS

Text Features   Use the headings in this article to write a summary of its contents. In your summary, cite the title and author of the article, and sum up the main points that the writer makes under each heading. At the end of your summary, explain the title "Tricky Science." Use the graphic organizer on the next page to gather details for your summary.

_____

_____

_____

_____

_____

_____

_____

_____

_____

_____

KEEPING TRACK

Personal Word List   Record the words you learned from this story in your Personal Word List. Circle one of the words. Write another word that means the same thing.

Personal Reading Log   Give yourself 3 points on the Reading Meter for reading this article.

Checklist for Standards Mastery   Use the Checklist for Standards Mastery to track your progress in mastering the standards.

Tricky Science ▪ *Interactive Reading,* page 19

Interact with Informational Text

Main-Idea Chart Prepare to write a summary of this article by filling out a chart that sums up the main topic of the article and lists the supporting details. Your supporting details should come from the three major sections of the article.

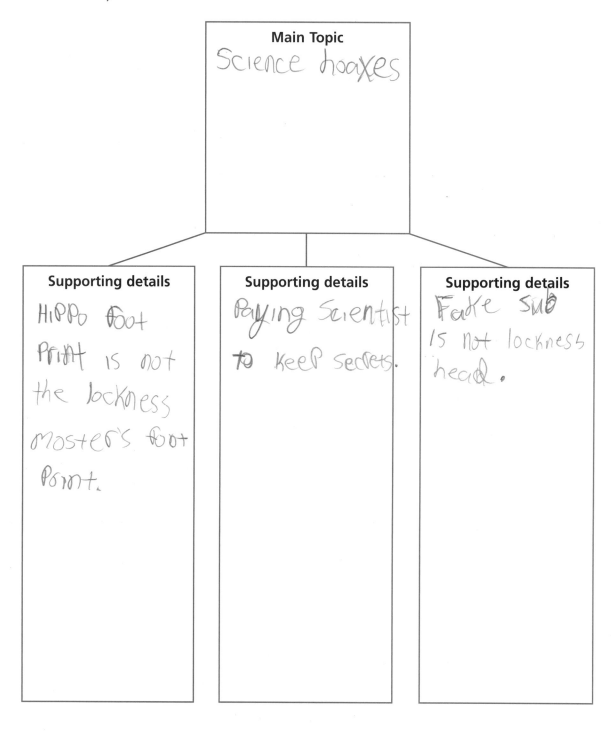

Main Topic

Science hoaxes

Supporting details

Hippo foot print is not the lockness moster's foot print.

Supporting details

Paying Scientist to keep secrets.

Supporting details

Fake Sub is not lockness head.

Literature

BEFORE YOU READ

Change a poor boy's outfit and he gets lucky—or does he? Well, *you* are about to get lucky. Get ready to read this classic tale, *The Prince and the Pauper,* in play form. Follow Tom Canty and the Prince of Wales as they experience a dramatic change of luck.

Here's what you need to know before you begin the play:

- The play is a version of Mark Twain's story *The Prince and the Pauper.*
- Characters' names appear in front of their lines of dialogue (the words that they speak).
- Stage directions appear in parentheses and italics. Stage directions tell the reader or actor about the characters' actions, thoughts, and feelings.
- Each scene starts with a description of the time and setting. The "At Rise" text describes what is happening onstage as the curtain rises.
- The Prince of Wales is the title given to the person next in line to the British throne.
- A pauper (pô′pər) is a very poor person.
- The Great Seal is the official insignia of the king, used to stamp important documents. The seal indicates the king's approval.

Reading Standard 3.3
Analyze the influence of setting on the problem and its resolution.

The Prince and the Pauper

Mark Twain
dramatized by **Joellen Bland**

TEXT STRUCTURE

Like most plays, this one begins with a cast of characters. Circle this list. Why is it important to include a cast of characters?

_____

_____

_____

_____

_____

_____

_____

_____

_____

_____

_____

_____

_____

_____

_____

Characters

EDWARD, Prince of Wales

TOM CANTY, the Pauper

LORD HERTFORD

LORD ST. JOHN

KING HENRY VIII

HERALD

MILES HENDON

JOHN CANTY, Tom's father

10 HUGO, a young thief

TWO WOMEN

JUSTICE

CONSTABLE

JAILER

SIR HUGH HENDON

TWO PRISONERS

TWO GUARDS

THREE PAGES

LORDS AND LADIES

20 VILLAGERS

Westminster Palace, London.

Scene 1

Time: 1547.

Setting: Westminster Palace, London. Gates leading to a courtyard are at right. Slightly to left, off the courtyard and inside the gates, the interior of a palace room is visible. There is a couch with a rich robe draped on it, a screen at rear, bell cord, mirror, chairs, and a table holding a bowl of nuts and a large golden seal. A piece of armor hangs on one wall. Exits rear and down stage.

30   **At Rise:** TWO GUARDS stand left and right of gates. Several VILLAGERS hover nearby, straining to see into the courtyard where the PRINCE is playing. TWO WOMEN enter right.

First Woman. I have walked all morning just to have a glimpse of Westminster Palace.

INFER

Pause at line 47. What can you tell about the prince from his actions? Circle the text that answers this question.

_____

_____

_____

_____

WORD KNOWLEDGE

In line 55 is the word *anteroom.* If you know that the prefix *ante-* means "comes before," what would you guess an anteroom is?

_____

_____

_____

_____

_____

_____

_____

VOCABULARY DEVELOPMENT

pantomime (pan′tə·mīm′) *v.:* use actions or gestures without words as a means of expression.

Second Woman. Maybe if we can get near enough to the gates, we can see the young prince.

[TOM CANTY, *dirty and ragged, comes out of crowd and steps close to gates.*]

Tom. I have always dreamed of seeing a real prince!
40 (*Excited, he presses his nose against gates.*)
First Guard. Mind your manners, you young beggar!
(*Seizes* TOM *by collar and sends him sprawling into crowd.*)

[VILLAGERS *laugh as* TOM *slowly gets to his feet.*]

Prince (*rushing to gates*). How dare you treat a poor subject of the king in such a manner! Open the gates and let him in!

[*As* VILLAGERS *see* PRINCE, *they remove hats and bow low.*]

Villagers (*shouting together*). Long live the Prince of Wales!

[GUARDS *open gates and* TOM *slowly passes through, as if in a*
50 *dream.*]

Prince (*to* TOM). You look tired, and you have been treated cruelly. I am Edward, Prince of Wales. What is your name?
Tom (*in awe*). Tom Canty, Your Highness.
Prince. Come into the palace with me, Tom. (PRINCE *leads* TOM *into anteroom.*)

[VILLAGERS **pantomime** *conversation, and all but a few exit.*]

Where do you live, Tom?

Tom. In Offal Court, Your Highness.

Prince. Offal Court? That's an odd name. Do you have

60   parents?

Tom. Yes, Your Highness.

Prince. How does your father treat you?

Tom. If it please you, Your Highness, when I am not able to beg for a penny for our supper, he treats me to beatings.

Prince (*shocked*). What! My father is not a calm man, but he does not beat me. (*Looks at* TOM *thoughtfully*) You speak well and have an easy grace. Have you been schooled?

Tom. Very little, Your Highness. A good priest who shares our house has taught me from his books.

70   **Prince.** Do you have a pleasant life in Offal Court?

Tom. Pleasant enough, Your Highness, save when I am hungry. We have Punch and Judy shows, and sometimes we lads have fights in the street.

Prince (*eagerly*). I should like that. Tell me more.

Tom. In summer, we run races and swim in the river, and we love to wallow in the mud.

Prince (*wistfully*). If I could wear your clothes and play in the mud just once, with no one to forbid me, I think I could give up the crown!

80   **Tom** (*shaking his head*). And if I could wear your fine clothes just once, Your Highness . . .

Prince. Would you like that? Come, then. We shall change places. You can take off your rags and put on my clothes— and I will put on yours. (*He leads* TOM *behind screen, and they return shortly, each wearing the other's clothes.*) Let's look in this mirror. (*Leads* TOM *to mirror*)

INTERPRET

Offal means "waste parts" or "garbage," usually the parts of butchered animals that are thrown away. What does this name suggest about the place Tom lives (line 60)?

_____

_____

_____

_____

_____

_____

RETELL

Pause at line 84. The prince has just reached a decision. Retell what he has decided to do. What does he want?

_____

_____

_____

_____

_____

_____

_____

_____

_____

_____

_____

_____

_____

_____

_____

_____

_____

INFER

Notice what the prince does as he exits. Circle his action. What do you predict it means?

_____

_____

_____

_____

_____

_____

_____

_____

_____

_____

_____

Tom. Oh, Your Highness, it is not proper for me to wear such clothes.

Prince (*excitedly*). Heavens, do you not see it? We look like

90   brothers! We have the same features and bearing. If we went about together, dressed alike, there is no one who could say which is the Prince of Wales and which is Tom Canty.

Tom (*drawing back, rubbing his hand*). Your Highness, I am frightened. . . .

Prince. Do not worry. (*Seeing* TOM *rub his hand*) Is that a bruise on your hand?

Tom. Yes, but it is slight thing, Your Highness.

Prince (*angrily*). It was shameful and cruel of that guard to

100   strike you. Do not stir a step until I come back. I command you! (*He picks up the golden seal and carefully puts it into a piece of armor. He then dashes out to gates.*) Open! Unbar the gates at once!

[SECOND GUARD *opens gates, and as* PRINCE *runs out,* FIRST GUARD *seizes him, boxes him on the ear, and knocks him to ground.*]

First Guard. Take that, you little beggar, for the trouble you have made for me with the prince.

[VILLAGERS *roar with laughter.*]

110   **Prince** (*picking himself up, turning on* GUARD *furiously*). I am Prince of Wales! You shall hang for laying your hand on me!

First Guard (*presenting arms, mockingly*). I salute Your Gracious Highness! (*Then, angrily shoving* PRINCE *aside*) Be off, you mad bag of rags!

[PRINCE *is surrounded by* VILLAGERS, *who hustle him off.*]

Villagers (*ad-lib as they exit, shouting*). Make way for His Royal Highness! Make way for the Prince of Wales! Hail to the prince!

120 **Tom** (*admiring himself in mirror*). If only the boys in Offal Court could see me! They will not believe me when I tell them about this. (*Looks around anxiously*) But where is the prince? (*Looks cautiously into courtyard.* TWO GUARDS *immediately snap to attention and salute. He quickly ducks back into anteroom as* LORDS ST. JOHN *and* HERTFORD *enter at rear.*)

Hertford (*going toward* TOM, *then stopping and bowing low*). My lord, you look distressed. What is wrong?

Tom (*trembling*). Oh, I beg of you, be merciful. I am no

130 prince, but poor Tom Canty of Offal Court. Please let me see the prince, and he will give my rags back to me and let me go unhurt. (*Kneeling*) Please, be merciful and spare me!

Hertford (*disturbed*). Your Highness, on your knees? To me? (*Bows quickly, then aside to* ST. JOHN) The prince has gone mad! We must inform the king. (*To* TOM) A moment, Your Highness.

[HERTFORD *and* ST. JOHN *exit rear.*]

Tom. Oh, there is no hope for me now. They will hang me

140 for certain!

TEXT STRUCTURE

Stage directions describe characters' actions or emotional states. They often appear in parentheses or brackets and are italicized. Circle the word that tells you how Tom feels when Lord Hertford begins speaking to him (line 129).

· · · · · · Notes · · · · · ·

FLUENCY

With a partner, read the boxed passage aloud. One partner should read the king's lines; the other, Tom's lines. Pay attention to the stage directions, and try to capture the tone that Tom and the king might use. When finished, switch roles.

INFER

Why is it possible that Tom can pass for the prince?

_____

_____

_____

_____

_____

_____

_____

_____

_____

_____

_____

_____

VOCABULARY DEVELOPMENT

heir (er) *n.:* person who inherits another's property or title upon the other's death.

[HERTFORD *and* ST. JOHN *reenter, supporting the* KING. TOM *watches in awe as they help him to couch, where he sinks down wearily.*]

King (*beckoning* TOM *close to him*). Now, my son, Edward, my prince. What is this? Do you mean to deceive me, the king, your father, who loves you and treats you so kindly?

Tom (*dropping to his knees*). You are the king? Then I have no hope!

King (*stunned*). My child, you are not well. Do not break 150 your father's old heart. Say you know me.

Tom. Yes, you are my lord the king, whom God preserve.

King. True, that is right. Now, you will not deny that you are Prince of Wales, as they say you did just a while ago?

Tom. Your Grace, believe me, I am the lowest of your subjects, being born a pauper, and it is by great mistake that I am here. I am too young to die. Oh, please, spare me, sire!

King (*amazed*). Die? Do not talk so, my child. You shall not die.

Tom (*gratefully*). God save you, my king! And now, may 160 I go?

King. Go? Where would you go?

Tom. Back to the alley where I was born and bred to misery.

King. My poor child, rest your head here. (*He holds* TOM*'s head and pats his shoulder, then turns to* HERTFORD *and* ST. JOHN.) Alas, I am old and ill, and my son is mad. But this shall pass. Mad or sane, he is my **heir** and shall rule England. Tomorrow he shall be installed and confirmed in his princely dignity! Bring the Great Seal!

Hertford (*bowing low*). Please, Your Majesty, you took the Great Seal from the chancellor two days ago to give to His Highness the prince.

King. So I did. (*To* TOM) My child, tell me, where is the Great Seal?

Tom (*trembling*). Indeed, my lord, I do not know.

King. Ah, your **affliction** hangs heavily upon you. 'Tis no matter. You will remember later. Listen, carefully! (*Gently but firmly*) I command you to hide your affliction in all ways that be within your power. You shall deny to no one that you are the true prince, and if your memory should fail you upon any occasion of state, you shall be advised by your uncle, the Lord Hertford.

Tom (*resigned*). The king has spoken. The king shall be obeyed.

King. And now, my child, I go to rest. (*He stands weakly, and* HERTFORD *leads him off, rear.*)

Tom (*wearily, to* ST. JOHN). May it please your lordship to let me rest now?

St. John. So it please Your Highness, it is for you to command and us to obey. But it is wise that you rest, for this evening you must attend the lord mayor's **banquet** in your honor.

[*He pulls the bell cord, and* THREE PAGES *enter and kneel before* TOM.]

Tom. Banquet? (*Terrified, he sits on the couch and reaches for a cup of water, but the* FIRST PAGE *instantly seizes the cup, drops to one knee, and serves it to him.* TOM *starts to take off*

170

180

190

VOCABULARY DEVELOPMENT

affliction (ə·flik′shən) *n.:* illness; pain; suffering.

IDENTIFY

We know what happened to the Great Seal. Where is it? (Lines 101–102.)

_____

_____

_____

_____

_____

WORD KNOWLEDGE

The word *pages* has multiple meanings. What do you guess it means in line 193?

_____

_____

_____

_____

_____

_____

VOCABULARY DEVELOPMENT

banquet (baŋ′kwət) *n.:* elaborate meal; feast.

impostor (im·päs′tər) *n.:*
person who pretends to be
someone or something that
he or she is not.

This is the end of the first
scene. Pause here to retell
what has happened so far in
the plot.

_____

_____

_____

_____

_____

_____

_____

_____

_____

_____

_____

_____

_____

_____

_____

his boots, but the SECOND PAGE *stops him and does it for him.*
He tries to remove his cape and gloves, and the THIRD PAGE
200 *does it for him.*) I wonder that you do not try to breathe for
me also! (*Lies down cautiously.* PAGES *cover him with a robe,*
then back away and exit.)

St. John (*to* HERTFORD, *as he enters*). Plainly, what do
you think?

Hertford. Plainly, this. The king is near death, my nephew
the Prince of Wales is clearly mad and will mount the
throne mad. God protect England, for she will need it!

St. John. Does it not seem strange that madness could so
change his manner from what it used to be? It troubles
210 me, his saying he is not the prince.

Hertford. Peace, my lord! If he were an **impostor** and
called himself the prince, that would be natural. But was
there ever an impostor who, being called prince by the
king and court, denied it? Never! This is the true prince
gone mad. And tonight all London shall honor him.

[HERTFORD *and* ST. JOHN *exit.* TOM *sits up, looks around*
helplessly, then gets up.]

Tom. I should have thought to order something to eat.
(*Sees a bowl of nuts on the table*) Ah! Here are some nuts!
220 (*Looks around, sees the Great Seal in the armor, takes it out,*
looks at it curiously) This will make a good nutcracker. (*He*
takes the bowl of nuts, sits on the couch, and begins to crack
nuts with the Great Seal and eat them as curtain falls.)

Scene 2

Time: Later that night.

Setting: A street in London near Offal Court.

At Rise: PRINCE limps in, dirty and untidy. He looks around wearily. Several VILLAGERS pass by, pushing against him.

Prince. I have never seen this poor section of London. I
230 must be near Offal Court. If only I can find it before I drop!

[JOHN CANTY *steps out of crowd, seizes* PRINCE *roughly.*]

Canty. Out at this time of night, and I warrant you haven't brought a farthing home! If that is the case and I do not break all the bones in your miserable body, then I am not John Canty!

Prince (*eagerly*). Oh, are you his father?

Canty. *His* father? I am *your* father, and—

Prince. Take me to the palace at once, and your son will be
240 returned to you. The king, my father, will make you rich beyond your wildest dreams. Oh, save me, for I am indeed the Prince of Wales.

Canty (*staring in amazement*). Gone stark mad! But mad or not, I'll soon find where the soft places lie in your bones. Come home! (*Starts to drag* PRINCE *off*)

Prince (*struggling*). Let me go! I am the Prince of Wales, and the king shall have your life for this!

Canty (*angrily*). I'll take no more of your madness! (*Raises stick to strike, but* PRINCE *struggles free and runs off.* CANTY
250 *runs after him.*)

Circle the words that describe the **setting** of Scene 2. How is it different from Scene 1?

_____

_____

_____

_____

_____

_____

_____

_____

What is the prince learning, as Scene 2 ends?

_____

_____

_____

_____

_____

_____

_____

INTERPRET

Pause at line 265. In what way do Tom's actions reveal who he truly is?

_____

_____

_____

_____

_____

_____

_____

_____

_____

IDENTIFY

Pause at line 277. What new problem has come up for Tom?

_____

_____

_____

_____

_____

_____

_____

_____

_____

Scene 3

Setting: Same as Scene 1, with addition of a dining table, set with dishes and goblets, on a raised platform. Thronelike chair is at the head of table.

At Rise: A banquet is in progress. TOM, in royal robes, sits at the head of table, with HERTFORD at his right and ST. JOHN at his left. LORDS and LADIES sit around the table, eating and talking softly.

Tom (_to_ HERTFORD). What is this, my lord? (_Holds up plate_)

260   **Hertford.** Lettuce and turnips, Your Highness.

Tom. Lettuce and turnips? I have never seen them before. Am I to eat them?

Hertford (_discreetly_). Yes, Your Highness, if you so desire.

[TOM _begins to eat food with his fingers. Fanfare of trumpets is heard, and_ HERALD _enters carrying scroll. All turn to look._]

Herald (_reading from scroll_). His Majesty, King Henry VIII, is dead! The king is dead!

[_All rise and turn to_ TOM, _who sits stunned._]

All (_together_). The king is dead. Long live the king! Long

270   live Edward, the king of England! (_All bow to_ TOM. HERALD _bows and exits._)

Hertford (_to_ TOM). Your Majesty, we must call the council. Come, St. John.

[HERTFORD _and_ ST. JOHN _lead_ TOM _off at rear._ LORDS _and_ LADIES _follow, talking among themselves. At gates, down right,_

VILLAGERS *enter and mill about.* PRINCE *enters right, pounds on gates, and shouts.*]

Prince. Open the gates! I am the Prince of Wales! Open, I say! And though I am friendless with no one to help me, I will not be driven from my ground.

280

Miles Hendon (*entering through crowd*). Though you be prince or not, you are indeed a gallant lad and not friendless. Here I stand to prove it, and you might have a worse friend than Miles Hendon.

First Villager. 'Tis another prince in disguise. Take the lad and dunk him in the pond!

[*He seizes* PRINCE, *but* MILES *strikes him with flat of his sword. Crowd, now angry, presses forward threateningly when the fanfare of trumpets is heard offstage.* HERALD, *carrying scroll,*

290

enters up left at gates.]

Herald. Make way for the king's messenger! (*Reading from scroll*) His Majesty, King Henry VIII is dead! The king is dead!

[*He exits right, repeating the message, and* VILLAGERS *stand in stunned silence.*]

Prince (*stunned*). The king is dead!

First Villager (*shouting*). Long live Edward, king of England!

Villagers (*together*). Long live the king! (*Shouting, ad-lib*)

300

Long live King Edward! Heaven protect Edward, king of England!

Circle the word *gallant* in line 283. Then underline lines in the dialogue above that help you figure out the meaning of the word. What might *gallant* mean?

_____

_____

_____

_____

· · · · · · Notes · · · · · ·

_____

_____

_____

_____

_____

_____

_____

_____

_____

_____

_____

_____

_____

Take time to picture the scene described in the **setting.** Draw a box around the descriptions. How is the setting different from Offal Court?

_____

_____

_____

_____

_____

_____

_____

_____

_____

Miles (*taking* PRINCE *by arm*). Come, lad, before the crowd remembers us. I have a room at the inn, and you can stay there. (*He hurries off with stunned* PRINCE.)

[TOM, *led by* HERTFORD, *enters courtyard up rear.* VILLAGERS *see them.*]

Villagers (*together*). Long live the king! (*They fall to their knees as curtains close.*)

Scene 4

310 **Setting:** MILES's room at inn. At right is table set with dishes and bowls of food, a chair at each side. At left is bed, with table and chair next to it, and a window. Candle is on table.

At Rise: MILES and PRINCE approach table.

Miles. I have had a hot supper prepared. I'll bet you're hungry, lad.

Prince. Yes, I am. It's kind of you to let me stay with you, Miles. I am truly Edward, king of England, and you shall not go unrewarded. (*Sits at table*)

320 **Miles** (*to himself*). First he called himself prince, and now king. Well, I will humor him. (*Starts to sit*)

Prince (*angrily*). Stop! Would you sit in the presence of the king?

Miles (*surprised, standing up quickly*). I beg your pardon, Your Majesty. I was not thinking. (*Stares uncertainly at* PRINCE, *who sits at table expectantly.* MILES *starts to uncover dishes of food, serves* PRINCE, *and fills glasses.*)

Prince. Miles, you have a gallant way about you. Are you nobly born?

330 **Miles.** My father is a baronet, Your Majesty.

Prince. Then you also must be a baronet.

Miles (*shaking his head*). My father banished me from home seven years ago, so I fought in the wars. I was taken prisoner, and I have spent the past seven years in prison. Now I am free, and I am returning home.

Prince. You must have been shamefully wronged! But I will make things right for you. You have saved me from injury and possible death. Name your reward and if it be within the compass of my royal power, it is yours.

340 **Miles** (*pausing briefly, then dropping to his knee*). Since Your Majesty is pleased to hold my simple duty worthy of reward, I ask that I and my successors may hold the privilege of sitting in the presence of the king.

Prince (*taking* MILES's *sword, tapping him lightly on each shoulder*). Rise and seat yourself. (*Returns sword to* MILES, *then rises and goes over to bed*)

Miles (*aside*). He should have been born a king. He plays the part to a marvel! If I had not thought of this favor, I might have had to stand for weeks. (*Sits down and begins*

350 *to eat*)

Prince. Sir Miles, you will stand guard while I sleep. (*Lies down and instantly falls asleep*)

Miles. Yes, Your Majesty. (*With a rueful look at his uneaten supper, he stands up.*) Poor little chap. I suppose his mind has been disordered with ill usages. (*Covers* PRINCE *with his cape*) Well, I will be his friend and watch over him. (*Blows out candle, then yawns and sits on chair next to bed, and falls asleep.*)

WORD KNOWLEDGE

What do you guess a *baronet* is (line 331)?

_____

_____

_____

_____

_____

_____

_____

INTERPRET

Is Miles serious here (line 343)?

_____

_____

_____

DECODING TIP

Circle the word *disordered* (line 355). The prefix *dis-* means "not." If the word *disinterested* means "not interested," what does the word *disordered* mean?

_____

_____

_____

_____

Circle the word *lead* (line 364). *Lead* (lēd), meaning "guide," and *lead* (led), meaning "the material pipes are made of," are **homographs**. Homographs are words that are spelled the same and often pronounced the same, but they mean different things.

RETELL

Retell what has happened in Scene 4. What new problems have come up for the prince?

_____

_____

_____

_____

_____

_____

· · · · · · **Notes** · · · · · ·

_____

_____

_____

_____

_____

_____

_____

360 [JOHN CANTY *and* HUGO *appear at window, peer around room, then enter cautiously through window. They lift the sleeping* PRINCE, *staring nervously at* MILES.]

Canty (*in a loud whisper*). I swore the day he was born he would be a thief and a beggar, and I won't lose him now. Lead the way to the camp, Hugo!

[CANTY *and* HUGO, *a thief, carry the* PRINCE *off right, as* MILES *sleeps on and curtain falls.*]

Scene 5

Time: Two weeks later.

Setting: Country village street. May be played before
370 curtain.

Before Rise: VILLAGERS walk about. CANTY, HUGO, and PRINCE enter.

Canty. I will go in this direction. Hugo, keep my mad son with you, and see that he does not escape again! (*Exits*)

Hugo (*seizing* PRINCE *by the arm*). He won't escape! I'll see that he earns his bread today, or else!

Prince (*pulling away*). I will not beg with you, and I will not steal! I have suffered enough in this miserable company of thieves!

380 **Hugo.** You shall suffer more if you do not do as I tell you! (*Raises clenched fist at* PRINCE) Refuse if you dare! (WOMAN *enters, carrying wrapped bundle in a basket on her arm.*) Wait here until I come back. (HUGO *sneaks along after* WOMAN, *then snatches her bundle, runs back to* PRINCE, *and thrusts it into his arms.*) Run after me and call "Stop, thief!" Be sure you lead her astray! (*Runs off.*)

[PRINCE *throws down bundle in disgust.*]

Woman. Help! Thief! Stop, thief! (*Rushes at* PRINCE *and seizes him just as several* VILLAGERS *enter*) You little thief!
390   What do you mean by robbing a poor woman? Somebody bring the constable!

[MILES *enters and watches.*]

First Villager (*grabbing* PRINCE). I'll teach him a lesson, the little villain!

Prince (*struggling*). Unhand me! I did not rob this woman!

Miles (*stepping forth and pushing man back with the flat of his sword*). Let us proceed gently, my friends. This is a matter for the law.

Prince (*springing to* MILES'*s side*). You have come just in
400   time, Sir Miles. Carve this rabble to rags!

Miles. Speak softly. Trust in me and all shall go well.

[CONSTABLE *enters.*]

Constable (*reaching for* PRINCE). Come along, young rascal!

Miles. Gently, good friend. He shall go peaceably to the justice.

Prince. I will not go before a justice! I did not do this thing!

Miles (*taking him aside*). Sire, will you reject the laws of the realm, yet demand that your subjects respect them?

WORD KNOWLEDGE

What do you guess a constable is (line 391)?

_____

_____

_____

INFER

Pause at line 401. What do you think will happen to the prince?

_____

_____

_____

_____

_____

_____

_____

_____

_____

_____

_____

_____

_____

_____

_____

_____

_____

_____

_____

WORD KNOWLEDGE

Circle the words *shilling* and *pence* (line 429). These coins were used in England at the time the story is set.

INTERPRET

What does this detail say about the laws in England at this time (lines 430–432)?

_____

_____

_____

_____

_____

_____

_____

410 **Prince** (*after a pause; calmly*). You are right, Sir Miles. Whatever the king requires a subject to suffer under the law, he will suffer himself while he holds the station of a subject.

[CONSTABLE *leads them off right.* VILLAGERS *follow.*]

Scene 6

Setting: Office of the justice. A high bench is at center.

At Rise: JUSTICE sits behind bench. CONSTABLE enters with MILES and PRINCE, followed by VILLAGERS. WOMAN carries wrapped bundle.

420 **Constable** (*to* JUSTICE). A young thief, your worship, is accused of stealing a dressed pig from this poor woman.

Justice (*looking down at* PRINCE, *then* WOMAN). My good woman, are you absolutely certain this lad stole your pig?

Woman. It was none other than he, your worship.

Justice. Are there no witnesses to the contrary? (*All shake their heads.*) Then the lad stands convicted. (*To* WOMAN) What do you hold this property to be worth?

Woman. Three shillings and eight pence, your worship.

430 **Justice** (*leaning down to* WOMAN). Good woman, do you know that when one steals a thing above the value of thirteen pence, the law says he shall hang for it?

Woman (*upset*). Oh, what have I done? I would not hang the poor boy for the whole world! Save me from this, your worship. What can I do?

Justice (*gravely*). You may revise the value, since it is not yet written in the record.

Woman. Then call the pig eight pence, your worship.

Justice. So be it. You may take your property and go.

440 [WOMAN *starts off and is followed by* CONSTABLE. MILES *follows them cautiously down right.*]

Constable (*stopping* WOMAN). Good woman, I will buy your pig from you. (*Takes coins from his pocket*) Here is eight pence.

Woman. Eight pence! It cost me three shillings and eight pence.

Constable. Indeed! Then come back before his worship and answer for this. The lad must hang!

Woman. No! No! Say no more. Give me the eight pence
450 and hold your peace.

[CONSTABLE *hands her coins and takes pig.* WOMAN *exits, angrily.* MILES *returns to bench.*]

Justice. The boy is sentenced to a fortnight in the common jail. Take him away, Constable! (JUSTICE *exits.*)

[PRINCE *gives* MILES *a nervous glance.*]

Miles (*following* CONSTABLE). Good sir, turn your back a moment and let the poor lad escape. He is innocent.

Constable (*outraged*). What? You say this to me? Sir, I arrest you in—
460 **Miles.** Do not be so hasty! (*Slyly*) The pig you have purchased for eight pence may cost you your neck, man.

Constable (*laughing nervously*). Ah, but I was merely jesting with the woman, sir.

· · · · · · · Notes · · · · · · ·

INTERPRET

Pause at line 444. What is the constable up to here?

INTERPRET

Why is no one looking for the prince (lines 476–477)?

_____

_____

_____

_____

_____

_____

_____

_____

_____

_____

_____

_____

_____

_____

Miles. Would the justice think it a jest?

Constable. Good sir! The justice has no more sympathy with a jest than a dead corpse! (*Perplexed*) Very well, I will turn my back and see nothing! But go quickly! (*Exits*)

Miles (*to* PRINCE). Come, my liege. We are free to go. And that band of thieves shall not set hands on you again.

470   I swear it!

Prince (*wearily*). Can you believe, Sir Miles, that in the last fortnight, I, the king of England, have escaped from thieves and begged for food on the road? I have slept in a barn with a calf! I have washed dishes in a peasant's kitchen and narrowly escaped death. And not once in all my wanderings did I see a courier searching for me! Is it not matter for commotion and distress that the head of state is gone?

Miles (*sadly, aside*). Still busy with his pathetic dream. (*To* PRINCE) It is strange indeed, my liege. But come, I will

480   take you to my father's home in Kent. There you may rest in a house with seventy rooms! I am all impatient to be home again!

[*They exit,* MILES *cheerful,* PRINCE *puzzled, as curtains close.*]

Scene 7

Setting: Village jail. Bare stage, with barred window on one wall.

At Rise: TWO PRISONERS, in chains, are onstage. JAILER shoves MILES and PRINCE, in chains, onstage. They struggle and protest.

490   **Miles.** But I tell you, I *am* Miles Hendon! My brother, Sir Hugh, has stolen my bride and my estate!

IDENTIFY

Where are the prince and Miles in Scene 7? What new complication has occurred?

_____

_____

_____

_____

Jailer. Be silent! Sir Hugh will see that you pay well for claiming to be his dead brother and for assaulting him in his own house! (*Exits*)

Miles (*sitting with head in hands*). Oh, my dear Edith . . . now wife to my brother, Hugh, against her will, and my poor father . . . dead!

First Prisoner. At least you have your life, sir. I am to be hanged for killing a deer in the king's park.

500   **Second Prisoner.** And I must hang for stealing a yard of cloth to dress my children.

Prince (*moved; to* PRISONERS). When I mount the throne, you shall all be free. And the laws that have dishonored you shall be swept from the books. (*Turning away*) Kings should go to school to learn their own laws and be merciful.

First Prisoner. What does the lad mean? I have heard that the king is mad, but merciful.

Second Prisoner. He is to be crowned at Westminster

510   tomorrow.

Prince (*violently*). King? What king, good sir?

First Prisoner. Why, we have only one, his most sacred majesty, King Edward VI.

Second Prisoner. Whether he be mad or not, his praises are on all men's lips. He has saved many innocent lives, and plans to destroy the cruelest laws that oppress people.

Prince (*turning away, shaking his head*). How can this be? Surely it is not that little beggar boy!

[SIR HUGH *enters with* JAILER.]

INTERPRET

What is the prince learning about the laws of his own country (lines 498–502)?

_____

_____

_____

_____

_____

_____

INTERPRET

Whom are the prisoners talking about (lines 507–513)?

_____

_____

_____

_____

_____

INTERPRET

What do you learn Tom is doing as king (lines 514–516)?

_____

_____

_____

_____

_____

_____

_____

RETELL

Retell what has happened to the prince and the pauper in Scene 7.

_____

_____

_____

_____

_____

_____

_____

_____

_____

_____

PREDICT

This scene takes place on coronation day. Who do you think will be crowned the king on this day?

_____

_____

_____

_____

_____

_____

_____

_____

_____

520 **Sir Hugh.** Seize the imposter!

[JAILER _pulls_ MILES _to his feet._]

Miles. Hugh, this has gone far enough!

Sir Hugh. You will sit in the public stocks, and the boy would join you if he were not so young. See to it, jailer, and after two hours, you may release them. Meanwhile, I ride to London for the coronation!

[SIR HUGH _exits and_ MILES _is hustled out by_ JAILER.]

Prince. Coronation! There can be no coronation without me!

530 [_Curtain._]

Scene 8

Time: Coronation Day.

Setting: Outside gates of Westminster Abbey. Throne is center. A bench is near it.

At Rise: LORDS and LADIES crowd abbey. Outside gates, GUARDS drive back cheering VILLAGERS, among them MILES.

Miles (_distraught_). I've lost him! Poor little chap! He has been swallowed up in the crowd!

[_Fanfare of trumpets is heard, then_ HERTFORD, ST. JOHN,
540 LORDS _and_ LADIES _enter slowly, followed by_ PAGES, _one of whom carries the crown on small cushion._ TOM _follows the_

procession, looking about nervously. Suddenly, the PRINCE,
in rags, steps from the crowd, his hand raised.]

Prince. I forbid you to set the crown of England upon that
head. I am the king!

Hertford. Seize the vagabond!

Tom. I forbid it! He *is* the king! (*Kneeling before* PRINCE)
Oh, my lord the king, let poor Tom Canty be the first
to say, "Put on your crown and enter into your own
550   right again."

[HERTFORD *and several* LORDS *look closely at both boys.*]

Hertford. This is strange indeed. (*To* TOM) By your favor,
sir, I wish to ask certain questions of this lad.

Prince. I will answer truly whatever you may ask, my lord.

Hertford. But if you have been well trained, you may
answer my questions as well as our lord the king. I need
definite proof. (*Thinks a moment*) Ah! Where lies the Great
Seal of England? It has been missing for weeks, and only
the true Prince of Wales can say where it lies.

560   **Tom.** Wait! Was the seal round and thick, with letters
engraved on it? (HERTFORD *nods.*) I know where it is, but it
was not I who put it there. The rightful king shall tell you.
(*To* PRINCE) Think, my king, it was the very last thing you
did that day before you rushed out of the palace wearing
my rags.

Prince (*pausing*). I recall how we exchanged clothes, but
have no recollection of hiding the Great Seal.

Tom (*eagerly*). Remember when you saw the bruise on my
hand you ran to the door, but first you hid this thing you
570   call the seal.

IDENTIFY

How does Hertford test
the prince to see if he is
the true king?

_____

_____

_____

_____

_____

_____

_____

_____

_____

_____

_____

_____

_____

_____

_____

_____

_____

_____

_____

_____

_____

_____

_____

_____

Prince (*suddenly*). Ah! I remember! (*To* ST. JOHN) My good St. John, you shall find the Great Seal in the armor that hangs on the wall in my chamber.

[ST. JOHN *hesitates, but at a nod from* TOM *hurries off.*]

Tom (*pleased*). Right, my king! Now the scepter of England is yours again.

[ST. JOHN *returns in a moment with Great Seal, holds it up for all to see.*]

All (*shouting*). Long live Edward, king of England!

580   [TOM *takes off cape and throws it over* PRINCE*'s rags. Trumpet fanfare is heard.* ST. JOHN *takes the crown and places it on the* PRINCE. *All kneel.*]

Hertford. Let the small impostor be flung into the tower!
Prince (*firmly*). I will not have it so. But for him, I would not have my crown. (*To* TOM) My poor boy, how was it you could remember where I hid the seal?
Tom (*embarrassed*). I did not know what it was, my king, and I used it to . . . to crack nuts.

[*All laugh.* MILES *steps forward, staring in amazement.*]

590   **Miles.** Is he really the king, the sovereign of England, and not the poor and friendless Tom o' Bedlam I thought he was? (*Sinks down on bench*) I wish I had a bag to hide my head in!

First Guard (*rushing up to him*). Stand up, you mannerless clown! How dare you sit in the presence of the king!

Prince. Do not touch him! He is my trusty servant, Miles Hendon, who saved me from shame and possible death. For his service, he owns the right to sit in my presence.

Miles (*bowing, then kneeling*). Your Majesty!

600   **Prince.** Rise, Sir Miles. I command that Sir Hugh Hendon, who sits within this hall, be seized and put under lock and key until I have need of him. (*Beckons to* TOM) From what I have heard, Tom Canty, you have governed the realm with royal gentleness and mercy in my absence. Henceforth, you shall hold the honorable title of king's ward! (TOM *kneels and kisses* PRINCE'*s hand.*) And because I have suffered with the poorest of my subjects and felt the cruel force of unjust laws, I pledge myself to a reign of mercy for all!

[*All bow low, then rise.*]

610   **All** (*shouting*). Long live the king! Long live Edward, king of England!

[*Curtain*]

THE END

IDENTIFY

"Tom o' Bedlam" is a term that refers to someone who is mentally ill. What does Miles discover?

_____

_____

_____

_____

_____

_____

INTERPRET

Why was it important for the prince to leave the court and live as a commoner?

_____

_____

_____

_____

_____

_____

_____

_____

_____

_____

OWN THE PLAY

Plot and Setting   Write a scene-by-scene summary of the play. Be sure to indicate where each scene is set. Before you begin writing, fill out the chart on the next page to gather your key events. At the end of your plot summary, tell what message you think is contained in this story about a king who lives for a time as a poor person. (What does he learn?)

_____

_____

_____

_____

_____

_____

_____

_____

_____

KEEPING TRACK

Personal Word List   Record the words you learned from this story in your Personal Word List. Then, say something to a partner using one of those words. Your partner can reply using another word from the list. Continue the conversation until one of you runs out of words— or ways to use them.

Personal Reading Log   Record this selection in your Personal Reading Log. Write a few sentences telling how you think the play would work as a TV series. Give yourself 10 points on the Reading Meter for reading the selection.

Checklist for Standards Mastery   Use the Checklist for Standards Mastery to track your progress in mastering the standards.

The Prince and the Pauper

SETTING & PLOT

Interact with a Literary Text

Plot and Setting Chart   Fill out the chart with details from *The Prince and the Pauper.* First, fill in the eight settings as described in the notes at the beginning of the scenes. Then fill in at least one key event that happened in each setting.

Settings	Play Events
Scene 1:	
Scene 2:	
Scene 3:	
Scene 4:	
Scene 5:	
Scene 6:	
Scene 7:	
Scene 8:	

Chapter 2

Characters
The People You'll Meet

Strategy Launch:
"Character Trace"

LITERARY FOCUS: CHARACTER

A **character** is a person or an animal in a story, play, or other literary work. In some works, such as fairy tales, a fantastic creature such as a dragon could be a character. Most often, however, the characters in literary works are ordinary human beings.

The way in which a writer reveals the personality of a character is called **characterization.** A writer can reveal character in six ways:

1. by describing how the character looks and dresses

2. by letting us "hear" the character speak

3. by showing us how the character acts

4. by letting us know the character's thoughts and feelings

5. by revealing what other people in the story think or say about the character

6. by directly describing the character's personality

A STRATEGY THAT WORKS: "CHARACTER TRACE"

A fun and effective way of tracing a character's development and actions is to color-code as you read. Follow these steps:

》》➡ As you read, highlight in a particular color all the clues that reveal the character traits of the story's main character.

》》➡ Then, use a different color to highlight the main character's actions throughout the story.

》》➡ Finally, choose a different color, and highlight the events that take place at the story's end, or resolution.

Review your work, and look for connections between the character's personality traits and actions. Then, look for connections between the character's actions and the story's ending.

Reading Standard 1.3
Recognize the origins and meanings of frequently used foreign words in English, and use these words accurately in speaking and writing.

Reading Standard 2.4
Clarify an understanding of texts by creating outlines, logical notes, summaries, or reports.

Reading Standard 3.2
Analyze the effect of the qualities of the character (for example, courage or cowardice, ambition or laziness) on the plot and resolution of the conflict.

Practice Read

Growing up can be tough, especially if your father is a karate expert. How can you possibly meet your dad's standards? How can you study martial arts if you hate to fight? The conflict in "Sparring" involves karate, but at the heart of this story is another kind of battle—a struggle we all must face as we learn who we really are.

Here's what you need to know before you begin the story:
- *Sparring* means "to practice fighting."
- *Karate* (kə·rät′ē) is a method of self-defense developed in Japan. Karate experts use their hands, elbows, knees, and feet as weapons.
- Ken's father is an eighth-degree black belt, which makes him a karate expert. He is also a *sensei,* a karate teacher.

Sparring

Richard Cohen

VOCABULARY DEVELOPMENT

karate (kə·rät′ē) *n.:* Japanese system of self-defense.

IDENTIFY

Pause at line 11. Who is telling this story? Circle the character's name. Write two things you have learned about this character.

Ken doe not like karate

"I keep having trouble tying this belt," I said.

"That's because it's still a white belt, Ken," my brother answered. "By the time it's yellow, you'll know how to tie it."

We were getting dressed for **karate** class, and as usual I was putting up a fuss. I hated putting on that stupid white belt every day. Mom washed it at least three times a week. She insisted that it be spotless for Dad. He was the *sensei,* so his kids had to be his best pupils. We had to make a

10 good impression for all the other kids and their parents. We had to show how effective Dad's teaching was.

I didn't feel the same way about it. I would think,
"Hey, I'm your son, why don't you treat me a little *better*
than your other students?" Of course I wouldn't have said
that out loud to Dad. I knew what he would say, and I even
knew that his reasons would be good ones.

I had tried to get out of taking karate in the first place.
"Dad, I don't like to fight. I just want everybody to be nice
to each other. I just want to read books and think. I'm

20 going to be a scientist when I grow up, not a **samurai.**"

Sometimes Dad has a way of smiling without showing
it. He looks like he's **glowering,** and his voice sounds like
an army sergeant's, but there's something behind his eyes
that tells me he's playing.

"In this world, people aren't always nice to each other,"
he scolded. "Even if you hate to fight, you must know how.
If your enemies know you can fight, you won't have to fight
so much."

"Enemies?" I asked. I tried to think of who my enemies

30 were. There were a few kids in school who teased me
because I got such good grades, but most kids I knew were
really nice. "I don't have enemies," I said. "Just friends and
people I'm **neutral** about."

"Ken, that's a good way to be," Dad said, more gently.
"I'm glad you don't like fighting. I hate fighting, too. Do I
ever get into a fight?"

I hadn't thought about that before. "No," I said.

"The only place I fight is in the *dojo.* And I don't fight
much there anymore, either. I just teach. Who would I

40 fight? Is there another eighth-degree black belt in town?"
No, of course there wasn't. There probably wasn't another
martial arts expert on Dad's level within fifty miles. Dad
had studied for something like thirty years to become an

CHARACTER TRACE

Pause at line 16. What does Ken reveal about his personality here? Highlight or circle details in the text that reveal this information.

He does not like Karate

VOCABULARY DEVELOPMENT

samurai (sam′ə·rī′) *n.:* warrior in feudal Japan.

glowering (glou′ər·iŋ) *v.:* staring with sullen anger; scowling.

neutral (noo′trəl) *adj.:* not favoring one side over another; impartial.

WORD KNOWLEDGE

What is the meaning of the word *dojo* (line 38)? Underline the context clues.

Why do you think Ken speaks to his father under his breath (line 54)?

_because It
Did not_

What does Ken mean when he says it "felt good in one way, but not another" (line 65)?

_Ken felt
good because
His_

Underline the clues in this paragraph that help you figure out the meaning of *kata*.

eighth-degree black belt. His knuckles had big calluses on them from doing hundreds of knuckle pushups every day since he was—well, since he was about my age.

"Okay, okay," I said. "I come to lessons every day, right? And I'm pretty good at it, right?"

"You're not bad," he admitted, "but your belt could

50 be tied better." He undid the knot in my belt and retied it. Magically, it was perfect: snug but not cramped, giving me just the right amount of breathing space. It felt like it wouldn't come untied in a thousand years.

"How do you do that?" I asked under my breath.

"Remember, I wanted to you to start learning years ago, when your younger brother did. But your mother said not to push you, and *I'd* started late anyway, so it was okay. When you were seven or eight you could handle Kevin because you were so much bigger than he was. But now he's

60 catching up to you and he's a brown belt. It's not right for the younger brother to beat the older one."

"I know," I nodded. The truth was, I sometimes liked to hang around with my brother in the schoolyard because I knew he could protect me if trouble ever broke out. That felt good in one way, but not another.

"Let's go to class," Dad said. And we walked barefoot in our uniforms from our house to Dad's storefront *dojo*, like they would do in Japan, me with my shiny white belt and Dad with his black one that was faded from years of wear.

70 In class, Dad put us through our paces as usual, starting with stretching exercises, then going on to basic punches and kicks and blocks, then simple combinations, then *kata*, the longer forms made up of many combinations of moves. Doing a *kata* is halfway between fighting and dancing, and that's the part I like. I'm in much better

shape than the average twelve-year-old who exercises mainly his fingertips at the remote control.

But after *kata,* I started to get nervous, as always. Sometimes I'm even afraid I'm going to get sick, although I never have. After *kata* comes *kumite*—sparring, practice fighting. You have to spar several two-minute rounds with whatever classmates Dad—I mean *sensei*—assigns you. And in Japan they don't believe in sparring by weight categories. You might have to fight someone much bigger than yourself, or smaller. You might have to fight someone with the same belt color as you, or a higher belt.

My **solution** is, I try not to hurt the other person and I hope he or she notices and doesn't try to hurt me either. I just try to get through two minutes. In a fight, time goes very slowly, especially if you're already exhausted from an hour's hard workout.

This time, Dad matched me against Juana, the green belt who had broken my toe a few months earlier. I don't really mean she broke my toe; I mean I broke my own toe kicking her. It was like trying to kick a tree. Dad let me sit out sparring for two weeks after that, but then he started me in again, simply telling me, "If the toe hurts, don't kick with that foot."

Juana and I circled each other slowly at the beginning of the round. I had seen the higher belts do that sometimes, circling each other to show how patient they were on defense, how they wouldn't just use any old punch or kick but would wait for the right moment to strike. It was a clever way to make ten or fifteen seconds pass harmlessly.

"Come on, make contact!" Dad shouted at us, circling us referee-style. "Try something! Use your combinations! Use what you learn in class!"

80

90

100

CHARACTER TRACE

Highlight or circle details that reveal Ken's feelings. What do his feelings reveal about his character?

_____

_____

_____

_____

WORD KNOWLEDGE

What does *kumite* mean (line 80)? Underline context clues.

_____

_____

VOCABULARY DEVELOPMENT

solution (sə·lo͞o′shən) *n.*: act, method, or process of solving a problem.

CHARACTER TRACE

Highlight or draw a box around Ken's actions during sparring. Highlight in another color or circle Ken's reasons for his actions. In what way do Ken's actions "fit" with his personality?

_____

_____

_____

_____

_____

_____

_____

_____

Why does Ken find it so hard to believe that his dad wants to fight him?

_____

_____

_____

_____

_____

_____

Which detail in the last paragraph reveals Dad's personality as a karate expert? Underline it. Which detail reveals Dad's ordinary personality? Circle it. How do the two differ?

_____

_____

_____

_____

Juana and I gave each other a sheepish smile. We both knew that Dad knew that we'd been slacking off. I punched

110   her with a series of three-punch combinations she could block easily, but it would look as if I was being aggressive. Then I tried an open-hand combination from one of my _kata_, but she just took a step to the side and let it go by. Then I kicked her—with the foot that didn't have the bro-· ken toe—and she caught my foot in midair. She held it there a few seconds, both of us grinning. Then she twirled me down gently to the polished wood floor.

"Time!" Dad called. He looked at us with mild annoyance. "Okay, Ken, now you and me."

120   "What?" I almost choked.

Usually, Dad sparred only with black belts. I remembered one time when he'd come home upset with himself because he'd accidentally bruised a black belt's ribs in sparring. "I used a special soft punch," he'd said. "I guess I misjudged how soft." After that, he became extracautious with students.

"Are you sure you want to do this?" I asked, putting a humorous little quiver into my voice to show that I was a nice guy and didn't want to get him angry. I was hoping

130   that the round had already started and that we could talk through most of it. My hands felt like jelly—extremely heavy jelly.

Dad barked, "_Kumite!_ Fight! Fists tight! Don't drop your arms!"

He called the start of the round, and we began circling. He glared fiercely, the way he always did in the ring. I searched for the look in his eyes that said he might be smiling underneath, but I couldn't find it.

As the senior opponent, he took defense, so he didn't
140 make any moves on me but waited to block whatever I did.
"Hit, hit!" he commanded. I was standing so far away from
him my kicks didn't even reach him.

Then he pulled me closer to him—pulled me by the
belt. The knot he had tied didn't loosen.

"If you don't want to attack," he said, "then defend."

Defend? Did that mean I didn't have to hit? I was
almost too shocked to move when he came toward me. He
punched me in the arm. It must have been the most super-
careful, supersoft punch he had, but it still hurt a little. He
150 punched me in the same place on the other arm. I couldn't
believe Dad really wanted to fight me.

I began shifting left and right to try to get out of his
way. Then he shot out his open hand in a move from one
of my *kata.* I saw the edge of his palm coming at me in
slow motion.

Then I saw his right foot swing upward toward my
chin. That bare, callused foot with its high arch seemed to
take forever in its flight. It took so long that I had time to
swing my arm up and catch his foot, grab it in midair.
160 I stood there, thinking: "I could trip him. I could shove
him backward."

Instead, I let go of his foot and knelt on my knees,
bowing my forehead to the clean, smooth planks of wood
in respect for him.

He pulled me up gently. "The round is over, son."

How had he known I would catch his foot?

Breathing hard, I followed Dad to the water cooler
after class. He handed me a paper cup of cold water. "You
know," he said, "my old teacher in San Francisco was very
170 strict, very traditional. One day he caught me smiling while

CHARACTER
TRACE

Re-read lines 156–183. What
do you learn about Ken
here? Highlight or circle
those details.

Highlight in a third color or put a star next to the events in the story's resolution. What has Ken discovered about himself and his dad?

_____

_____

_____

_____

_____

_____

_____

_____

_____

_____

_____

_____

_____

_____

_____

_____

_____

_____

_____

_____

_____

I was sparring. He blew a fuse. 'No smile, no smile in _kumite!_' As punishment, he made me fight him. Of course he was careful not to hurt me seriously. But he said, 'You think you have no more enemies? _I_ am your enemy!'"

"You're not my enemy," I told Dad.

"I hope not."

"No, really, you're not."

He nodded. "You know something else? You're very talented on defense. Anyone your size, you could have beat
180 with those moves. And you would have beat him without hurting him. Anyone can hurt someone else; it's no trick. Only a master can beat someone without hurting him. How about next week you test for yellow belt?"

I broke into a smile. "Yes!"

"One thing, though. You've got to learn how to tie it right."

He put his arm around me. That evening, for the first time ever, I stayed late to help him lock the school.

OWN THE STORY

PRACTICING THE STANDARDS

Character   Review Ken's character traits that you marked as you read this story. Then, fill out the Character Cluster Chart on the next page. Write a paragraph using that information to analyze Ken's character. Open your paragraph with a statement telling what kind of person you believe Ken is (cruel, kind, peaceful, respectful, cowardly, sneaky, and so on). Then, describe two incidents in the story that support your characterization of Ken.

_____

_____

_____

Write a second paragraph in which you imagine another kind of boy in Ken's place, facing a karate lesson he hates, taught by his father. Tell how the story might have ended if a different kind of boy had been the main character in the story. Here is a framework to follow:

   If the main character had been a kid who was _____, then these events might have happened: _____
   _____.

KEEPING TRACK

Personal Word List   Record the words you learned from this story in your Personal Word List. Circle the words you like the most and want to use in everyday conversation.

Personal Reading Log   As you record this story in your Personal Reading Log, tell whether or not you would recommend it to a friend. Give yourself 4 points on the Reading Meter for completing this story.

Checklist for Standards Mastery   Check your progress in mastering the standards, using the Checklist for Standards Mastery.

Sparring ▪ *Interactive Reading,* page 58

CHARACTER

Interact with a Literary Text

Character Cluster Complete this cluster after you read "Sparring." In the face, write down Ken's character traits. In each box, write down a detail from the story that illustrates each trait.

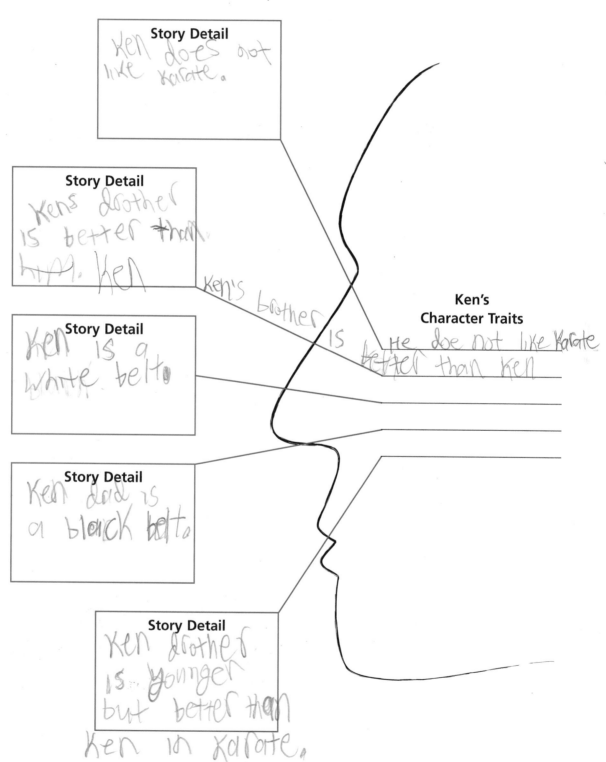

Story Detail

Ken does not like karate.

Story Detail

Kens brother is better than him. Ken

Ken's brother is better than Ken

Story Detail

Ken is a white belt

Ken's Character Traits

He doe not like karate

Story Detail

Ken dad is a black belt.

Story Detail

Ken brother is younger but better than Ken in karate.

Ta-Na-E-Ka

Interact with a Literary Text

Character-and-Conflict Chart Fill out this Character-and-Conflict Chart after you read "Ta-Na-E-Ka." Then, analyze how the main character's personality affects the story's resolution.

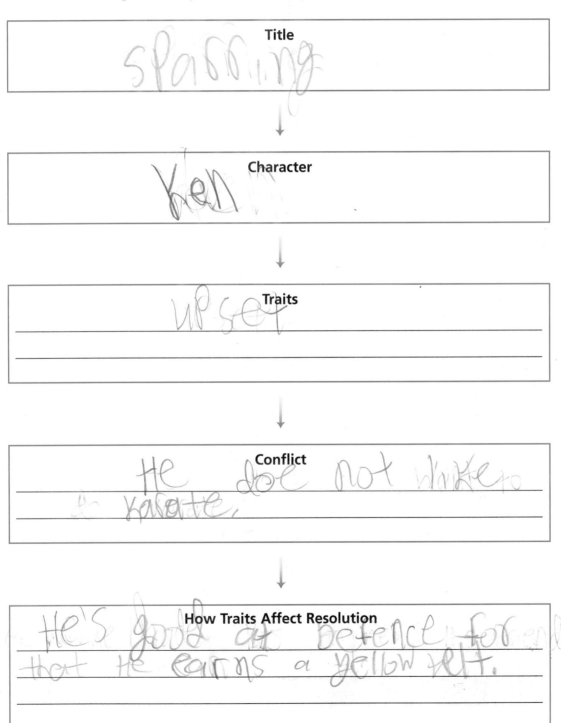

Title

sparring

Character

Ken

Traits

upset

Conflict

He doe not want to karate.

How Traits Affect Resolution

He's good at defence, for that he earns a yellow belt.

The Wind People

Interact with an Informational Text

Outline Organizer   Good readers often outline informational texts to be sure they understand the facts. Complete the outline below. Note the topic, subtopics, and supporting details in "Facts About the Kaw." Each topic is represented by Roman numerals (I, II, III, etc.). Subtopics are shown by capital letters (A, B, C, etc.). Supporting details are shown by Arabic numerals (1, 2, 3, etc.). The first section has been done for you.

Title: "Facts About the Kaw: The Wind People"
I. April 23, 2000, news story
    A. William Mehojah died
        1. Last of the Kaw
        2. 82 years old
    B. Kaw people gone forever
II.
    A.
        1.
        2.
    B.
        1.
        2.
III.
    A.
        1.
        2.
    B.
        1.
        2.
IV.
    A.
        1.
        2.
    B.
        1.
        2.
    C.
        1.
        2.

The Bracelet

Interact with a Literary Text

Character Map   "The Bracelet" is told from the point of view of a particular character. During the course of the story, you learn about that character's actions and her thoughts and feelings. After you read "The Bracelet," fill in this Character Map with details that describe what you learn about the narrator.

Details showing her thoughts:
_____
_____
_____
_____
_____
_____

Details showing her emotions:
_____
_____
_____
_____
_____
_____

Details revealing her actions:
_____
_____
_____
_____
_____
_____
_____

Wartime Mistakes, Peacetime Apologies

Interact with an Informational Text

Time Line   A **time line** is a kind of chart that shows events in time order. In a time line main events are listed from the beginning to the end. As you read "Wartime Mistakes, Peacetime Apologies," fill out this time line with events from the article.

Time Line

Go for Broke

for use with
Holt Literature and Language Arts,
page 88

CLARIFYING
TEXT

Interact with an Informational Text

Notes Organizer Effective notes include only the main idea and key supporting details in a passage. As you take notes, put the information in your own words. You can use the author's words, too—but be sure to put quotation marks around them to show that you have copied them directly from the text.

As you read "Go for Broke," fill out the following note cards.

Main Idea
442nd Regimental Combat Team
Details
• **What?**

• **Who?**

• **When?**

Main Idea
Friction between mainland and Hawaiian soldiers
Details
• **Mainland attitude:**

• **Hawaiian attitude:**

Main Idea
Men work together
Details
• **What?**

• **How?**

Main Idea
442nd was a very special unit
Details
• **What?**

• **How?**

Main Idea
About Frank Hachiya
Details
• **Who?**

• **What?**

• **Direct quote:**

Graphic Organizer 71

Blanca Flor

Interact with a Literary Text

Story Frame and Character Chart   After you read *Blanca Flor,* complete the following chart to review the play's plot. In item 5, note how the outcome of the story would have been different if the characters had been different kinds of people.

1. In this story the main characters are: (1) _____

   (2) _____

   (3) _____

2. Their character traits are:

   Character 1: _____

   _____

   Character 2: _____

   _____

   Character 3: _____

   _____

3. The problem starts when:

   _____

   _____

4. The problem is resolved at the end because:

   _____

   _____

   _____

5. If the main characters had been different, the following endings could have occurred:

   Ending 1: _____

   _____

   Ending 2: _____

   _____

Literature

AUTHOR STUDY

Yoshiko Uchida wrote two books about her experiences in internment camps during World War II. She also wrote versions of traditional Japanese folk tales as well as novels for young adults.

Uchida was born in California to Japanese parents. Her firsthand account of life in an internment camp during World War II opened the eyes of many Americans to the unfair treatment of Japanese Americans during the war.

In her writing, Uchida often explored the issue of Asian American identity. She explained it this way: "Through my books I hope to give young Asian Americans a sense of their past and to reinforce their self-esteem and self-knowledge. At the same time, I want to dispel the stereotypic image still held by many non-Asians about the Japanese and write about them as real people."

BEFORE YOU READ

Have you ever wondered what it would be like to visit the land of your ancestors? Would you like to know how it feels to live in a culture other than the one you were born into? In "Foreigner in Japan," you will read a true story of someone who tries to find her place in another world.

Here's what you need to know before you begin the story:
- This is a true story. It takes place in 1933.
- Before airplane travel became commonplace, U.S. citizens traveled to Europe, Asia, and the Pacific by ocean liner.
- World War II disrupted travel between Europe, Asia, and the United States. As a result, years passed before many people were able to see their family and friends who lived abroad.
- This selection is a chapter from an autobiography, the story of a writer's own life. This autobiography is called *The Invisible Thread.*

**Reading
Standard 3.2**
Analyze the effect of the qualities of the character (for example, courage or cowardice, ambition or laziness) on the plot and resolution of the conflict.

Foreigner in Japan

Yoshiko Uchida

IDENTIFY

Pause at line 13. Underline at least three details that tell you about the narrator.

_____

_____

_____

_____

_____

_____

_____

_____

_____

I was twelve when we sailed on the *Chichibu Maru* to visit my Grandmother Umegaki in Japan. My parents had taken me once before when I was two, but since I didn't remember that visit, I felt it didn't count. This time we were taking along our Los Angeles grandmother for her first visit to Japan since her departure so many years before.

I considered this my first ocean voyage, although I had gone often with my parents to see friends off at the drafty San Francisco piers. We would be among dozens

10 of well-wishers crowding on board the ship to visit friends in staterooms bursting with luggage, flowers, and baskets of fruit. Caught up in the festive excitement, I used to wish *I* were the one sailing off to Japan.

When one of the cabin boys traveled through the corridors beating the brass **gong,** however, I always felt a cold chill run down my spine.

VOCABULARY DEVELOPMENT

gong (gäŋ) *n.:* slightly convex metallic disk that gives a loud, resonant tone when struck. This word comes from the Malay language.

FLUENCY

Read the boxed passage aloud. As you read, capture the excitement of the scene by emphasizing words like *hurried* and *shriek*.

"Come on, Papa," I would urge. "That's the 'all ashore that's going ashore' gong. Let's go."

But Papa continued talking with his friends, totally

20 ignoring the urgent banging of the gong. By the time the passengers moved to the deck to throw rolls of colored tape to their friends below, the rest of us hurried down the narrow gangplank.

Papa, however, was still on board, smiling and waving from the upper deck. He would throw a roll of blue tape to my sister and a pink one to me.

"Come on, Papa!" we would shriek. "Hurry up!"

"Foreigner in Japan" from *The Invisible Thread* by Yoshiko Uchida. Copyright © 1991 by Yoshiko Uchida. Reprinted by permission of *Simon & Schuster Books for Young Readers, an imprint of Simon & Schuster Children's Publishing Division.*

Finally, minutes before the gangplank was pulled up, he would **saunter** down, calmly saying, "Don't worry, they would never sail with me still on board."

30

Papa had a permanent dock pass to board the ships, and he came so often to meet friends or to see people off that he seemed to know everybody. For him the ships were familiar territory, but to me they were exotic, majestic, and slightly mysterious.

But this time, at last, I didn't have to worry about Papa getting caught on board a departing ship. This time we were passengers. *We* were the ones sailing to Japan. *We* were the ones everybody had come to see off. The baskets of fruits

40

and flowers in the stateroom from Papa's business friends were for *us*. So were the gardenia corsages and the bouquets of flowers.

Now *I* was the one throwing rolls of tape down to our friends on the pier and waving and calling goodbye.

As the ship slowly eased out into San Francisco Bay, the wind tugged at the streamers I held in my hand. But I wouldn't let go. I hung on until the ship snatched them from the hands of the friends we'd left behind, and I watched as they fluttered off into the sky looking like a

50

flying rainbow.

"Hey, we're really going!" I said to Keiko. "We're really going to Japan!"

But ten minutes after we had sailed through the Golden Gate, the ship began to pitch and roll, and my happy grin soon disappeared. The ever-present smell of **bouillon** I'd found so inviting earlier now made me turn green. All of us except Papa took to our bunks and stayed there for the next four days.

Yoshiko Uchida **75**

VOCABULARY DEVELOPMENT

saunter (sôn′tər) v.: walk about idly; stroll.

WORD KNOWLEDGE

The words *corsages* (kôr·sazh′əs) and *bouquets* (bō·kāz′) (line 41) are from the French language.

· · · · · · Notes · · · · · ·

_____

_____

_____

_____

_____

_____

_____

VOCABULARY DEVELOPMENT

bouillon (bool′yän′) n.: clear broth, usually of beef. This word also originated in the French language.

CHARACTER TRACE

Circle or highlight all the words in lines 59–76 that describe Yoshiko and her sister, Keiko.

WORD KNOWLEDGE

Sukiyaki (line 70) is a Japanese dish that is cooked quickly and can be prepared right at the table.

DECODING TIP

Chopsticks (line 76) is a compound word, a word made up of two or more smaller words. Break this word into its parts to define it. Then, check your definition in the dictionary.

DECODING TIP

You can often figure out the pronunciation and meaning of a new word by looking at its prefix or suffix. Draw a line underneath the word *puppet* (line 88). Circle the word *puppeteer.* The suffix *-eer* changes its meaning. Say this word aloud. What do you think it means?

_____

_____

_____

_____

_____

_____

When we were finally able to join Papa in the dining salon, our waiters were so pleased to have a full table to serve, they broke into applause as we appeared.

By this time all shipboard activities were in full swing, and Keiko and I worked hard to catch up. We played shuffleboard and deck tennis. We had hot bouillon served by white-coated boys who rolled the soup cart up and down the decks each morning at ten o'clock. We went to every afternoon tea, stuffing ourselves with little cakes and fancy sandwiches, and amazingly had room for a big dinner in the evening.

One night there was a sukiyaki party on the lantern-festooned deck. For once I didn't have to set the table and neither Mama nor Papa had to cook. *We* were the company, and I was delighted that the ship's waiters did all the work. The deans of women of Mills College and the University of California in Berkeley happened to sit at our table, and we showed them how to use chopsticks and eat Japanese food.

"You'll have to send one of your daughters to each of us," they teased Mama and Papa. And that is exactly what happened. Keiko went to Mills College and I went to UC Berkeley.

The day a costume party was scheduled, Keiko and I worked all day to prepare for it. She wore a pair of Papa's pants and suspenders, drew a mustache on her face, and squashed one of his hats on her head.

I dressed up like a doll, painting round circles of rouge on my cheeks. We tied strings to my wrists and ankles, attached them to two sticks, and went to the costume party as Tony the puppeteer and his doll puppet. We were beside ourselves when we won first prize.

90   By the time we neared Yokohama, I was so charmed with the good life on board the *Chichibu Maru,* I didn't want to get off.

Mama, on the other hand, could hardly wait. The morning we docked, she was up early. As our ship slid noiselessly alongside the pier, she impulsively pushed open one of the cabin's portholes to scan the faces on the pier.

Suddenly I heard her shout, "Oka San! Mother!"

It was a voice I had never heard before—filled with the longing and anguish of years of separation and a joy
100   mingled with tears.

This was a Mama I'd never known before. For the first time in my life, I saw her not just as Mama who cooked and washed and sewed for us, but as someone's daughter. She was a person with a life and feelings of her own quite apart from mine.

For a fleeting moment I thought I understood the **turmoil** of her uprooted soul. But in the excitement of landing, the feeling passed, and she became once more the Mama I had always known.

110   None of us ever dreamed then of the terrible war that would separate her from her family and homeland forever.

It was a wonder to me how Mama could have left behind such a nice family and so many good friends. We met them all while we were in Japan.

Grandmother Umegaki was a plump, friendly woman with a quiet manner that **belied** her strength. It was that hidden strength that gave her the courage to send her oldest daughter to America, and I believe my mother had a good measure of it in herself as well.

INFER

Pause at line 105. How does Yoshiko's view of Mama change? How does Yoshiko now see her mother?

_____

_____

_____

_____

_____

VOCABULARY DEVELOPMENT

turmoil (tʉr′moil′) *n.:* commotion; upset.

belied (bə·līd′) *v.:* gave a false idea of; misrepresented; disguised.

INFER

What might be the "turmoil" in Mama's "uprooted soul" (line 107)? What can't she have?

_____

_____

_____

_____

_____

_____

INFER

What does Yukio's choice of a gift for Yoshiko suggest (line 122)?

_____

_____

_____

_____

_____

_____

_____

_____

_____

WORD KNOWLEDGE

The word *tatami* (ta·ta′mē) is italicized because it comes from the Japanese language. In traditional Japanese households, *tatami* mats are used for sleeping.

VOCABULARY DEVELOPMENT

mosquito (mə·skēt′ō) *n.:* any of a large family of two-winged insects, the females of which have skin-piercing mouth parts used to extract blood from animals. *Mosquito* comes originally from the Spanish language.

120   Mama's brother Yukio was a silversmith who made all sorts of beautiful gifts for us—a copper hanging engraved with my mother's favorite wildflower, a silver pin of my dog for me, and an engraved silver buckle for Keiko.

Another brother, Minoru, was a college professor who was writing several scholarly books and also painted quite well. I wasn't sure how to behave in front of Seizo, the brother who had become a priest, but he turned out to be the most fun of all and a skilled artist as well.

All three uncles wrote wonderful illustrated letters to
130   my sister and me until the war ended their correspondence, and the life of one uncle as well.

Mama's only sister, Kiyo, was a widow who had lost a baby son and lived with her only daughter. They both seemed permanently saddened by their losses and had none of the easy laughter that dwelled in Mama and her brothers.

We were surrounded by family in Japan, since two of Papa's sisters had returned to live there as well. One lived in Osaka and the other in Tokyo. Wherever we went, we
140   seemed to have a place to stay. Our relatives simply spread out some quilts for us on the *tatami* mat, enclosed us in great billowing **mosquito** netting, and we were set for the night.

One of the happiest times for my parents and Grandma Uchida was our stay in Kyoto, with its temples and hills and their beloved Doshisha University. The first friends Obah San wanted to visit were Dr. and Mrs. Learned, for whom she had worked so long ago.

They seemed so old and frail to me, like pale white
150   shadows in a sea of Japanese faces. They showered us with love and affection, and gave Keiko and me the American

names we had long wanted to have. Keiko was named Grace, and I was given the name Ruth. But somehow it didn't make me as happy as I thought it would. I just didn't feel like a Ruth, and I never used the name.

Keiko and I tolerated innumerable long dinners and lunches with our parents' many friends, but when things got too boring, we would count the number of times people bowed to each other. In Japan no one hugged or shook hands. They just bowed. And bowed. And bowed some more. My mother set the record, with thirteen bows exchanged in one encounter.

What I liked best was going to temples and shrines on festival days, when the celebration, with costumed dancers and booming drums, was like a holiday parade and carnival rolled into one.

But I liked the celebration of Obon (All Souls' Day), too. That was when the spirits of the dead were believed to return home, and some families lit tiny bonfires at their front gate to welcome them at dusk. Inside, there were tables laden with all sorts of delicious dishes, prepared especially for the returning spirits.

In Japan the dead seemed to blend in with the living, as though there were no great black separation by death. And I found that a comforting thought.

Sometimes we climbed wooded hills that rose behind ancient temples to visit graveyards filled with moss-covered tombstones. And one day we went to pay our respects to our samurai grandfathers whom we had never known. Using small wooden scoops, we poured cold water on their tombstones to refresh their spirits, and left them handfuls of summer lilies.

INFER

For a long time, Yoshiko had wanted to have an American name. Why, then, isn't she happy when she finally gets one (lines 152–155)?

_____

_____

_____

_____

_____

INTERPRET

Pause at line 162. How does Yoshiko seem to regard the custom of bowing? What does her attitude reveal about her character?

_____

_____

_____

_____

_____

_____

_____

_____

_____

_____

_____

kimonos (kə·mō′nəz) *n.:*
loose outer garments with
short, wide sleeves and a
sash, part of the traditional
costume of Japanese men
and women.

The word *kimono* is now
commonly used in English.

CHARACTER
TRACE

What was the conflict
Yoshiko faced as she was
growing up? How does she
seem to resolve it? Highlight
or circle the details giving
you this information.

_____

_____

_____

_____

_____

_____

_____

_____

_____

_____

_____

_____

_____

_____

I wondered what they thought of us—their grandchildren from far-off America, dressed in strange clothing
and babbling in a foreign tongue. I hoped they liked us.

Once we stayed with an uncle and some cousins at a
rural inn, where at the end of the day, we all went to the
communal tub to have a pleasant soak together.

Then, wearing cool cotton **kimonos** provided by the
190   inn, we gathered around the low table, where the maids
brought us miso soup, broiled eel, and slivered cucumber
on individual black lacquer trays.

After dinner we sat on the veranda and had sweet
bean-paste cakes and tea, watching a full moon rise over
the mountains. The talk was gentle, and whenever it
stopped, we could hear the swarms of cicadas in the pine
trees buzzing in unison like some demented chorus.

As I sat watching the fireflies darting about in the
darkness, I thought maybe I could get quite used to living
200   in Japan. Here, at least, I looked like everyone else. Here, I
blended in and wasn't always the one who was different.

And yet, I knew I was really a foreigner in Japan. I had
felt like a complete idiot when an old woman asked me to
read a bus sign for her, and I had to admit I couldn't read
Japanese.

Deep down inside, where I really dwelled, I was thor-
oughly American. I missed my own language and the casual
banter with friends. I longed for hot dogs and chocolate
sodas and bathrooms with plumbing.

210   But the sad truth was, in America, too, I was perceived
as a foreigner.

So what was I anyway, I wondered. I wasn't really totally American, and I wasn't totally Japanese. I was a mixture
of the two, and I could never be anything else.

OWN THE STORY

PRACTICING THE STANDARDS

Character   Re-read the final paragraph of "Foreigner in Japan." Then, fill out the chart below, showing those parts of Yoshiko's character that she feels are American and those that seem Japanese.

Yoshiko

American Traits	Japanese Traits

KEEPING TRACK

Personal Word List   As you read this selection, you collected several words that come from other languages. Add them to your Personal Word List. In addition, add other words from the selection that you particularly liked.

Personal Reading Log   Did you enjoy this true story? Write your reaction to it as you enter it in your Personal Reading Log. You've just earned 4 points on the Reading Meter for completing it.

Checklist for Standards Mastery   You're making progress. Use the Checklist for Standards Mastery to see how far you have come in mastering the standards.

Foreigner in Japan ■ *Interactive Reading,* page 74

Go Beyond a Literary Text

Author Time Line   As you learned from "Foreigner in Japan,"
Yoshiko Uchida had a rich, interesting, and sometimes difficult life.
Create a time line showing at least ten key events in her life, including
her birth, her education, her deportation to an internment camp, the
publication of her major books, and her death. You can find
information about Yoshiko Uchida in the reference text *Something
About the Author* or on-line at *Contemporary Authors On-line.*

Year/Event	Year/Event	Year/Event	Year/Event

Year/Event	Year/Event	Year/Event	Year/Event

Year/Event	Year/Event	Year/Event	Year/Event

Information

BEFORE YOU READ

You've probably come across the term *samurai* before. Maybe you know that it has something to do with warriors, or with martial arts, or with Japan. But did you know that the samurai go all the way back to the tenth century? If you're wondering why a way of life *that* old is still a part of Japanese culture, you'll appreciate this informative article.

Reading Standard 2.4
Clarify an understanding of texts by creating outlines, logical notes, summaries, or reports.

from Faces: The Magazine About People

The Samurai

Paul Varley

A **samurai** is "one who serves." In ancient times, the term described lowly servants supplied to the households of elderly people by the Japanese government. Later it became one of several terms used for members of the warrior class that developed in the **provinces** of Japan during the tenth century. Although the word *bushi* ("military gentry") appears most often in old official records, the term *samurai* has become widely known among people outside Japan. Today the Japanese themselves also use this word when
10 they refer to the fighting men of their country before modern times.

   The samurai first appeared in the eastern provinces of Japan—that is, in the Kantō plain that contains the modern city of Tokyo. In the tenth century, the central government consisted of court officials in the service of the emperor in Kyoto, then the capital city. The samurai arose because these officials paid little attention to affairs in the provinces

TEXT STRUCTURE

Locate the author's name and the captions in this article. Circle them.

VOCABULARY DEVELOPMENT

samurai (sam′ə·rī′) *n.:* Japanese warriors. Note the meaning of the word given in the text.

provinces (präv′ins·əz) *n.:* administrative divisions of a country.

· · · · · · Notes · · · · · · ·

_____

_____

_____

DECODING TIP

You can often find a clue to the meaning of an unfamiliar new word by breaking it up into smaller words that you know. Look at the word *oversight* (line 19). What smaller words do you see? Circle the words. Use the meanings of the smaller words to help you define *oversight*.

VOCABULARY DEVELOPMENT

frontier (frun·tir′) *n.:* developing, often still uncivilized or lawless region of a country.

shogun (shō′gun′) *n.:* any of the military governors of Japan who, until 1868, had absolute rule.

WORD KNOWLEDGE

Underline the definitions of these words, which are given right in context on this page: *vassals; shogunate; serfs.*

FLUENCY

Read the boxed passage aloud as if you were reading to a group of classmates who are taking notes as you read. Make sure you emphasize the words and phrases that are given special treatment in the paragraph—those in italics, in parentheses, and within quote marks.

except for making sure that they received the income from their agricultural estates. Without effective oversight from the Kyoto court, men in the provinces took up arms to become a professional military class.

In that period, the Kanto was a **frontier** area, rich in farmland and especially in need of men to maintain order as the territory developed. The samurai in the Kantō and elsewhere organized themselves into bands whose members were joined together as lords and vassals (followers under a lord's protection), much like the knights of medieval Europe.

Although Japan is far from Europe and had no contact with Europeans until the mid-sixteenth century, the Japanese developed a system of organizing society remarkably similar to that of medieval Europe. This system, known as feudalism, took root in Japan with the founding of its first military government, or shogunate (government headed by a ***shogun,*** or "great general"), in 1185. As in Europe, feudalism in Japan was based almost entirely on agriculture. Land divided into estates, or manors, was worked by peasants called serfs who had to remain on the land and could not move about freely. Feudalism also featured a ruling warrior or military class made up of lords and their vassals.

In samurai society, a vassal was supposed to give absolute, unquestioning loyalty to his lord and even be prepared to die for him in battle. In fact, the relationship between a lord and vassal went both ways: In return for performing military service, a vassal expected rewards and protection from his lord. The idea of the loyal, self-sacrificing vassal was often ignored. Many vassals,

Frightening the enemy was part of the strategy of the samurai. In battle, these warriors wore fierce-looking masks and fought fiercely, too.

50 especially in the **tumultuous** fifteenth and sixteenth centuries, betrayed or rebelled against their lords.

The samurai continued to rule Japan until the beginning of the modern period in 1868. During the time of the last military government, the shogunate of the Tokugawa family (1600–1867), Japan remained almost entirely at peace. Deprived of their profession of warfare, many

VOCABULARY DEVELOPMENT

tumultuous
(tōō·mul′chōō·wəs) *adj.:* full of disturbance or upheaval; unsettled.

IDENTIFY

Re-read lines 51–60. According to the article, what happened to the samurai during the shogunate of the Tokugawa family? Underline this information. How did this historical happening contribute to the development of the martial art that is still practiced today?

_____

_____

_____

_____

_____

_____

_____

_____

_____

_____

_____

_____

_____

_____

_____

_____

samurai lived idly on payments provided by their lords. Others entered government service or professions such as teaching. As a substitute for actual fighting, the samurai of the Tokugawa period developed the martial arts still

60   practiced by many people in Japan and elsewhere.

Members of the samurai class overthrew the Tokugawa shogunate and brought Japan into the Western-dominated modern world in the late nineteenth century. Although samurai status was officially dissolved in the 1870s, many people of samurai background continued to provide leadership in modernizing Japan. Moreover, samurai values remained deeply ingrained in the behavior of many Japanese at least through World War II.

This samurai was photographed in 1860.

PRACTICING THE STANDARDS

Clarify the Text   Re-read "The Samurai." As you read, highlight with a marker or circle the most important information revealed in the article. Then, use another color highlighter to call out or draw a box around supporting details. Create an outline of the article on which you plot its main ideas and details. Your outline should follow this style:

    I. Major topic
       A. Main idea
          1. Detail
          2. Detail
       B. Main idea
          1. Detail
          2. Detail

KEEPING TRACK

Personal Word List   Record new words in your Personal Word List. Put a star next to words you might use in a conversation.

Personal Reading Log   As you add this selection to your Personal Reading Log, tell whether or not you'd like to read more about the samurai. Give yourself 1 point on the Reading Meter for completing the article.

Checklist for Standards Mastery   You've just clarified a text by using the skill of outlining. Now, track your progress by using the Checklist for Standards Mastery.

The Samurai ▪ *Interactive Reading,* page 83

Go Beyond an Informational Text

Research Template   The samurai of long ago provide a fascinating topic for research. Use the template below to learn more about these warriors of feudal Japan.

Project Samurai

Questions for Research	Resource
Who were the samurai?	
When did they live?	
What was their purpose?	
Why were they so feared?	
Why did they cease to exist?	

Literature

BEFORE YOU READ

Folk tales often provide fanciful explanations for everyday events. We don't really believe these explanations—or do we? Both "The Spider Weaver" and "The Grateful Statues" describe strange, wonderful happenings. Whether you believe these stories or not, there's something valuable to be learned.

Here's what you need to know before you begin these folk tales:

- Jizo is a Japanese Buddha who is the protector of children.
- Traditionally Japanese people celebrate the new year by eating special foods. Sweet, sticky rice cakes are a traditional new year's food.

Reading Standard 3.2
Analyze the effect of the qualities of the character (for example, courage or cowardice, ambition or laziness) on the plot and resolution of the conflict.

Two Japanese Folk Tales

retold by **Florence Sakade**

The Spider Weaver

Long ago there was a young farmer named Yosaku. One day he was working in the fields and saw a snake getting ready to eat a spider. Yosaku felt very sorry for the spider. So he ran at the snake with his hoe and drove the snake away, thus saving the spider's life. Then the spider disappeared into the grass, but first it seemed to pause a minute and bow in thanks toward Yosaku.

IDENTIFY

What amazing event is related in this paragraph? Underline it.

_____

_____

_____

_____

_____

_____

IDENTIFY

In many folk tales a person is helped or promised something, but on some condition. What rule does the girl say Yosaku must obey? Underline it.

IDENTIFY

Why is Yosaku's curiosity aroused by the girl's response to his question? What does he do about it?

_____

_____

_____

_____

_____

_____

_____

_____

WORD KNOWLEDGE

Like many folk tales, this one includes a _metamorphosis_ (met·ə·môr′fə·sis), a marvelous change from one form to another. Circle the description of a metamorphosis.

IDENTIFY

Why did the spider take a human form? Underline the passage that tells you why.

One morning not long after that, Yosaku was in his house when he heard a tiny voice outside calling: "Mr. Yosaku, Mr. Yosaku." He went to the door and saw a beautiful young girl standing in the yard.

"I heard that you are looking for someone to weave cloth for you," said the girl. "Won't you please let me live here and weave for you?"

Yosaku was very pleased because he did need a weaving girl. So he showed the girl the weaving room and she started to work at the loom. At the end of the day Yosaku went to see what she'd done and was very surprised to find that she'd woven eight long pieces of cloth, enough to make eight kimonos. He'd never known anyone could weave so much in just a single day.

"How ever did you weave so much?" he asked the girl.

But instead of answering him, she said a very strange thing: "You mustn't ask me that. And you must never come into the weaving room while I am at work."

But Yosaku was very curious. So one day he slipped very quietly up to the weaving room and peeped in the window. What he saw really surprised him! Because it was not the girl who was seated at the loom, but a large spider, weaving very fast with its eight legs, and for thread it was using its own spider web, which came out of its mouth.

Yosaku looked very closely and saw that it was the same spider which he'd saved from the snake. Then Yosaku understood. The spider had been so thankful that it had wanted to do something to help Yosaku. So it had turned itself into a beautiful young girl and come to weave cloth for him. Just by eating the cotton in the weaving room it could spin it into thread inside its own body, and then with

its eight legs it could weave the thread into cloth very,
40 very fast.

Yosaku was very grateful for the spider's help. He saw
that the cotton was almost used up. So next morning he set
out for the nearest village, on the other side of the mountains, to buy some more cotton. He bought a big bundle of
cotton and started home, carrying it on his back.

Along the way a very terrible thing happened. Yosaku
sat down to rest, and the same snake that he'd driven away
from the spider came up and slipped inside the bundle of
cotton. But Yosaku didn't know anything about this. So he
50 carried the cotton home and gave it to the weaving girl.

She was very glad to get the cotton, because she'd now
used up all the cotton that was left. So she took it and went
to the weaving room.

As soon as the girl was inside the weaving room, she
turned back into a spider and began eating the cotton very,
very fast, just as though it were something very delicious,
so she could spin it into thread inside her body. The spider
ate and ate and ate, and then suddenly, when it had eaten
down to the bottom of the bundle—the snake jumped out
60 of the cotton. It opened its mouth wide to swallow the
spider. The spider was very frightened and jumped out
of the window. The snake went wriggling very fast after it.
And the spider had eaten so much cotton that it couldn't
run very fast. So the snake gradually caught up with the
spider. Again the snake opened its mouth wide to gulp the
spider down. But just then a wonderful thing happened.

Old Man Sun, up in the sky, had been watching what
was happening. He knew how kind the spider had been to
Yosaku and he felt very sorry for the poor little spider. So
70 he reached down with a sunbeam and caught hold of the

IDENTIFY

Pause at line 50. What new
problem has come up?
Underline it.

FLUENCY

Read aloud the boxed pas-
sage. As you read, vary your
volume, rate of speech, and
pitch to help your listeners
feel the scene's excitement.
Then, re-read the passage to
improve the smoothness of
your delivery.

· · · · · · Notes · · · · · ·

Why did Old Man Sun save the spider?

_____

_____

What natural feature of our world is explained in the story?

_____

_____

Underline words in lines 1–10 that describe the old man. Circle passages that tell what he wants. Box passages that tell what he does.

· · · · · · Notes · · · · · ·

_____

_____

_____

_____

_____

end of the web that was sticking out of the spider's mouth, and he lifted the spider high up into the sky, where the snake couldn't reach it at all.

The spider was very grateful to Old Man Sun for saving him from the snake. So he used all the cotton that was inside his body to weave beautiful fleecy clouds up in the sky. That's the reason, they say, why clouds are soft and white like cotton, and also that is the reason why both a spider and a cloud are called by the same name
80   in Japan—*kumo.*

"Fine Wind, Clear Morning," hand-colored woodblock print by Katsushika Hokusai, 1831.

The Grateful Statues

Once upon a time an old man and an old woman were living in a country village in Japan. They were very poor and spent every day weaving big hats out of straw. Whenever they finished a number of hats, the old man would take them to the nearest town to sell them.

One day the old man said to the old woman: "New Year's is the day after tomorrow. How I wish we had some rice cakes to eat on New Year's Day! Even one or two little cakes would be enough. Without some rice cakes we can't
10   even celebrate New Year's."

"Well, then," said the old woman, "after you've sold these hats, why don't you buy some rice cakes and bring them back with you?"

So early the next morning the old man took the five new hats that they had made, and went to town to sell them. But after he got to town, he was unable to sell a single hat. And to make things still worse, it began to snow very hard.

The old man was very sad as he began trudging weari-
20 ly back toward his village. He was going along a lonesome mountain trail when he suddenly came upon a row of six stone statues of Jizo, the protector of children, all covered with snow.

"My, my! Now isn't this a pity," the old man said. "These are only stone statues of Jizo, but even so just think how cold they must be standing here in the snow."

"I know what I'll do!" the old man suddenly said to himself. "This will be just the thing."

So he unfastened the five new hats from his back and
30 began tying them, one by one, on the heads of the Jizo statues.

When he came to the last statue, he suddenly realized that all the hats were gone. "Oh, my!" he said, "I don't have enough hats." But then he remembered his own hat. So he took it off his head and tied it on the head of the last Jizo. Then he went on his way home.

When he reached his house, the old woman was wait-ing for him by the fire. She took one look at him and cried: "You must be frozen half to death. Quick! Come to the fire.
40 What did you do with your hat?"

The old man shook the snow out of his hair and came to the fire. He told the old woman how he had given all the

CHARACTER TRACE

Pause at line 36. Box the passage that tells what the old man does for the statues. What do the old man's actions reveal about his character?

_____

_____

_____

_____

_____

_____

_____

_____

_____

_____

_____

_____

_____

_____

_____

_____

_____

_____

_____

_____

CHARACTER TRACE

Circle what the old woman says to the old man. What does her reaction tell you about her character?

_____

_____

_____

_____

_____

PREDICT

Pause at line 53. What "very wonderful thing" might happen?

_____

_____

_____

_____

_____

IDENTIFY

How are the old man and the old woman rewarded for their actions?

_____

_____

_____

_____

_____

_____

new hats, and even his own hat, to the six stone Jizo. He told her he was sorry that he hadn't been able to bring any rice cakes.

"My! That was a very kind thing you did for the Jizo," said the old woman. She was very proud of the old man, and went on: "It's better to do a kind thing like that than to have all the rice cakes in the world. We'll get along without

50 any rice cakes for New Year's."

By this time it was late at night, so the old man and woman went to bed. And just before dawn, while they were still asleep, a very wonderful thing happened. Suddenly there was the sound of voices in the distance, singing:

"A kind old man walking in the snow
Gave all his hats to the stone Jizo.
So we bring him gifts with a yo-heave-ho!"

The voices came nearer and nearer, and then you could hear the sound of footsteps on the snow.

60 The sounds came right up to the house where the old man and woman were sleeping. And then all at once there was a great noise, as though something had been put down just in front of the house.

The old couple jumped out of bed and ran to the front door. When they opened it, what do you suppose they found? Well, right there at the door someone had spread a straw mat, and arranged very neatly on the mat was one of the biggest and most beautiful and freshest rice cakes the old people had ever seen.

70 "Whoever could have brought us such a wonderful gift?" they said, and looked about wonderingly.

They saw some tracks in the snow leading away from their house. The snow was all tinted with the colors of dawn, and there in the distance, walking over the snow, were the six stone Jizo, still wearing the hats which the old man had given them.

The old man said: "It was the stone Jizo who brought this wonderful rice cake to us."

80   The old woman said: "You did them a kind favor when you gave them your hats, so they brought this rice cake to show their gratitude."

The old couple had a very wonderful New Year's Day celebration after all, because now they had this wonderful rice cake to eat.

COMPARE & CONTRAST

What would you say is the "lesson" of this folk tale? Compare this lesson to the lesson in "The Spider Weaver."

OWN THE SELECTIONS

Comparing Characters and Events   Complete the Venn diagram below. Show how the characters and events in the two folk tales are the same and how they are different. Then, share your work with a partner, and comment on each other's work.

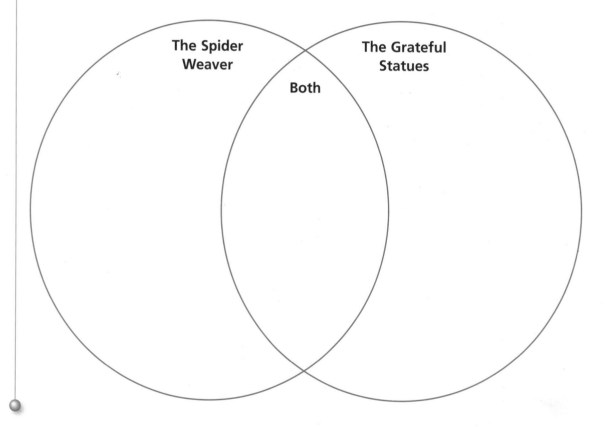

The Spider Weaver

Both

The Grateful Statues

KEEPING TRACK

Personal Word List   Record this academic term in your Personal Word List: *metamorphosis.*

Personal Reading Log   As you add this selection to your Personal Reading Log, indicate whether you would like to read more Japanese folk tales. Give yourself 3 points on the Reading Meter.

Checklist for Standards Mastery   Use the Checklist for Standards Mastery to see how much you have learned.

Two Japanese Folk Tales ▪ *Interactive Reading,* page 89

Interactive Reading, page 89

Go Beyond Literary Texts

Story Map   The folk tales you have read have a great deal in common. Both folk tales are about ordinary people who do kind deeds and receive great rewards for their actions. Both folk tales contain strong moral messages about the kind of people we should all try to be.

Tell a "folk tale" of your own. Include some of these characteristics of a folk tale:

- characters who want something very much
- supernatural characters
- a moral lesson
- a condition or test
- an explanation of how something in our world came to be
- a marvelous metamorphosis

Before you write your folk tale, gather your details in a story map like the one that follows:

Characters	Setting

What characters want

Why they can't get it

What happens

Event 1:   Event 2:   Event 3 (and so on):

Resolution

Moral:

Chapter 3

The Heart of the Matter
Themes and Conclusions

Chapter Preview In this chapter you will—

Strategy Launch:
"Most Important Words"

LITERARY FOCUS: THEME

Stories reveal truths about our lives. This revelation is known as **theme.** Sometimes a story's theme is stated directly, but more often it is not. You have to decide yourself what the story reveals to you about our human experience. To find a story's theme, you think about what the characters (and you) have discovered in the story and what you have learned from sharing their experience.

A STRATEGY THAT WORKS: "MOST IMPORTANT WORDS"

Identifying the most important words in a story can help you find the story's theme. "Most important words" may be found in the story's descriptions, in the characters' dialogue, or in general comments about life made by the narrator. "Most important words" could also be words or ideas that are repeated in the story. Sometimes important words are found in a story's title and in its opening and closing paragraphs.

TIPS FOR USING "MOST IMPORTANT WORDS"

➤ As you read, circle or underline story passages that seem to say something important or interesting.

➤ When you're finished reading the story, re-read it, paying special attention to the passages you marked.

➤ Think about the story's title.

➤ Think about what the characters have experienced and what the story seems to be "telling" you. Then, write down in your own words what you think the theme of the story is.

Reading Standard 1.2
Identify and interpret figurative language in prose text.

Reading Standard 2.6
Determine the adequacy and appropriateness of the evidence for an author's conclusions.

Reading Standard 3.6
Identify and analyze features of themes conveyed through characters, actions, and images.

Practice Read

BEFORE YOU READ

Do you ever wonder what your life would be like if you switched responsibilities with someone else? In this story a mom and a dad switch jobs for a week to figure out whose life is easier. As you read this story, see if you can predict how they'll feel as the week draws to a close.

Reading Standard 3.6 Identify and analyze features of themes conveyed through characters, actions, and images.

Walk a Mile in Someone Else's Shoes

Richard Cohen

VOCABULARY DEVELOPMENT

smirked (smʉrkt) *v.:* smiled in a conceited, knowing, or annoying way.

IDENTIFY

What is the **conflict** or problem in the story?

_____

_____

_____

MOST IMPORTANT WORDS

Re-read lines 1–10. Circle the word or words you think are most important.

"*I* know how to do this," Dad said. "I'm not one of those dads you see in the movies who can't change a diaper or fry a burger."

"Yeah, right," I **smirked.** Dad helped Mom in the house when he could—but I couldn't say he knew for sure where we keep the butter.

Today, however, he was the one cooking dinner. For the next week, Dad was going to do Mom's job, and Mom was going to do Dad's. They want to see whose job is harder.

10   Today was Day 1 of the Great Experiment.

"Where are the pickles around here?" Dad complained, rooting around in the refrigerator. "People should put things in the right places, the logical places where they belong. You don't put—oh, here it is. See? That's just what I was saying. You don't put the pickles near the taco shells.

It's like if you had a zoo and you put the elephants near the—I don't know, the penguins. It just doesn't make sense."

"Yes, Dad," I sing-songed.

20 "Never you mind, Donnelle. I'm just not used to things yet. You know what I did today? I got you off to school. I fed Tara and got her dressed. I took her to the playground and then to the dry cleaners and the supermarket. I made the beds and straightened up the house. After which I did two loads of laundry. And that was just *before* lunch. After lunch, it was more of the same, except I lugged you across town to your dance class. I worked like the Little Engine That Could. I worked like a—like a—*microchip.*"

30 I laughed. From the bedroom came the sound of Tara crying. She was up; she was hungry; she wanted to play.

"Uh-oh, here goes," Dad said. "Time for her dinner. You get Tara, I'll get the grub." He **peered** into the cabinet and took out a jar of baby food that looked more like the stuff we feed the cat.

In real life, Dad was the managing editor of the newspaper in our town, *The Journal Courier,* which has a circulation of almost 60,000. Mom was in the news business, too—at least she used to be. Dad and Mom 40 met when they were both reporters for the paper. He stayed with the paper, and Mom got into TV news.

Mom was just starting out in her career when I came along. She took three months' leave, and then went back. It was hard for her to juggle everything—the job, a new baby, the household chores. When she could, she worked at home or took me to the office with her. I would spend hours at

IDENTIFY

Who is telling you this story? Circle her name.

WORD KNOWLEDGE

Dad uses **similes,** or comparisons between two unlike things using a word such as *like* or *as.* The similes describe how hard he works. What does Dad compare his work situation to?

_____

_____

_____

_____

_____

VOCABULARY DEVELOPMENT

peered (pird) *v.:* looked closely.

INTERPRET

Why do you think the narrator uses the word *juggle* in line 44? How is Mom like a juggler?

_____

_____

_____

_____

VOCABULARY DEVELOPMENT

grief (grēf) *n.*: trouble; difficulty; problems. (The narrator is exaggerating here!)

IDENTIFY

Pause at line 64. What does Dad say that angers Mom?

_____

_____

_____

_____

MOST IMPORTANT WORDS

Re-read lines 58–64. Circle the words in this paragraph that you think are important.

VISUALIZE

Circle the words "he was trying to save a sinking ship." What picture does it put in your mind? In using the comparison, what is the writer saying about Dad?

_____

_____

_____

_____

_____

_____

_____

her computer, giving her **grief,** hammering away at the keys while she frantically tried to keep me from crashing the hard drive.

50   Anyway, by the time Tara was born, Mom felt differently about her job. She had steadily climbed the ladder—now she produced the weekend news—but she was tired. Taking a year or two off to raise a baby sounded like a vacation.

So Mom began an unpaid leave of absence. The chief of the news department thought the world of her. He assured her she could come back whenever she wanted.

But Mom got itchy. She felt stuck. She wanted to go back to work. She loved the excitement of a busy news-
60   room. She began to talk about finding someone to look after Tara. Dad was all for that, but one evening he said something that really got to Mom. He predicted that after a while, she'd be sorry she gave up her "life of leisure" for the tough, exhausting life of a TV news producer.

"What do you mean 'life of leisure'?" Mom practically shouted. "You think raising two children and keeping house is *easy*?"

"Now, dear," he said trying to calm Mom down. "I know you work hard around here. I'm just saying that the
70   pressure of producing a news show might be greater than the pressure of running a household. I mean, if the baby's wet, you can change her diaper five minutes later and it's no tragedy. But the news can't wait."

"Oh, now I've heard *everything,*" Mom said. "The news is more important than a baby."

"That's not what I said," Dad said, but he was trying to save a sinking ship.

"The simple fact is," Mom said icily, "my job is harder than yours." She can be pretty **inflexible** sometimes.

80   "Oh, *really,*" Dad returned.

That's when Mom proposed the exchange and Dad got a brainstorm. They could turn it into a news story! They could combine their talents and write a daily column about the experience. They even got a title for their column; based on some old saying about not knowing another person till you walked a mile in his (or her) moccasins (sandals, whatever!). *The Journal Courier* would print the column. Mom could spend a week working at her old job at the TV station and write about her half of the project.

90   When Mom came home from work on that first day, the kitchen was a mess. Food spilled over countertops; measuring cups, frying pans, baby food, crayons, and toy parts were mixed together on the floor. If Mom noticed, she didn't seem to care. She went into the living room, kicked off her shoes, and threw herself onto the couch. She let out a huge sigh. She looked like a balloon with the air let out.

"Rough day?" Dad teased.

"Oh, nothing I couldn't handle," Mom said breezily.
100 Her voice sounded a little different, though.

"I know how it is," Dad said. He eyed her as if looking for signs of distress.

"What's for dinner?" she asked brightly.

"I thought we'd go out," Dad said. "To celebrate the first day of our Experiment," he added.

She eyed him suspiciously. "It couldn't be you don't have the *energy,* could it?"

"Do *you* always have the energy?" he responded.

She stuck out her tongue at him.

VOCABULARY
DEVELOPMENT

inflexible (in·fleks′ə·bəl) *adj.:* cannot be bent; stiff; rigid. An inflexible person won't give in.

INFER

Pause at line 97. What do Mom's actions reveal about the day she has had?

_____

_____

_____

_____

_____

_____

_____

_____

_____

_____

_____

_____

_____

_____

_____

_____

_____

_____

IDENTIFY

Pause at line 136. How has the conflict in the story been resolved?

_____

_____

_____

_____

_____

_____

_____

_____

_____

_____

_____

_____

_____

_____

_____

_____

110 Honestly, these people are my *parents.*

Well, we ate at our favorite Cal-Mex place, which was probably a lot better than whatever Dad might have cooked. That night, Mom gave Tara her bath, just like Dad always did when he came home. He put Tara to bed, just like she always did, and then they both helped me with my English report.

After I polished off my homework, I went in to say goodnight. "'Night, sweetie," Mom called, over the noise of the TV. Dad was stretched out on the rug, snoring. Mom
120 and I rolled our eyes at each other and smiled. Mom was obviously having an easier time than Dad was. It looked like she was winning.

But as the week wore on, Mom ran into trouble. The second day, she complained about a reporter who didn't want an assignment he said was "fluff." The third day, the mayor ducked Mom's calls. The fourth day, the station sent around a memo about declining ratings. The fifth day, the computers went down. At home, Mom complained about all these misfortunes. But Dad could not help her out. He
130 was too tired. He could only mutter, "The laundry . . . the telephone . . . the bills . . . the baby," and things like that. He had quite a long list.

And so the big week ended. No, it wasn't a draw. Dad did admit that staying home with a baby all day was way harder than a day at the newspaper.

"So you win," he said.

Then they hugged and kissed, and all that married-people stuff I find particularly icky.

So what's the result of their Great Experiment? Now
140 that each one knows how tough the other one has it, they talk to each other about their jobs constantly. But I think I

hear more, well, respect coming from them. I think that walking a mile in someone else's shoes taught them something.

There's another result. Mom decided to continue working part-time. She met this really nice older lady, Mrs. Ecchivera, who takes care of little kids during the day, so Tara is happy enough. Of course, Dad and I help out a lot, too.

150   "And now I'm working twice as hard as before," Mom often says. But she smiles when she says it.

And guess what? Now Dad knows where the butter is.

MOST IMPORTANT WORDS

Circle any word or words you think are important at the end of the story. Then tell what the story says about our lives.

_____

_____

_____

_____

_____

_____

_____

_____

_____

_____

_____

MOST IMPORTANT WORDS

How does the title of the story point to its theme? Where is the title explained?

_____

_____

_____

_____

OWN THE STORY

Theme Fill out the "Most Important Words" Table on the next page. Then, write a paragraph explaining what you think is the story's theme. Then, answer this question: Why is this theme an important one for people to think about? Have you ever had an experience like this—when you "walked a mile in someone else's shoes"?

_____

_____

_____

_____

_____

_____

_____

_____

_____

_____

_____

_____

_____

KEEPING TRACK

Personal Word List Record the words you learned from this story in your Personal Word List. Put a star next to words you might use in conversation. Make a point to use one of those words today.

Personal Reading Log As you record this story in your Personal Reading Log, indicate whether or not you would recommend it to a friend. Give yourself 3 points on the Reading Meter for completing this selection.

Checklist for Standards Mastery Keep track of your progress using the Checklist for Standards Mastery.

Walk a Mile in Someone Else's Shoes ■ *Interactive Reading,* page 100

Interact with a Literary Text

"Most Important Words" Table   After you finish "Walk a Mile in Someone Else's Shoes," go back and review the words and phrases you found important. In the chart below, write each word or phrase in the left-hand column. In the right-hand column, give a reason explaining why you feel that entry is important.

Important Words	Why This Passage Is Important
1.	
2.	
3.	
4.	

After thinking about each of your choices, choose the passage that you feel best reveals the story's **theme.** Explain why below.

_____

_____

_____

_____

The All-American Slurp

Interact with a Literary Text

Pyramid   A **theme** is an idea about our human experience that is revealed through stories. We discover theme by thinking about the story's characters and what they learned or discovered in the story.

After you read "The All-American Slurp," complete this pyramid. In the top section, write a word from the story you feel has captured the story's essence. (Remember that no one word is right. There are many possibilities.) In the next section, describe how this word is related to the characters and their actions. Finally, in the bottom section of the pyramid, write the truth about life that is revealed in the story.

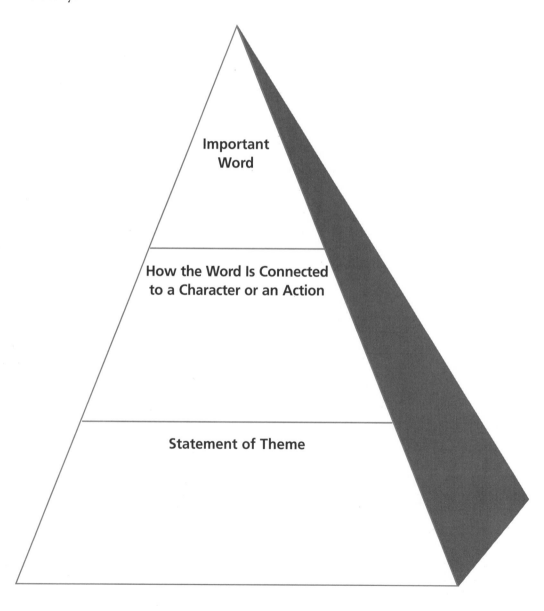

Important
Word

How the Word Is Connected
to a Character or an Action

Statement of Theme

Everybody Is Different, but the Same Too

for use with
Holt Literature and Language Arts,
page 131

CONCLUSIONS

Interact with an Informational Text

Evidence Flow Chart   As you read the interview called "Everybody Is Different, but the Same Too," you'll see that Nilou comes to a conclusion about life in America. Read the evidence listed below that leads up to her conclusion. Then look for her conclusion at the end of the interview. Restate Nilou's conclusion in your own words. Evaluate the evidence and tell whether or not you feel it adds up to the conclusion.

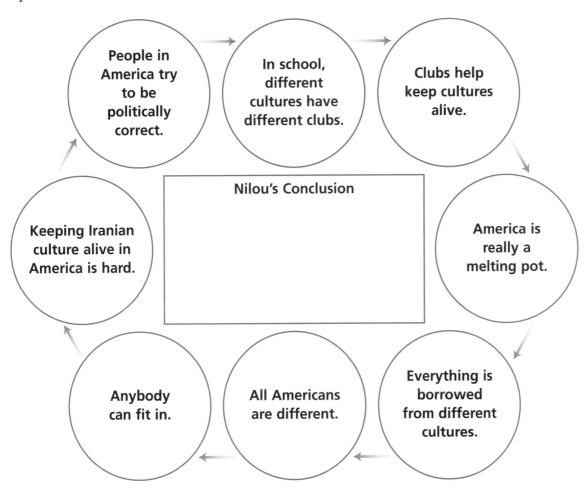

People in America try to be politically correct.

In school, different cultures have different clubs.

Clubs help keep cultures alive.

Keeping Iranian culture alive in America is hard.

Nilou's Conclusion

America is really a melting pot.

Anybody can fit in.

All Americans are different.

Everything is borrowed from different cultures.

Does Nilou give enough evidence to form her conclusion? Why or why not? Explain.

_____

_____

_____

_____

The Emperor's New Clothes

for use with
Holt Literature and Language Arts,
page 137

Interact with a Literary Text

Theme Chart   The revelation a story makes about our lives is its **theme.** One way to find a story's theme is to examine what we and the characters discover in the course of the story. That discovery is usually the same as the story's theme.

Complete this graphic organizer after you read "The Emperor's New Clothes."

> **Main character(s):**
> _____

> **Key experiences:**
> _____
> _____
> _____
> _____

> **What we discover from those experiences:**
> _____
> _____
> _____
> _____

> **Statement of theme:**
> _____
> _____
> _____
> _____

Uniform Style

Interact with an Informational Text

Support Chart   When writers want to persuade us to accept their opinion about an issue, they must provide support for their conclusions. The writer of "Uniform Style" feels that there are many benefits to be gained from wearing school uniforms. Fill in each section of the chart below with details you found in the article.

Question: Should students wear uniforms?

Conclusion: Uniforms have benefits.

Supporting Evidence:

1. Statistics _____
_____
_____
_____
_____
_____

2. Direct Quotations _____
_____
_____
_____
_____
_____

3. Logic and Reasoning _____
_____
_____
_____
_____
_____

Baucis and Philemon

for use with
Holt Literature and Language Arts,
page 150

Interact with a Literary Text

"Most Important Word" Chart Although "Baucis and Philemon" is a very old story, its **themes** are timeless. Completing this chart will help you identify at least one of the themes in this myth. Re-read the myth, and select what you think is the most important word or phrase. Then, tell how that word or phrase relates to the story's plot and characters. Finally, state what the word or phrase tells you about the story's theme.

How it relates to plot:

_____
_____
_____
_____
_____
_____
_____
_____

How it relates to characters:

_____
_____
_____
_____
_____
_____
_____
_____

Most Important Word

_____

Theme:

_____
_____
_____
_____

One Child's Labor of Love

Interact with an Informational Text

Evidence Cards   The writer of this essay makes conclusions about Craig Kielburger, a teen who fights against child labor. Before you agree with those conclusions, you must be sure that the writer has provided enough supporting evidence. The cards below will help you evaluate the evidence. Read each conclusion. Then, list evidence from the article to see if there is enough to support each conclusion.

Conclusion I
Craig Kielburger is passionate about his belief that child labor and slavery cannot be tolerated.

Evidence

- _____
- _____
- _____
- _____
- _____

Conclusion II
Craig Kielburger refuses to let wrongs go unchallenged.

Evidence

- _____
- _____
- _____
- _____
- _____

Literature

MYTH

GREEK MYTH STUDY

The Greek myth "Baucis and Philemon" appears on page 150 in *Holt Literature and Language Arts.* In that myth we learn how two old people are rewarded by the gods for their generosity. Now you will read another Greek myth. This one is about two young people, Atalanta (at·ə·lan′tə) and Hippomenes (hi·päm′i·nēz). This myth, like the myth about Baucis and Philemon, ends with a **metamorphosis** (met′ə·môr′fə·sis), a marvelous change in form. Notice that though one metamorphosis is a reward, the other is a dreadful punishment.

BEFORE YOU READ

Have you ever forgotten to thank someone? In the Greek myth "Atalanta and Hippomenes," you'll see what happens when a young man forgets to thank a goddess of love for the help she gave him.

Here's what you might want to know before you begin the story:
- Myths often teach important lessons about life.
- Venus is the goddess of love.
- Atalanta and Hippomenes are mortals, or humans.

Reading Standard 3.6 Identify and analyze features of themes conveyed through characters, actions, and images.

Atalanta and Hippomenes

A Greek Myth

Atalanta was a Greek maiden who could run faster than anyone on earth. She could outrun the winds, Boreas and Zephyr. Only Mercury, with his winged sandals, ran more swiftly.

Besides being so fleet-footed, Atalanta was very beautiful, and many Greek youths from every part of the kingdom wished to marry her. But Atalanta did not wish to marry anyone and turned them all away, saying, "I shall be the bride only of him who shall outrun me in the race, 10 but death must be the penalty of all who try and fail."

In spite of this hard condition there still were a few brave **suitors** willing to risk their lives for a chance of winning Atalanta.

For one of the races the runners chose the youth Hippomenes for judge.

Hippomenes felt both pity and **scorn** for the runners. He thought they were foolish to risk their lives, and bade them go home. He reminded them that the land was full of lovely maidens who were kinder and more gentle than 20 Atalanta.

> "But you have not yet seen Atalanta," said one of the suitors to Hippomenes. "You do not know all her beauty and loveliness. See, she comes!"
>
> Hippomenes looked, and saw Atalanta as she drew near. She laid aside her cloak and made ready for the race.

"Atalanta and Hippomenes" from *A Child's Book of Myths and Enchantment Tales* by Margaret Evans Price. Copyright 1924 by Rand McNally & Company; copyright renewed 1952 by Margaret Evans Price. Reprinted by permission of **Lucy Eddins on behalf of the Estate of Margaret Evans Price.**

DECODING TIP

Many names in Greek myths are difficult to pronounce. *Zephyr* will be easier to read if you remember that *ph* makes the *f* sound. Try breaking difficult names into syllables and sounding them out. For example, At/a/lan/ta or Hi/ppom/e/nes.

IDENTIFY

Circle the words in the first two paragraphs that describe an important characteristic of Atalanta.

VOCABULARY DEVELOPMENT

suitors (sōōt′ərz) *n.:* men who are courting, or wish to marry, a woman.

scorn (skôrn) *n.:* feeling that someone or something is worthless, or not worthy of notice.

FLUENCY

Improve your fluency by reading the boxed passage aloud. Read it once slowly and carefully. Then, read it again, with more speed. Read it a third time, and add expression to the description of Atalanta.

envious (en'vē·əs) *adj.:*
jealous; wanting something
that someone else has.

penalty (pen'əl·tē) *n.:*
punishment.

· · · · · · Notes · · · · · ·

For a moment she stood poised like a graceful white bird about to fly.

The suitors who stood beside her trembled with fear and eagerness.

30 At a word from Hippomenes the runners were off, but at the first step Atalanta flew ahead. Her tunic fluttered behind her like a banner. Her hair, loosened from its ribbon, blew about her shoulders in bright waves.

As she ran, Hippomenes thought her very beautiful and became **envious** of the runner who might win her. He shouted praises when she reached the goal far ahead of her poor suitors.

Hippomenes forgot that the **penalty** of failure was death. He did not remember the advice he had given the 40 other runners to go home and forget the loveliness of Atalanta. He knew only that he loved her and must himself race with her.

Raising his head toward Mount Olympus, he prayed to Venus, the goddess of love, and asked her to help him.

Atalanta and Hippomenes (detail) by
Sebastiano Marsili (1572). Palazzo Vecchio, Florence.

As he stood beside Atalanta, waiting for the signal for the race to start, Venus appeared to him and slipped three golden apples into his hands.

"Throw them one by one in Atalanta's path," whispered Venus.

50 The goddess was invisible to everyone but Hippomenes. No one saw her as she gave him the apples, nor heard her as she told him what to do with them.

Atalanta looked pityingly at the handsome youth as he stood ready to run. She was sorry for him, and for a moment she hesitated and almost wished that he might win the race.

The signal was given, and Atalanta and Hippomenes flew swiftly over the sand. Atalanta was soon ahead, but Hippomenes, sending up a prayer to Venus, tossed one of 60 his golden apples so that it fell directly in front of Atalanta.

Astonished at the beautiful apple which seemed to fall from nowhere, she **stooped** to pick it up.

That instant Hippomenes passed her, but Atalanta, holding the apple firmly in her hand, at once darted ahead. Again she outdistanced Hippomenes. Then he threw the second apple.

Atalanta could not pass without picking it up, and then, because of the apple in her other hand, paused a moment longer. When she looked up, Hippomenes was 70 far ahead.

But gaining, she overtook and passed him. Then, just before she reached the goal, he threw the third apple.

"I can win easily," thought Atalanta, "even though I stoop for this other apple." As she was already holding an apple in each hand, she paused just for an instant as she wondered how to grasp the third.

IDENTIFY

What does Venus tell Hippomenes to do with the golden apples?

_____

_____

_____

_____

_____

_____

_____

_____

VOCABULARY DEVELOPMENT

stooped (sto͞opt) v.: bent over.

· · · · · · Notes · · · · · ·

_____

_____

_____

_____

_____

_____

_____

_____

_____

_____

_____

_____

_____

EVALUATE

Although Hippomenes wins the race, has he really outrun Atalanta? Explain.

_____

_____

_____

_____

_____

_____

MOST IMPORTANT
WORDS

Underline the word *thoughtless* in line 90, used to describe Hippomenes. What important theme in the myth is reflected in this word?

_____

_____

_____

_____

_____

_____

That moment Hippomenes shot past, reaching the goal before Atalanta.

Amid the wild shouts of those who watched, he
80 wrapped the maiden's cloak around her shoulders and led her away. Hippomenes was so happy that he forgot to thank the goddess Venus, who followed them to the marriage feast.

Invisible, she moved among the wedding guests. She saw Atalanta place the golden apples in a bowl of ivory and admire their beauty, but Hippomenes, in his delight, thought no more of the apples or of the goddess who had given them to him.

Venus was angry with Hippomenes for being so
90 thoughtless, and instead of blessing the lovers she caused them to be changed into a lion and a lioness, doomed forever to draw the chariot of Cybele,° the mother of Jupiter, through the heavens and over the earth.

_____

° **Cybele** (sib′ə·lē).

OWN THE STORY

Theme   Complete the following If/Then Chart to see how the story's theme would differ if Atalanta or Hippomenes had acted differently.

If	Then
Atalanta had . . .	
Hippomenes had . . .	

Metamorphosis   A metamorphosis (met′ə·môr′fə·sis) is a marvelous change in form. Greek myths are full of metamorphoses. What metamorphosis rewards Baucis and Philemon? What metamorphosis punishes Atalanta and Hippomenes?

_____

_____

KEEPING TRACK

Personal Word List   The names of several gods and goddesses are mentioned in "Atalanta and Hippomenes." Write their names in your Personal Word List, and tell who they are.

Personal Reading Log   What did you think of the cruel ending of this myth? If you could change the ending, what would you want to happen? Write your response in your Personal Reading Log. Give yourself 2 points on the Reading Meter for completing this myth.

Checklist for Standards Mastery   Use the Checklist for Standards Mastery to determine your skill in identifying theme.

Atalanta and Hippomenes ◾ *Interactive Reading,* page 115

Interact with a Literary Text

Word-and-Theme Diagram   Use this word-and-theme diagram to record important ideas from "Atalanta and Hippomenes." First, select several words from the myth you think are important. Then, explain how each word reveals a theme in the myth.

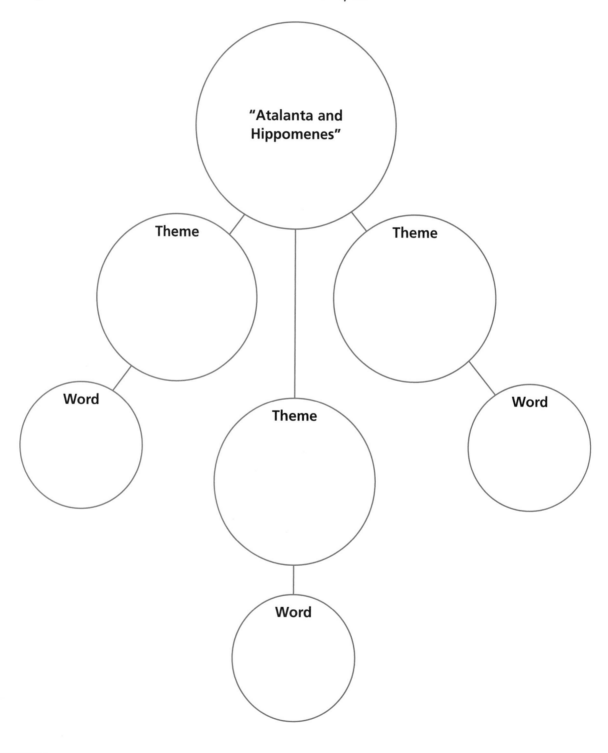

Information

Reading Standard 2.6 Determine the adequacy and appropriateness of an author's conclusions.

Myths in Our Lives

Joseph Bruchac

Myths Make Us Human

Probably the first stories people ever told were myths—stories that explain people's relationships with the gods and with the powers of creation. Myths are central to human experience. All over the world—in Europe and Asia, in Australia and Africa, in North America and South America, on the many Pacific Islands—we find great bodies of myths.

Although the myths may differ greatly in their details, all of them explain how, long ago, things came to be.
10　Polynesian people tell how the god Maui goes fishing and catches the Hawaiian Islands on his magical hook, pulling them up out of the deep. Lakota Indian people tell how life on earth began with Tunka-shila, "Grandfather Rock," rising up out of fire to create dry land and clouds. The Greeks tell how, out of **Chaos,** Earth, and Sky were born.

TEXT STRUCTURE

This article is divided into sections, introduced by headings. Underline each heading.

IDENTIFY

Underline the definition of *myth* in the first paragraph. Underline the topic of the second paragraph.

VOCABULARY DEVELOPMENT

chaos (kā′äs) *n.:* disordered formless matter, supposed to have existed before the universe took its present orderly shape. In the selection, *chaos* is capitalized because it is personified as a living force. In ordinary usage, *chaos* is not capitalized.

ritual (rich′ oo·əl) *n.:* form or
system of rites, religious or
otherwise. Church services
are rituals, as are graduation
ceremonies and marriages.

ancient (ān′chənt) *adj.:*
belonging to long ago.

essential (ē·sen′shəl) *adj.:*
basic; fundamental.

foundations (foun·da′shənz)
n.: fundamentals or begin-
nings of something.

IDENTIFY

Re-read lines 21–31. Circle
a conclusion that Joseph
Bruchac makes about myths.
Underline the evidence he
presents to explain his
conclusion.

EVALUATE

Pause at the end of the essay
on the next page. Is there
enough evidence to support
the writer's statement that
our lives are like the lives
of the heroes in Greek
mythology (lines 37–39)?
Underline the evidence
you find.

Myths may also explain such big questions as why
we suffer, why seasons change, why a religious **ritual** is
practiced, or what happens after death. These are serious
matters, so it is wise to treat all myths with respect.

Myths of Greece and Rome

20

In the Western world the best-known myths are from
ancient Greece and Rome. There are a number of reasons
for that. First, these myths are great stories that contain
essential truths about life. Second, Western civilization is
based largely on the social and cultural **foundations** of
ancient Greece. Most European languages, including
English, contain words from Greek and Latin. (*Myth*, for
example, comes from the Greek *mythos*, "story.") Third,
tales of the Greek and Roman gods and goddesses have
been written down for more than two thousand years.
We have had a long time to become familiar with them.

30

It's important to remember that the myths of ancient
Greece and Rome are only one small part of the body of
myths. There are thousands of different cultures, and myths
are part of every one.

The Myths of Our Lives

Medusa

40

In many ways our own lives echo the
great mythic tales about journeys of
heroes. Like those heroes, we are
born, we must grow and learn how
to overcome problems, we are given
advice by those who are older and
wiser, and we must all, finally, face the challenge of death.

Whether it is the story of Perseus guided by a wise goddess as he seeks to defeat the monster Medusa or it is the Native American Ojibway tale of Manabozho taking the advice of his wise grandmother as he fights the Fever Monster, a great myth helps us to understand the joys and challenges of our own lives.

from The Greek Gods

Word Origins

Bernard Evslin

A great many words we use today are derived from Greek myths. It is interesting to trace the origin of some of these words and to see how we have adapted them for our own use.

Arachne (ə·rak′nē), meaning "spider" in Greek, was adopted to describe in science the spider family, which includes scorpions, mites, and ticks: *arachnida* or *arachnoidea*.

Athene was also known as Pallas Athene. *Pallas* signifies "brandisher," that is, as a spear. An asteroid was named Pallas as well as a very rare metallic element called palladium, which was named after the asteroid.

Calliope

Calliope (kə·lī′ə·pē) is the name of a musical instrument. The mother of Orpheus was named Calliope because she was the muse of eloquence and heroic poetry. The name comes from two words meaning "beauty" and "voice."

10

In this list on pages 123–126, entry words appear in alphabetical order. The words in italicized type, found within the explanation, contain the same root as the entry word. Choose one word from the list, and identify two other words related to it.

Here are some common **euphemisms** (words that try to hide something unpleasant): "armed conflict," "controlled-substance abuser," "termination of employment." How would you translate each one into plain English?

_____

_____

_____

_____

_____

_____

_____

_____

Cronos refers to the old god who ruled the universe before Zeus, his son, overthrew him. From this word we have the noun *chronology,* which describes an arrangement of events in order of occurrence. *Chronic* describes something that continues over a long period of time. A *chronicler* is one who records a historical account of events in the order of time. A timepiece of great accuracy is called a *chronometer.*

The Cyclops (detail) by Odilon Redon (1840–1916).

Cyclops (sī′kläps) is derived from two Greek words meaning "circle" and "eye." We have adopted *cyclops* in the field of biology to describe the group of tiny, free-swimming crustaceans which have a single eye. The word has been used as a root to describe a wheel in such words as *tricycle, bicycle,* and *motorcycle.* It is used to describe a violent storm which moves in a circle: *cyclone.* It also appears in the word *encyclopedia* to describe circular (or complete) learning.

Elysian (i·lizh′ən) **Fields,** which means a "place of great happiness," inspired the French to call their famous boulevard in Paris the Champs Elysées.

Erinyes (i·rin′ē·ez) or the **Furies,** punished people for their crimes on the earth. They were called the *Eumenides* (yoo·men′ə·dēz), which meant "the kindly ones." This name reveals the Greek habit of calling unpleasant things by pleasant names. We use the word *euphemism* (yoo′fə·miz′m) to describe words which do not say the unpleasant idea intended.

Hades is used today to describe the home of the dead. **Hades** comes from the Greek word meaning "the unseen."

50 Hades was also known in Roman mythology as Pluto, the god of wealth—from the Greek word *plutus,* meaning "wealth." We use the word *plutocracy* to describe a government run by wealthy people.

Jove, one of the names for Jupiter and Zeus, has come to mean "born under a lucky planet" and therefore "happy and healthy." The adjective *jovial* derives from the word *Jove.* The planet Jupiter is the largest body in the solar system, except the sun.

Muses refers to the nine goddesses of dancing, poetry,
60 and astronomy. We use the verb *muse* to describe the act of pondering or meditating. The words *music, musician,* and *musical* all come from this word.

Narcissus is the name of a family of flowers which includes daffodils and jonquils. The word *narcissist* is a psychological term meaning "a person who loves himself."

Olympus was the home of the Greek gods. The term has come to mean "something which is grand, imposing, or heavenly." The great festival of games in ancient Greece was called the Olympian Games, and today we call the
70 world-famous athletic contest the *Olympics.*

Oracle (ôr′ə·k′l) is derived from the Greek word meaning "to pray." It is used to refer to places where people pray *(oratories);* to great speakers *(orators);* and even to great speeches *(orations).* A person who seems to possess great knowledge or intuition is called an *oracle.*

Pandora has the same prefix as *Pantheon* and means, of course, "all." The root, *doron,* is a Greek word for "gift;" therefore, Pandora was all-gifted.

· · · · · · · · Notes · · · · · · · ·

INFER

Often an artist refers to another person as his or her "muse." What do you think a muse is, in this sense?

IDENTIFY

What is a *narcissist*? Look for the definition in the word's context (lines 63–65).

INTERPRET

Given that *pan-* is a prefix meaning "all," what would you say a Pan-American conference would be?

_____

_____

_____

_____

_____

_____

_____

_____

INTERPRET

How would you explain what a titan of industry is?

_____

_____

_____

_____

_____

_____

_____

_____

_____

_____

_____

_____

Pantheon is made up of two Greek words: *pan,* meaning "all," and *theos,* meaning "god," or "having something to do with gods." The prefix *pan* is used in such words as *panacea* and *Panama.* The root *theos* is used in such words as *theology* and *theocracy.*

Prometheus means "forethinker." It has come to mean "something that is life-giving, daringly original, or creative." An element which is a fission product of uranium is called *promethium.* The prefix *pro-* is used in countless words today.

Python

Python, which comes from the Greek word "to rot," is used to describe snakes such as the boa, which kills its prey by crushing it.

Titan, the name for a mythical race of giants, has been used to describe anything which is enormous in size or strength. The famous ship which sank when it hit an iceberg was called the *Titanic.*

OWN THE TEXT

Evidence Practice identifying conclusions and looking for evidence in informational texts by filling out the evidence organizer on the following page. When you're finished, exchange charts with a class-mate, and compare the evidence you found.

Research "Word Origins" explains how many words commonly used in English today can be traced back to the old Greek myths. Use a library or online information to do research on the following mythic characters mentioned in the article. Then, report to the class on your findings. You will find stories of all these characters in a collection of Greek myths:

Arachne   Pandora

Cyclops   Prometheus

Narcissus

_____

_____

_____

_____

KEEPING TRACK

Personal Word List You have been introduced to many new words and their definitions. Choose five words that you particularly like or think you would like to use when you write or speak. Add them and their definitions to your Personal Word List.

Personal Reading Log Do word origins interest you? Explain why or why not. Then, give yourself 3 points on the Reading Meter for completing these selections.

Checklist for Standards Mastery Discover how much you've learned by filling out the Checklist for Standards Mastery.

Myths in Our Lives ■ *Interactive Reading,* page 121

Interact with an Informational Text

Evidence Organizer   In "Myths in Our Lives" Joseph Bruchac draws several conclusions about mythology. Determine whether or not Bruchac's conclusions are sound by filling in the chart below with supporting evidence you find in the article.

Conclusion
"Myths are central to human experience."

Evidence (Find Examples):

_____

_____

_____

_____

_____

Conclusion
"In the western world the best-known myths are from ancient Greece and Rome."

Evidence (Find Reasons or Explanations):

_____

_____

_____

_____

_____

Conclusion
"Our own lives echo the great mythic tales about journeys of heroes."

Evidence (Find Examples):

_____

_____

_____

_____

_____

Word Origins ▪ *Interactive Reading,* page 123

Interact with an Informational Text

Word Tree   Select a word from this article, and put it into a word tree. To make a word tree, you write the root, or core part, of the word in the tree's roots. Then, for the branches, write the words and definitions that come from that root word.

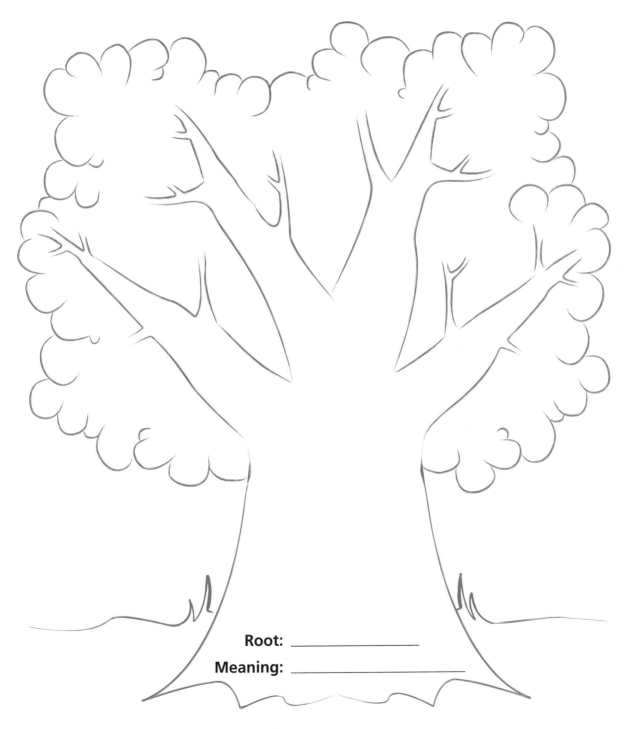

Root: _____

Meaning: _____

Literature

BEFORE YOU READ

Do you believe that love is blind? Does a person in love sometimes overlook the beloved's less-than-perfect appearance? In stories, does the handsome prince ever fall in love with a princess who is *not* a great beauty? You'll read about the meaning of real beauty in this folk tale from the Hispanic Southwest in North America.

Reading Standard 3.6 Identify and analyze features of themes conveyed through characters, actions, and images.

FABIANO AND REYES

A Hispanic Folk Tale, retold by Rudolfo A. Anaya

IDENTIFY

Circle the phrases from the second paragraph that tell about the kind of relationship Fabiano and Reyes have.

· · · · · · Notes · · · · · ·

Once there lived two kings and their wives who were very good friends. When one of the queens gave birth to her first child, the neighboring king and queen were asked to be godparents, and they named the baby boy Fabiano. Two years later the other queen gave birth to a baby girl, and she and the king, in turn, invited their friends to be godparents, and they named the girl Reyes.

Fabiano and Reyes grew up like brother and sister, and they loved each other very much. When they were growing
10 up, they would visit each other, spending one week in one palace and the next in the other. And later when they went to study at school, Fabiano always took care of Reyes, because he cared for her as if she were his sister.

Fabiano grew to be a very handsome young man, one without equal in the region. When he was only fifteen, he

"Fabiano and Reyes" from *Cuentos: Tales from the Hispanic Southwest,* selected and adapted in Spanish by José Griego y Maestas, retold in English by Rudolfo A. Anaya. Copyright © 1980 by the *Museum of New Mexico Press.* Reprinted by permission of the publisher.

began writing love notes to his many girlfriends, and he shared all his secrets with Reyes because she was his **confidante.** When he showed her a letter from a girl whose heart he had broken, he would say, "My dear Reyes, I only want a beautiful girl. If I had to marry an ugly girl, I'd rather be blind."

And Reyes, who didn't consider herself a beautiful girl, would bow her head in shame and answer, "Fabiano, you deserve the most **virtuous** woman on this earth, one who is as beautiful as you."

Time passed and Fabiano continued his flirtations, and he always told Reyes everything, including his dislike for ugly girls. When school was over, they returned home, and they still visited each other as before—one week in one palace and the next in the other.

In those days the kings often entertained people by holding big fiestas at their palaces. There were dances, bullfights, and many other diversions. And as usual, Fabiano and Reyes were always together. Fabiano always found the most beautiful girls to dance with, and when he introduced them to Reyes he would always whisper, "I'll never marry an ugly girl, better to be blind than that!"

One summer, after the dances had come to an end in the palace of Fabiano's family, the entertainment was moved to the palace of Reyes's father. Her father had vowed to outdo his compadre—he was going to bring singers and bullfighters from across the sea!

And so it was at a dance at Reyes's home that Fabiano found a pretty American girl. When he introduced her to Reyes, he said, "Look, I have finally found my sweetheart. This is the kind of girl for me—is she not a beauty?"

20

30

40

VOCABULARY DEVELOPMENT

confidante (kän'fə·dant') *n.*: close, trusted friend whom one can share things with.

INFER

Pause at line 21. What do Fabiano's words to Reyes tell you about his character?

_____

_____

_____

_____

VOCABULARY DEVELOPMENT

virtuous (vʉr'chō͞o·əs) *adj.*: honorable and good.

DECODING TIP

In Spanish, unlike English, all vowel sounds are pronounced. Fiestas, in line 32, is pronounced (fē·es'təz). Underline the word *compadre* (line 41). It has three syllables and is pronounced (kəm·pä'drā').

· · · · · · Notes · · · · · ·

_____

_____

_____

_____

_____

INFER

Pause at line 49. What do you make of the fact that Reyes has said this before?

_____

_____

_____

_____

_____

_____

_____

_____

INFER

In this conversation (lines 53–64), what is revealed about the characters of Fabiano and Reyes?

_____

_____

_____

_____

_____

_____

_____

_____

_____

_____

_____

_____

"I agree," Reyes answered courteously. "Also, the woman who marries you should be the most virtuous woman in the world."

50 The following night Fabiano saw that Reyes was not dressed in her silk dress and jewelry; instead she had made a very simple linen dress for herself.

"Reyes!" Fabiano exclaimed, "Why aren't you dressed in your silk dress! That simple linen dress doesn't become a rich princess who has all the virtues of the world."

"Fabiano," she answered, "a woman as ugly as myself doesn't deserve to wear silk and fine apparel. I should wear only the most simple dress."

"I will be ashamed," he said, "for you to be seen with 60 my American sweetheart; she will be dressed in her best silks and you in simple linen."

"Oh, she deserves the best," Reyes answered. "She is a lovely woman. But I don't deserve silk as I am ugly. So I will dress in a simple manner."

The following night, which was the last night of entertainment at the palace of Reyes's father, the singers who had been invited failed to arrive. Fabiano, who was eager to show off his new sweetheart, waited for them all afternoon but there was no sign of the singers. Finally a 70 servant arrived with the message that there had been a shipwreck and the singers had drowned.

Reyes grew very worried. "I don't want my father to be ashamed in front of his guests because he has no entertainment," she said. "Perhaps I can take their place."

"Oh, no!" Fabiano objected. "It would be a disgrace to have you, a princess, sing in public!"

Nevertheless Reyes decided to sing for the sake of her father. Even as Reyes began to sing, Fabiano continued to insist that she should not. It wouldn't look right, he said, for such a handsome man as he to be seen with a plain and common singer.

But Reyes sang and when Fabiano heard her he was astonished. Never had he heard such a beautiful voice. He then became so **enamored** of Reyes that he didn't know what to do. When Reyes finished singing, Fabiano was immediately at her side telling her how beautifully she had sung, but Reyes reminded him that she was an ugly woman and unworthy of his attention.

That evening when the festivities were concluded, Fabiano could hardly bear to leave. He had fallen completely in love with Reyes. The next day he told his parents that they should go and arrange for him to have Reyes's hand in marriage. The king and queen were overjoyed to hear of this plan.

But Reyes refused the offer by sending back a pumpkin, which according to the custom of that time meant a refusal. She also sent a letter in which she told Fabiano that she didn't deserve a man like him. She reminded him he had often **derided** ugly women, and since she was not beautiful and didn't wish him to be blind he should marry someone else. Fabiano waited a month but then became impatient and sent a friend to again ask Reyes to marry him. The friend went to Reyes but she explained that a marriage with Fabiano was impossible because of his conceit. It was true, she loved Fabiano, but as things were, the situation was impossible.

When Fabiano heard Reyes's answer, he was brokenhearted. To try to forget his love, he left his parents and moved to a foreign country. But he couldn't forget Reyes, and every week he wrote her of his love.

enamored (en·a′mərd) v.: filled with love.

INFER

Do you think Fabiano really loves Reyes? Why or why not?

_____

_____

_____

_____

_____

_____

_____

_____

_____

_____

_____

_____

_____

_____

VOCABULARY DEVELOPMENT

derided (di·rīd′id) v.: put down or mocked.

INFER

Pause at the top of this page. What is the basic **conflict,** or problem, in the story?

_____

_____

_____

_____

_____

_____

_____

_____

_____

_____

_____

_____

_____

_____

FLUENCY

Read the boxed passage aloud, and time yourself. When you read the passage a second time, try to read more smoothly and quickly.

VOCABULARY DEVELOPMENT

consolation (kän′sə·lā′shən) *n.:* comfort; something that makes one less sad.

Now it so happened that one afternoon Fabiano went hunting. He fired at a rabbit and the gun exploded. The gunpowder burned his eyes and blinded him. To make matters worse, while Fabiano was recovering from the accident his parents died, and shortly afterwards he heard that Reyes's parents had died also.

120 Later, when Fabiano returned home, he found himself alone. He had kept all of the letters he had written to Reyes but had never sent in a small box, but since he was now blind he was unable to read them as he used to. Now his only companion was a friend who came to visit him. His friend saw that Fabiano was very sad because he was alone and blind. One afternoon when he was visiting Fabiano, the friend inquired about Reyes.

"Has Reyes come to see you?" he asked.

"No," Fabiano answered, "she doesn't come to see me because of the way I treated her, but I know that without her I will die. She doesn't know that I truly love her and that she is my only **consolation** in life."

130 Then the friend went to see Reyes, and she asked about Fabiano.

"As you know, he is home, and he is blind, but you are such a hard woman it seems you have forgotten you grew up together."

"You are wrong, sir," Reyes answered. "The love I have for Fabiano cannot be destroyed by death itself."

"He doesn't know that," the friend said. "He thinks you don't love him. His life is very difficult. Because he is blind, his servants take advantage of him and feed him only when 140 they want to. The food is poorly prepared and he is neglected. He needs someone to care for him. Would you be willing to be his nurse?"

"I will be Fabiano's nurse on one condition," Reyes answered, "and that is if you swear not to tell him it is I. I still believe he fell in love with me only because he heard me sing. Perhaps this way I will discover if he truly loves me."

"You have my word that I won't tell him anything," the friend said, "and you can see for yourself if his love is real."

150   The friend went back to Fabiano and asked him if he could bring a nurse to care for him. "Yes," Fabiano agreed, "but bring me a nurse who can read, one who will care kindly for me and see that I am fed."

So the friend brought Reyes to Fabiano's palace, and she was so overjoyed to see him again that she turned away and wept secretly. Then with great care she prepared his bath, and after he had bathed she helped him dress in the clothes of a prince. She fed him well and took good care of him because she loved him very much.

160   One day after she had been there a month, Fabiano asked her for a favor.

"Nurse," he asked, "can you keep a secret?"

"I believe I can," Reyes answered.

"Then go to the storage room near my bedroom. There you will find a small box. Bring it to me. But remember, this is a secret only you and I will share."

Reyes brought the box, and when Fabiano opened it she saw it was full of his old love letters to her. He asked her to read the letters, and when she read them Fabiano grew
170   very sad and his eyes grew wet with tears. Reyes, too, wept silently, but because Fabiano was blind he could not see the tears which rolled down her cheeks.

IDENTIFY

What test is Reyes going to put Fabiano to?

_____

_____

_____

_____

_____

_____

_____

PREDICT

Pause at line 166. What do you think will happen when Reyes brings the box to Fabiano?

_____

_____

_____

_____

_____

_____

_____

_____

_____

_____

Why does Reyes now believe that Fabiano's love for her is real?

_____

_____

_____

_____

_____

_____

_____

_____

_____

_____

_____

_____

_____

_____

_____

_____

_____

_____

_____

_____

The next day Fabiano's friend came to visit and he found Reyes in the kitchen, her eyes red from crying. He asked Reyes what was the matter.

"Yesterday I discovered that Fabiano's love for me is real," she said, "and I cried all night after reading the letters he wrote to me."

"What do you plan to do?" the friend asked.

180   "I must put aside the mistakes of the past and marry Fabiano," she answered. "I have always loved him, and I love him even more now and want to care for him."

The friend was overjoyed. He immediately went to Fabiano and said, "My friend, I believe you should be married. You have many good years of life left; perhaps you should consider marrying this good woman who is your nurse."

Fabiano sighed. "Who would love a blind man?" he said. "And although the nurse is a good woman, the only

190   love in my heart is for Reyes."

"Then I shall go and ask her for you," the friend said.

Fabiano shook his head. "She refused me when I was young and handsome. Why should she accept me now that I am blind?"

"I will ask her anyway, and we shall see if she loves you or not!" the friend insisted.

For a moment hope stirred in Fabiano's heart. "Oh, if Reyes would marry me I would give you half of all I own, my friend!"

200   So the wedding was arranged, and the next day the friend and his wife, who were to be the witnesses, brought Reyes to Fabiano.

As they left for the church, Fabiano, who still didn't know that it was Reyes who had been his nurse, called for the nurse and told her to prepare a banquet table for the wedding feast.

Then the wedding party went to the chapel and Fabiano and Reyes were married. When they returned, everyone was happy and excited. Fabiano called his nurse to come and serve them. Only then did his friend turn to him and tell him that the nurse who had served him so loyally all that time was Reyes herself: "Don't call for your nurse, for she is in truth Reyes. She is the bride at your side!"

Fabiano then took Reyes in his arms and understood at last that the real beauty of a woman lies in her soul.

210

What does this folk tale say about love? To find out, skim the story again, and circle the words or passages that you feel say something important. Then, think about all the circled words, and state the story's theme—the overall message about life that it reveals.

_____
_____
_____
_____
_____
_____
_____
_____
_____
_____
_____
_____
_____
_____
_____
_____
_____

OWN THE STORY

Theme Write a few sentences explaining what Fabiano and Reyes each learn about love. You may find it helpful to review the story to make sure your explanation is accurate. Exchange sentences with a partner, and give feedback on each other's work.

_____

_____

_____

_____

_____

_____

KEEPING TRACK

Personal Word List Record three new vocabulary words from this tale in your Personal Word List. Choose one of the words to use in a sentence.

Personal Reading Log Did you enjoy reading this folk tale? Why or why not? Write your answer in your Personal Reading Log. Give yourself 5 points on the Reading Meter for completing it.

Checklist for Standards Mastery Track your progress toward academic success. Use the Checklist for Standards Mastery to see how much you have learned.

Fabiano and Reyes ▪ *Interactive Reading, page 130*

Go Beyond a Literary Text

Song Lyrics   The folk tale "Fabiano and Reyes" conveys a powerful **theme.** Identify that theme by analyzing what the characters learned as a result of their experiences. Then, create a "theme song" for a movie based on this story. You may choose to write only the song lyrics, or words, or you may choose to write the music as well.

Story Theme:

_____

_____

_____

♫ ♪ **Song Lyrics** ♫ ♪

_____

_____

_____

_____

_____

_____

_____

_____

_____

_____

_____

_____

_____

Chapter **4**

Forms and Patterns
Stories and Explanations

"From Form to Prediction"

LITERARY FOCUS: FORMS OF FICTION

Fiction is a type of story that has made-up events and characters. Here are some of the different forms that fiction takes:

A **novel** is a long work of fiction with a complex plot, subplots, many characters, several settings, and several themes. A **short story** is a short work of fiction and usually focuses on one major character, one major event, one setting, and one theme. A **novella** is shorter than a novel and longer than a short story; it has the same elements of fiction.

Fiction can also be categorized as science fiction, historical fiction, mysteries, and so on. You may also know these other, older categories:

A **myth** is a very old story about gods and superheroes that often explains the workings of the world. A **fable** is a teaching story with a practical moral, often with animal characters. A **legend** is a story handed down from the past that is loosely based on a historical event. A **folk tale** is an entertaining, popular story that is remembered and shared generation after generation.

A STRATEGY THAT WORKS: "FROM FORM TO PREDICTION"

As we read any kind of fiction, we use our knowledge of the form to evaluate the text critically and to predict what will happen. Here are some pointers for using the "From Form to Prediction" strategy:

⟩⟩⟩⟶ Think about what you know about the various forms of fiction. What are the characteristics of a short story? of a novel? What will you expect to find in a myth or fable?

⟩⟩⟩⟶ Before you start this chapter from a novella, predict the story details you'd expect to find in a novella.

⟩⟩⟩⟶ When you finish reading, check your predictions.

Reading Standard 1.2
Identify and interpret words with multiple meanings.

Reading Standard 2.2
Analyze text that uses the compare-and-contrast organizational pattern.

Reading Standard 3.1
Identify the forms of fiction, and describe the major characteristics of each form.

Practice Read

The text that follows is Chapter 2 from a novella called *May Hope Never Die*. A **novella** is a form of fiction that is shorter than a novel and longer than a short story. As in most fiction, a novella has a plot in which characters want something badly enough to take action to get it. Complications develop until we reach the plot's climax, which reveals how the problems in the story will work out. The resolution ends the story.

May Hope Never Die is an example of *historical fiction,* which means that even though the story is not true, it is based on actual historical events. Sometimes historical fiction even includes historical figures as story characters.

Keep the following in mind as you begin to read:
- The Nazis came to power in Germany in 1933. World War II began in 1939. By 1945, Germany was in ruins, the war in Europe was over, and about 34 million people were dead.
- Between 1941 and 1945, the Nazis hunted down and murdered 6 million European Jews.
- As this part of the novella opens, we are in Warsaw, Poland.
- The Horowitz family is hiding out in a church basement until Father Stanislaus can find a way to get them out of Poland. The family will go anywhere that is safe from the Nazis—Montreal, London, Buenos Aires, New York. Through the grapevine in the ghetto in Warsaw, they had heard of and met Father Stanislaus, who, through his network, is helping Jews escape from Poland. After the last Nazi roundup of Jews in the ghetto, the family begged Father Stanislaus for help.

Chapter 2 *from* May Hope Never Die: A Novella

The Cellar

Richard Cohen

The first night in the cellar was damp and cold. Father
Stanislaus led the family into the windowless church
storage room. "Remember—no loud noises," he cautioned.
"It's not likely that anyone would hear, but it's best not to
take chances."

Together, Father Stanislaus and Mr. Horowitz removed
the heaviest books from the bookcase and filled it with
pamphlets, hymnals—anything that was lighter in weight.
Then they pushed it against the far wall so that the door

10 to the storage room was completely hidden from **view.**
After the family was moved in, Father Stanislaus would
move the bookcase only to deliver food or information to
the family inside.

"I know this isn't a pleasant way to spend the night,"
he said. "The **quarters** are small and not very clean."

"Please," Mrs. Horowitz said. "You are saving us from
the Nazis. Don't apologize for the conditions. We are
putting you in danger. It is *we* who must apologize."

For a few moments, the priest was silent.

20 "No," he said finally, shaking his head slowly from side
to side, like he was trying to wake himself up from a bad
dream. "It is them—the Nazis—who must apologize."

"We just hope this brings you no trouble," Mr.
Horowitz said. "You are taking such a risk."

Father Stanislaus looked away. "The risk would be in
not helping." He cleared his throat. "I'll be down here in the

IDENTIFY

"The Cellar" is a chapter
from a longer work. Circle
the title of that work.

IDENTIFY

What do you know about
the **setting** of this part of
the story? Underline the
words that give the answer.

VOCABULARY
DEVELOPMENT

view (vyo͞o) *n.:* sight or
vision.

View can also mean
"judgment" or "opinion."

quarters (kwôrt′ərz) *n.:* rooms
in which people live or work.

Quarters may also refer to
coins equal to twenty-five
cents.

INTERPRET

What do you think the priest
means in saying "The risk
would be in *not* helping"
(lines 25–26)?

_____

_____

_____

PREDICT

What prediction could you make based on lines 27–33?

_____

_____

_____

_____

DECODING TIP

When you see a long and complicated word, divide it into syllables. Use vertical lines to divide the word *circumstances* (line 37) into four syllables. Then, say the word.

VOCABULARY DEVELOPMENT

match (mach) *n.:* slender piece of wood or cardboard tipped with a composition that catches fire by friction.

A *match* may also refer to "two or more persons or things that go together" or "one of a pair."

WORD KNOWLEDGE

Onomatopoeia is a literary device in which words are used to imitate sounds. Re-read lines 49–52. Circle the word or words that are examples of onomatopoeia.

morning to bring you your rations. It will have to be just me, I'm afraid. I wish I could take Magda into my confidence, but no—not yet anyway. She is a good woman,

30 but I have no idea what her politics are. It shocks me how many of the people I thought were decent and honest have been swayed by that madman. Nowadays, it's wise not to trust anyone you're not absolutely sure of."

"Of course," Mr. Horowitz said. "We understand. And now we bid you good night."

"Good night and sleep well—as well as you can under the circumstances."

Mr. Horowitz lit a **match,** which he used to light the single candle that would be the family's only source of

40 light. With the candle in hand, he led his family into the stuffy storage room. The room had no window—that was one of the peculiarities that made it a perfect hiding place. The room's existence was known only to Father Stanislaus and his housekeeper, Magda. The family—Saul Horowitz, his wife, Tekla, their thirteen-year-old daughter, Katya, and their little boy, Berel—would have only one another now— and, of course, the good priest who had agreed to hide them.

The family watched as Father Stanislaus shut the door.

50 They heard the *skreak, skreak!* of the bookcase as Father Stanislaus dragged it along the floor, the dull thud when it made contact with the wall.

If German soldiers happened to pass through the church on a routine search, and happened to descend into the cellar, they would not see the door frame behind the tall piece of furniture. There was no reason to suspect that anything was out of the ordinary. There was only one way they could know that Jews were hiding there—if someone told them.

60   In the tiny room, on a small makeshift table, the
candle burned steadily. There was no wind to make it
flicker. Only once in a while, if Berel walked by too quickly
or Katya reached out her hand too suddenly, the flame
would switch once or twice like a horse's tail in summer.
In this room, though, there was no summer.

      Above their heads, the Horowitzes could hear faint
rumblings. The sounds seemed distant, as if they came
from a truck far down the street, but in fact they were the
sounds of pedestrian traffic directly overhead. The storage
70   room had been dug under the sidewalk. Over the family's
heads, ordinary life was going on—that is, as ordinary as
life could be under Nazi occupation. That it was the
season of **spring** did not give to daily life the pleasantness
we often associate with springtime. Police were directing
traffic, hospitals were treating patients, janitors were
cleaning office buildings, taxis were picking up passengers.
Some people had **dates**—at theaters, cafes, or their friends'
and relatives' houses. Maybe they were coming home after
a long day's work.

80   But real life was forbidden to the Horowitzes and to
the other Jews who still remained in Warsaw. Any Jew
found on the streets was in danger. Police officers directing
traffic would be legally bound to arrest him and hand him
over to the Germans. Jews who fell ill could not go to the
hospital for treatment, nor could they buy food if they
were hungry.

      "How long do we have to stay here, Mama?"
Berel asked.

      "I don't know, sweetheart. The priest—"
90   "Father Stanislaus, Mama," Katya said.

      "Yes. Father Stanislaus. A good man. He said he would
find a way to get us out of Poland. But who knows?"

VOCABULARY
DEVELOPMENT

spring (spriŋ) *n.*: that season
of the year in which plants
begin to grow after lying
dormant all winter.

The word *spring* has many
meanings. It may, for
instance, refer to a coil of
wire that returns to its
original shape after being
pulled. A *spring* is also a flow
of water from the ground.

dates (dāts) *n.*: appointments
for a set time, especially for a
social engagement.

Sweet, fleshy fruits from the
date palm are also called
dates.

IDENTIFY

As a work of historical
fiction, "The Cellar" blends
factual, historical details with
fictional ones. Re-read the
story through the bottom of
page 145. Circle factual
details about Jews in
Warsaw.

· · · · · · Notes · · · · · ·

PREDICT

Given your knowledge of the Holocaust and of the elements of fiction, what conflict do you predict might arise in this story?

_____

_____

_____

_____

_____

INFER

In line 112, the ellipses show a pause in Mr. Horowitz's thinking. Why do you think he paused?

_____

_____

_____

_____

INFER

Why do you think not wearing a prayer shawl is "forgivable" (line 116)?

_____

_____

_____

_____

_____

_____

"Don't you trust him, Mama?" Katya asked.

"I didn't say that. It's just—who knows anything anymore? The world has gone insane. Who knows how long the priest himself will be a free man?"

Disturbed by her last comment, they all fell silent. But the storage room was unbearable if people weren't talking. Words filled up the space.

100 "Well, Tekla," Mr. Horowitz said, trying to joke, "perhaps you could sew some curtains for our new home. We could at least _pretend_ there's a window."

"Curtains with no windows! Don't make me laugh."

"A nice laugh wouldn't hurt any of us," her husband observed.

"A nice laugh could be fatal if a Nazi heard it," she said.

"Let's not worry too much," said Mr. Horowitz. "Before we know it, we may find ourselves in Montreal or London or Buenos Aires."

110 "I want to go to New York," Berel stated.

"All right, Berel, we'll keep that in mind," Mr. Horowitz said tenderly. "But when the time comes, we may just have to go, wherever it is they take us . . . And now," he turned to his wife, "If you will light the candle, I will put on my hat."

He was putting his hat on to pray, of course. He had no prayer shawl with him, but that was forgivable. He sat in a corner on one of the folding chairs and murmured rapidly in Hebrew—the ancient, holy language that was not used in everyday life. Then, stopping, he nodded to his 120 wife. She blew out the candle, and the room was plunged into darkness.

"Papa?" Katya said. In the pitch darkness, a person's voice seemed to come from everywhere and nowhere at the same time. The family was not yet used to locating the source of one another's voice. "If you don't mind my asking, what were you praying for?"

"For four people who are very dear to me," he said.

"Four?" Berel asked.

"Actually, *boychik*," his father explained affectionately,

130   "I was referring to my beloved wife and two children—and Father Stanislaus."

PREDICT

"The Cellar" ends with Mr. Horowitz praying for his family and Father Stanislaus. Given what you know about the Holocaust, do you think the Horowitzes have a good chance of escaping? How about Father Stanislaus?

_____

_____

_____

OWN THE STORY

PRACTICING THE STANDARDS

Forms of Fiction   Complete the "From Form to Prediction" Chart that appears on the next page. How did the writer use historical facts and the readers' knowledge of history to create suspense?

_____

_____

_____

_____

KEEPING TRACK

Personal Word List   Record the words with multiple meanings from this story in your Personal Word List.

Personal Reading Log   As you record this story in your Personal Reading Log, explain whether or not you would like to read the rest of the novella. Give yourself 3 points on the Reading Meter.

Checklist for Standards Mastery   Track the progress you've made on the Checklist for Standards Mastery.

The Cellar ▪ *Interactive Reading,* page 143

Interact with a Literary Text

"From Form to Prediction" Chart   Complete the following chart.
Look back at the story to find the details you need. Then work with
a partner to compare charts.

What I Know About Historical Fiction

What I Expected to Find in the Story

What I Actually Found in the Story

The Gold Cadillac

Interact with a Literary Text

Form-Analysis Map Fill out the following map by answering the questions about "The Gold Cadillac." What form of fiction is this story?

1. How long is "The Gold Cadillac"? _____
_____

2. Who are the characters? _____
_____

3. What is the main conflict in the plot? _____
_____

4. Is there a subplot? If so, describe it. _____
_____
_____
_____

5. Where and when is the story set? _____
_____

6. Does the story include real historical events and/or real historical people? _____
_____

7. Does the story have gods and heroes as characters, or does it explain some
   natural phenomenon? _____

8. Is the story an old tale passed on anonymously from generation to generation,
   and does it contain fantastic events? _____
_____

9. Is the story very, very short, with animal characters and with a moral stated at
   its end? _____
_____

Conclusion: _____
_____
_____

Separate but Never Equal

for use with
Holt Literature and Language Arts,
page 190

Interact with an Informational Text

Comparison Chart   In the chart below, list characteristics of the education of African American children in 1949 as opposed to those of white children, as described in "Separate but Never Equal." In the middle part of the chart, list characteristics of education common to both white and black children in 1949. On the left and right parts of the chart, list characteristics unique to each category.

Education for Black Children	BOTH	Education for White Children

La Bamba

Interact with a Literary Text

Short-Story Map Mapping the specific characteristics of a short story can help you understand its unique form. Complete the following short story map with details from Gary Soto's short story "La Bamba."

Title: Author:	Setting:
Main Character:	

Problem

↓

Event 1

↓

Event 2

↓

Event 3

↓

Event 4

↓

Resolution

Goodbye Records, Hello CDs

for use with
Holt Literature and Language Arts,
page 204

Interact with an Informational Text

Compare-and-Contrast Frame   When you *compare,* you see how two things are the same; when you *contrast,* you see how they are different. Complete the following compare-and-contrast frame as you read "Goodbye Records, Hello CDs." Write your conclusion in the box at the bottom of the frame.

Central Issue: CDs and records have many similarities and differences.

Records	CDs
1.	
2.	
3.	
4.	
5.	
6.	

Conclusion:

Medusa's Head; Perseus and the Gorgon's Head

Interact with a Literary Text

Myth Chart   Myths, an early form of fiction, have their own unique characteristics. Show that "Medusa's Head" and "Perseus and the Gorgon's Head" are myths by filling this chart with details from the stories.

Characteristics of Myths	Examples from "Medusa's Head"/ "Perseus and the Gorgon's Head"
Heroes often have supernatural power.	
Gods and goddesses are characters.	
Monsters threaten the hero.	
Explanations are provided for natural occurrences.	
Metamorphoses take place.	
Cultural values are expressed.	

He Lion, Bruh Bear, and Bruh Rabbit

for use with
Holt Literature and Language Arts,
page 225

Interact with a Literary Text

Folk-Tale Grid   A **folk tale** is a story that has been passed on anonymously from generation to generation. Folk tales usually teach lessons, which is why they are often told to children. The same character types tend to show up in folk tales: the handsome prince, the all-good princess, the clever trickster, the evil giant. Complete the following graphic organizer to see how "He Lion, Bruh Bear, and Bruh Rabbit" qualifies as a folk tale.

A Quest, a Problem to Be Solved	**Trickster Character**
Animals set off to prove to He Lion that he is not most powerful, to stop his roaring.	
Use of Number Three and Other Repetition	**Lesson Taught**

"He Lion, Bruh Bear, and Bruh Rabbit"

The Fox and the Crow; The Wolf and the House Dog

Interact with Literary Texts

Fable Chart   Fables are a special type of folk tale. **Fables** usually have animal characters that talk and act like people. Most fables teach a practical lesson about how to get along in life. They tend to be much shorter than most folk tales.

Complete the following chart to analyze "The Fox and the Crow" and "The Wolf and the House Dog."

Characteristics of Fables	Fable: "The Fox and the Crow"	Fable: "The Wolf and the House Dog"
Animals that talk and act like people		
Animal characters who represent types: tricksters, vain people, gullible people, sly people		
Moral lesson		

Literature

AUTHOR STUDY

 In the early 1980s, **Virginia Hamilton,** who had already published many novels and biographies, decided to try her hand at writing folk tales. In 1985, she published *The People Could Fly*, a collection of African American folk tales dating from the time of slavery. Hamilton went on to publish three more collections of folk tales: *In the Beginning: Creation Stories from Around the World* (1988); *Her Stories, African American Folktales, Fairy Tales, and True Tales* (1995); and *When Birds Could Talk & Bats Could Sing* (1996).

Speaking of her four volumes of folk tales, Hamilton notes: "None of these stories was ever written for children. They were just told; so I redid them, brought them out of the musty old manuscripts where nobody ever saw them." She often finds the stories in old manuscripts or out-of-print materials in libraries.

BEFORE YOU READ

Here's what you might like to know before you begin these two versions of "Little Red Riding-Hood":

- Like many folk tales, the story of Little Red Riding-Hood is found in different cultures around the world. Each culture puts its own unique spin on the story.
- Virginia Hamilton uses **dialect** in her version of the folk tale to describe her characters and setting. *Dialect* is the way people in a certain region, or even in a certain age group, speak. When dialect appears in print, the words are often spelled and pronounced differently from the way they are in standard English.

Reading Standard 3.1 Identify the forms of fiction, and describe the major characteristics of each form.

A Wolf and Little Daughter

An African American folk tale retold by Virginia Hamilton

One day Little Daughter was pickin some flowers. There was a fence around the house she lived in with her papa. Papa didn't want Little Daughter to run in the forest, where there were wolves. He told Little Daughter never to go out the gate alone.

"Oh, I won't, Papa," said Little Daughter.

One mornin her papa had to go away for somethin. And Little Daughter thought she'd go huntin for flowers. She just thought it wouldn't harm anythin to peep through

10 the gate. And that's what she did. She saw a wild yellow flower so near to the gate that she stepped outside and picked it.

Little Daughter was outside the fence now. She saw another pretty flower. She skipped over and got it, held it in her hand. It smelled sweet. She saw another and she got it, too. Put it with the others. She was makin a pretty bunch to put in her vase for the table. And so Little Daughter got farther and farther away from the cabin. She picked the flowers, and the whole time she sang a sweet song.

20 All at once Little Daughter heard a noise. She looked up and saw a great big wolf. The wolf said to her, in a low, gruff voice, said, "Sing that sweetest, goodest song again."

So the little child sang it, sang:

"*Tray-bla, tray-bla, cum qua, kimo.*"

And, *pit-a-pat, pit-a-pat, pit-a-pat, pit-a-pat,* Little Daughter tiptoed toward the gate. She's goin back home. But she hears big and heavy, PIT-A-PAT, PIT-A-PAT, comin

---

PREDICT

Underline the words in the first paragraph that help you predict that this is a Red Riding-Hood story.

FLUENCY

"A Wolf and Little Daughter" is written to imitate a storyteller's voice. Read the boxed passage aloud. Remember that the words are spelled the way they are pronounced.

TEXT STRUCTURE

Sometimes the typeface will tell how to read the text— for example, *pit-a-pat* and *PIT-A-PAT.* How do you think these words should be read?

_____

_____

_____

_____

_____

_____

_____

_____

_____

The storyteller uses nonstandard English here. Underline the word in lines 32–33 that would not be found in the dictionary. Write the standard English word that means the same thing above it.

_____

_____

_____

_____

· · · · · · Notes · · · · · ·

_____

_____

_____

_____

_____

_____

_____

_____

_____

_____

_____

_____

_____

behind her. And there's the wolf. He says, "Did you move?" in a gruff voice.

30   Little Daughter says, "Oh, no, dear wolf, what occasion have I to move?"

"Well, sing that sweetest, goodest song again," says the wolf.

Little Daughter sang it:

"*Tray-bla, tray-bla, cum qua, kimo.*"

And the wolf is gone again.

The child goes back some more, *pit-a-pat, pit-a-pat, pit-a-pat,* softly on tippy-toes toward the gate.

But she soon hears very loud, PIT-A-PAT, PIT-A-PAT,
40   comin behind her. And there is the great big wolf, and he says to her, says, "I think you moved."

"Oh, no, dear wolf," Little Daughter tells him, "what occasion have I to move?"

So he says, "Sing that sweetest, goodest song again."

Little Daughter begins:

"*Tray-bla, tray-bla, tray-bla, cum qua, kimo.*"

The wolf is gone.

But, PIT-A-PAT, PIT-A-PAT, PIT-A-PAT, comin on behind her. There's the wolf. He says to her, says,
50   "You moved."

She says, "Oh, no, dear wolf, what occasion have I to move?"

"Sing that sweetest, goodest song again," says the big, bad wolf.

She sang:

"*Tray bla-tray, tray bla-tray, tray-bla-cum qua, kimo.*"

The wolf is gone again.

And she, Little Daughter, *pit-a-pat, pit-a-pat, pit-a-pat*tin away home. She is so close to the gate now. And this

60 time she hears PIT-A-PAT, PIT-A-PAT, PIT-A-PAT comin
on *quick* behind her.

Little Daughter slips inside the gate. She shuts it—
CRACK! PLICK!—right in that big, bad wolf's face.

She sweetest, goodest safe!

PREDICT

Were you surprised by the ending of this tale? Why or why not?

_____

_____

_____

Little Red Riding-Hood

retold by Patricia Pierce

Once upon a time there was a little village girl, the prettiest ever seen; her mother doted upon her, and so did her grandmother. She, good woman, made for her a little red hood which suited her so well, that everyone called her Little Red Riding-Hood.

One day her mother, who had just made some cakes, said to her: "My dear, you shall go and see how your grandmother is, for I have heard she is ailing; take her this cake and this little pot of butter. Go quickly, and don't talk

10 to strangers on the way."

Little Red Riding-Hood started off at once for her grandmother's cottage, which was in another village.

While passing through a wood she walked slowly, often stopping to pick flowers. She looked back and saw a wolf approaching, so she stopped and waited. The wolf, who would very much liked to have eaten her, dared not,

PREDICT

Circle the phrase "Once upon a time." What do you predict the story will be like?

_____

_____

_____

_____

PREDICT

Folk and fairy tales often include a warning to the hero or heroine. Underline the warning in paragraph 2. Do you predict it will be obeyed?

_____

_____

"Pull the bobbin, and the latch will go up!"

IDENTIFY

In lines 20–23, what warning is Little Red Riding-Hood forgetting?

because some woodcutters were nearby in the forest. So he said, "Good morning, Red Riding-Hood. Where are you going?"

20   The poor child, who did not know it was dangerous to talk to a wolf, answered, "I am going to see my grand-mother, to take her a cake and a little pot of butter that my mother sends her."

"Does she live a great way off?" said the wolf.

"Oh, yes!" said Little Red Riding-Hood, "she lives beyond the mill you see right down there in the first house in the village."

"**Well,**" said the wolf, "I shall go and see her too. I shall take this road, and you take that one, and let us see who will get there first!"

The wolf set off at a gallop along the shortest road; but the little girl took the longest way and amused herself by gathering nuts, running after butterflies, and plucking daisies and buttercups.

The wolf soon reached her grandmother's cottage; he knocked at the door—*rap, rap.*

"Who's there?"

" 'Tis your grand-daughter, Little Red Riding-Hood," said the wolf in a shrill voice, "and I have brought you a cake and a little pot of butter that my mother sends you."

The good old grandmother, who was ill in bed, called out, "Pull the bobbin, and the latch will go up!"

The wolf pulled the bobbin and the door opened. He leaped on the old woman and gobbled her up in a minute; for he had had no dinner for three days **past.**

Then he shut the door and rolled himself up in the grandmother's bed, to wait for Little Red Riding-Hood.

In a while she came knocking at the door—*rap, rap.*

"Who's there?"

Little Red Riding-Hood, who heard the gruff voice of the wolf, was frightened at first, but thinking that her grandmother had a cold, answered, " 'Tis your grand-daughter, Little Red Riding-Hood, and I have brought you a cake and a little pot of butter that my mother sends you."

30

40

50

VOCABULARY DEVELOPMENT

well (wel) *inter.:* here, *well* is used as an interjection, a word that expresses emotion. *Wow!* is a common interjection.

Well can also be a noun, meaning "hole in the earth from which comes water, gas, or oil." *Well* can also be an adverb meaning "in good health."

PREDICT

Pause at line 30. What do you predict will happen next?

_____

_____

WORD KNOWLEDGE

Circle the word *bobbin* (line 42), an old-fashioned term. Look at the illustration on page 160. Find the *bobbin,* and write a definition.

_____

_____

WORD KNOWLEDGE

past (past) *adj.:* time that has gone by.

Don't confuse *past* with the verb *passed. Past* means "time that has gone by." *Passed* is the past tense of *pass,* which means "go from one place to another" or "go through a test successfully."

interest (in'trist) *n.*: concern or curiosity about something.

Interest can also mean "money paid for the use of money," as in "The bank charged 5 percent interest on the student loan."

FLUENCY

This is one of the best-loved folk-tale passages in the world. Read the boxed passage aloud with a partner as if you were performing for a roomful of children. See how scary you can sound.

• • • • • • Notes • • • • • •

_____

_____

_____

_____

_____

_____

_____

_____

_____

_____

_____

_____

_____

Then the wolf called to her in as soft a voice as he could, "Pull the bobbin, and the latch will go up." Little Red Riding-Hood pulled the bobbin and the door opened.

When the wolf saw her come in, he covered himself up with the sheets, and said, "Put the cake and the little pot of 60 butter on the chest, and come and lie down beside me."

Little Red Riding-Hood went over to the bed; she was surprised to see how strange her grandmother looked in her nightcap. But she took off her cloak and hung it up, then went back and sat down by the bed. She looked at her grandmother again with great **interest.**

She said to her, "Oh, grandmamma, grandmamma, what great arms you have got!"

"All the better to hug you with, my dear!"

"Oh, grandmamma, grandmamma, what great legs 70 you have got!" she said.

"All the better to run with, my dear!"

"Oh grandmamma, grandmamma, what great ears you have got!" said the little girl.

"All the better to hear you with, my dear!"

"Oh grandmamma, grandmamma, what great eyes you have got!" she said, beginning to get frightened.

"All the better to see you with, my dear!"

"Oh, grandmamma, grandmamma, what great *teeth* you have got!" said Little Red Riding-Hood.

80 "All the better to gobble you up!" said the wicked wolf, suddenly sitting up in the bed, drooling with hunger.

Little Red Riding-Hood screamed with terror and leapt up from her chair. Then a shot from a gun was heard, and the wicked wolf dropped back in the bed—dead.

A woodcutter who was passing had heard the cries of Little Red Riding-Hood, popped his gun through the window, and shot the wolf in time to save her. The wood-cutter rushed into the cottage and picked up Little Red Riding-Hood, who was trembling with fright. She was able to tell the woodcutter, between her tears, that the wolf had eaten up her grandmother. Quick as a wink, the woodcutter cut open the wolf's stomach and rescued the old lady, who soon recovered from her dreadful experience. She thanked the woodcutter for his timely arrival, and for saving both her and Little Red Riding-Hood. They both waved goodbye, when he left to go back to his work in the forest.

The old lady hugged her dear little grand-daughter and asked if she might have a cup of tea, please.

"Yes, of course," said Little Red Riding-Hood. She put the kettle on and put out the cake her mother had made on a pretty little plate. While she was waiting for the kettle to boil, she made her grandmother comfortable once more.

All Little Red Riding-Hood really wanted to do was to go home to her mother, for she was still very frightened by all that had happened. So she kissed her grandmother goodbye and ran all the way home. When she came to the cottage, she found her mother waiting for her at the door.

The mother **drew** Little Red Riding-Hood in, and listened to her story of all that had happened. She was delighted to have her little girl home safely again, and Little Red Riding-Hood was so happy to be out of danger that she promised her mother never to be disobedient any more.

90

100

110

OWN THE STORIES

Forms of Fiction   Make a list of at least four different folk-tale characteristics used in these two versions of "Little Red Riding-Hood." Give specific examples from each tale. Compare your folk-tale characteristics in class.

_____

_____

_____

_____

_____

_____

KEEPING TRACK

Personal Word List   You collected several words with multiple meanings as you read these folk tales. Now, add the words to your Personal Word List.

Personal Reading Log   Which version of the Little Red Riding-Hood folk tale did you enjoy more? Why? Write your reasons. You've just earned 3 points on the Reading Meter for completing these two folk tales.

Checklist for Standards Mastery   Use the Checklist for Standards Mastery to see how far you have come in mastering the standards.

A Wolf and Little Daughter;
Little Red Riding-Hood ■ *Interactive Reading,* page 157

Go Beyond Literary Texts

Author Profile   Virginia Hamilton has been called America's most honored writer of books for children. Use the Internet and library to gather more information about this popular writer. Enter your findings on the chart below.

Virginia Hamilton's Life and Art

Virginia Hamilton's Life Story	Most Famous Books

Fascinating Fact

In the Author's Own Words (Quote)

Information

FOLK TALE

BEFORE YOU READ

How many folk tales do you know? Five? Ten? You probably know even more than that. If someone in your family keeps telling the same funny story about the time Grandma . . . , that story becomes a kind of folk tale. You'll find out more about folk tales from Virginia Hamilton's informational article "Telling Tales."

Reading Standard 2.2
Analyze text that uses the compare-and-contrast organizational pattern.

Telling Tales

Virginia Hamilton

IDENTIFY

Locate and circle the section headings in this article. What do they tell you about the article's topic?

Who tells stories where you live? Is it your mother or father? Is it your uncle or aunt? Your cousin or your friend? Is it you?

"Nobody I know tells stories," I answered when my English teacher asked that question. "At my house, everybody just talks."

Now I realize that both my father and mother were storytellers. I simply did not recognize that what they were "talking" were stories. My four brothers and sisters and I, and our parents, talked about everything, all the time. We had only the radio for entertainment—there wasn't television until I was twelve—and we got used to hearing talking. It was natural for us to listen to stories and then do some telling ourselves.

Mother would begin a story with "That reminds me" or "I remember when." Once she began, "That reminds me of the time all of the Boston ivy fell from Mrs. Pinton's house."

"All of it? All at once—when did that happen?" my oldest sister, Nina, asked. And Mother was off and running with the tale about "the day the ivy fell." It is a story, part true, part fiction, and part tragic, that found its way into my novel *Sweet Whispers, Brother Rush.*

My mom and dad loved telling stories and remembering their pasts. We don't know for certain, but perhaps folk tales—"tells"—began in a similar way.

How Folk Tales Grow

Folk tales are stories passed on by word of mouth, often over many centuries. Each time the tale is told, it is changed a bit because no two people tell a story exactly the same way.

Some of these folk tales travel; that is, as they are told and retold, they move out of their original environments into other times and other places. Although traditional folk tales reflect the particular culture and people that created them, common features, called motifs, can be found in folk stories from many parts of the world. You'll find that many

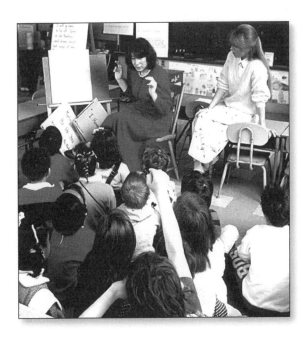

Classroom storytelling.

IDENTIFY

What does Hamilton mean by "tells" (line 26)? Check the context.

_____

_____

_____

_____

IDENTIFY

Underline Hamilton's definition of *folk tales.*

IDENTIFY

Underline the definition of *motifs* (line 35). On page 168, underline six examples of motifs.

• • • • • • Notes • • • • • •

_____

_____

_____

_____

_____

_____

PREDICT

Skim the information in lines 44–70. What do you expect this section to be about?

_____

_____

_____

_____

_____

_____

_____

_____

WORD KNOWLEDGE

Elaborate (ē·lab′ə·rit) is an adjective meaning "complex."

Elaborate (ē·lab′ə·rāt) can also be a verb, meaning "add more details." Note the difference in pronunciation.

IDENTIFY

Circle the term *escape story* (line 61). What is an escape story?

_____

_____

_____

_____

_____

folk tales include motifs like grateful beasts, tests of the hero, magic, false parents, fairy godmothers, and brave youngest sons and daughters.

40   Handed down from generation to generation, told over and over again, these "tells" become familiar stories—"They say the people could fly . . ." "Once upon a time . . ." They have become tales of the folks.

American Folk Tales: Keeping Cultures Alive

When the first Europeans came with their folk tales, the Native Americans already had an **elaborate** and rich folklore tradition. Other folk tales traveled to the New World from other countries. For example, Africans who

50   were brought to America as slaves carried with them their unique folk-telling traditions. Over generations they passed on tales about their lives on the plantations and about their relationships with the white men and women who owned them as slaves.

In fact, the African American storyteller developed the animal tale into a highly individual form. In this animal tale the social order of the plantation is broken down into animal elements, which symbolize the people in the plantation community. The African folk-tale tellers who

60   were slaves fantasized about freedom and so developed another kind of folk tale, an escape story, about flying away from slavery.

In America, people from Ireland, Denmark, Germany, France, Italy, Poland, Turkey, the Middle East, Russia, China, Japan, Korea, Vietnam, Cambodia, the Philippines, Brazil, Haiti, Puerto Rico, Nigeria, Jamaica, and practically everywhere else have told their children folk tales from their old homelands. These stories, as well as their dances, songs, and folk art, help these people stay together and

70 keep their beliefs and cultures alive.

Folk Tales and Community

Some folk tales are simple stories and others are complex. But the basic situation of the taleteller weaving his or her magic for a community of listeners is found everywhere, in every society.

For generation after generation, folk tales keep alive and close what we regard as important. They reveal who we are. As they instruct us in living, they show us our weaknesses and strengths, our fears and joys, our

80 nightmares and wishes. Folk tales are our self-portraits.

"Tells" and Tale Givers

All over America there are folk-tale-telling festivals, in which taletellers stand up and give "tells" to the listeners. In New London, Connecticut, the National Congress on Storytelling is held every June at Connecticut College. Festivals take place in Michigan, Ohio, Kentucky, and other states. The National Association for the Preservation and Perpetuation of Storytelling is based in Tennessee.

Storytelling is an ancient and wonderful custom. I have

90 grown out of the tale-giving tradition and so, perhaps, have some of you. As you read these folk tales and fables from around the world, think about those early folk-tale tellers who committed tales to memory in order to tell them aloud. Try to picture what those early tellings must have

DECODING TIP

Circle the word *taleteller* (line 73). If this word is unfamiliar to you, break it into two smaller words. Draw a line between the words, and then say the whole word aloud.

WORD KNOWLEDGE

Perpetual (pər·pech′ōō·əl) is an adjective, meaning "continuing." Knowing this, what does *perpetuation* in line 88 mean?

_____

_____

_____

_____

_____

_____

_____

_____

_____

_____

_____

_____

_____

_____

_____

been like—imagine the smoky underground kivas° of the Pueblos, the dusty village squares in Nigeria.

Sitting or standing there, surrounded by the community of listeners, the teller calls softly, "Time was when the animals could talk . . ." The listeners respond.

100 They lean forward, absolutely quiet now, eager to hear, to be entertained, to learn.

° **kiva** (kē′və) *n.:* in Pueblo Indian dwellings, a kiva is a large underground room used basically for religious purposes.

OWN THE TEXT

PRACTICING THE STANDARDS

Forms of Fiction   Make a list of six folk tales that are part of your tradition or that are popular in the United States. You can get your information from your own experience, from interviews with other people in your family or community, from an encyclopedia, or even from a visit to a library or bookstore. After each title, write a few sentences summing up the folk tale's plot.

KEEPING TRACK

Personal Word List   In your Personal Word List, record any new words you learned from this article. Put a star next to the words that have more than two meanings.

Personal Reading Log   As you add this article to your Personal Reading Log, describe one folk tale you would like to share with Virginia Hamilton. Give yourself 2 points on the Reading Meter for completing the article.

Checklist for Standards Mastery   See how much progress you have made by using the Checklist for Standards Mastery.

Telling Tales ■ *Interactive Reading,* page 166

Go Beyond an Informational Text

Research on Storytelling   Virginia Hamilton mentions several folk-tale festivals in America. Do research on the festivals she mentions, and make a report on them. You should see if any new festivals have arisen since Hamilton wrote this article. Pay special attention to storytelling festivals near where you live. You can use this graphic to keep your notes.

Names of Festivals

Locations

Purposes

Famous Storytellers

Sources of My Information

Literature

TALL TALE

"I caught a mouse the size of a dog. I'm not kidding!" How many storytellers use wild overstatement like this? A form of folk tale that uses exaggeration for comic effect is called the **tall tale**. Tall tales are so-called because as each reteller adds more exaggeration, the story gets taller, and taller, and . . . We don't really believe the exaggerations in a tall tale, but they make a whale of a good yarn! Enjoy this tall tale about Papa John, who did everything bigger and faster—and with more style—than anybody else.

You might want to know the following before you start reading "Papa John's Tall Tale":

• This story was first told by Africans held in slavery, who worked on plantations in the American South. The story was adapted and set down in print by Virginia Hamilton.

• The story contains the following specialized vocabulary:

  big house: plantation owner's house.

  Missus: plantation owner or the owner's wife.

  House Jim: title meaning that Jim works in the big house rather than in the field.

Reading Standard 3.1
Identify the forms of fiction, and describe the major characteristics of each form.

Papa John's Tall Tale

Virginia Hamilton

Papa John was an old-timer and we did what he told us. Jake was his son, and after he had his dinner, Papa John told Jake to find a horse that was fastest. Jake went to the big house, asked for the horse that was fastest.

House Jim says, "Take Missus' ridin horse, that the one is fastest."

So Jake rode Missus' mare on back over to Papa John. He got there before he left, too. And he says, "Papa, here's Fastest."

10 "Who the mare belong to?" asked Papa John.

"Belong to Missus," Jake says.

"How you know she is Fastest?" Papa John says.

"I know she is Fastest because I'm here before I'm gone," says Jake. And it was the truth, he had got **back** before he'd left. Any fool could see that.

"Well," Papa John says, "take that mare and take this pumpkin seed on your back. Don't drop it—it's heavy. Carry it on over to the **field.** Take a shovel and make a hole a quarter mile wide and drop that pumpkin seed in."

20 "That all?" asked Jake.

"No," said Papa John. "You got to get out of there as fast as you can. That's why you ridin the horse that's fastest. Don't look back, just get out of there once you drop that pumpkin seed."

So Jake did what he was told. And we was all watchin. That mare run as best she knew how, which was fastest. But it wasn't good enough.

"Papa John's Tall Tale" from *The People Could Fly: American Black Folktales* by Virginia Hamilton. Copyright © 1985 by Virginia Hamilton. Reprinted by permission of **Alfred A. Knopf Children's Books, a division of Random House, Inc.**

IDENTIFY

Pause at line 9. Circle the expression "He got there before he left, too." Why would you expect to hear this sort of thing in a tall tale?

_____

_____

_____

_____

_____

VOCABULARY DEVELOPMENT

back (bak) *adv.:* to or toward a former position or location.

Back can also be a verb, meaning "provide financial support," or a noun that refers to the part of a body, or a book opposite the front part.

field (fēld) *n.:* wide stretch of open land. What would a baseball player mean by *field* (think of a noun and a verb).

_____

_____

FLUENCY

Put down your book, and tell a partner what's going on in the boxed passage. Then, read it aloud.

DECODING TIP

This writer uses **dialect** to re-create the way the storyteller would speak. Use context clues and sound clues to guess at what *ofum* (line 34) means.

_____

_____

IDENTIFY

You expect to find outrageous exaggeration in a tall tale. Underline the comical exaggeration on this page.

VOCABULARY DEVELOPMENT

hands (handz) *n.*: workers who labor with their hands; staff or crew. What other meaning of *hands* are you familiar with?

_____

_____

_____

_____

_____

_____

Jake said, "Git-up-and-gone, Fastest!" He looked back, what he wasn't spose to do, which slowed him down some, 30 and saw the pumpkin seed was growin vines, and the vines was after that fastest mare.

The mare and Jake had to climb across the leaves to keep goin. And then there were pumpkins house high. The hogs was eatin inside ofum and livin in there. So Jake and the horse ridin on through. Get on back to Papa John. Real upset, Jake was, and told him what happen.

Papa John soothes him, "That's all right, that's all right. Nothin gone get you next to me here," Papa John said. "That wasn't much of a pumpkin seed to begin with. You 40 shoulda been around when I was a turnip grower."

"You a turnip grower, Papa?" asked Jake.

"Was one time," Papa John said. "I plowed me two acre. I got me a mountain of manure and spread it on thick. Then I put down the turnip seed."

"What happened?" Jake asked him.

"Well, all a sudden," Papa John says, "that manure was slopped up. That turnip grew so, a herd of cows would get under a turnip leaf and sleep all day. So I had to fence it. Keep all out. Took me six months to fence around that 50 turnip, too.

"When that turnip growed up," Papa John continued, "I had to find some way to cook it. I went down there to a man could make things. I say, 'I need a pot big and high as a hill.'

"Man says, 'I can do it. Hire me some **hands** to help me.'

"That's what he did," Papa John says. "He hires up a hundred hands. They dug up that hill for the clay. Then they was a-moldin and castin that hill into a pot. When it

60　was done they had them a clay pot hill high. Then the man could make things got another hundred hands to help roll that pot atop the turnip. Wasn't no use tryin to get the turnip in the pot. So that's how we had to cook it, with the fire above the pot and the turnip under it."

"Take you long?" asked Jake.

"Well, it took about a year to get it boiled through. But it cooked up real fine, that turnip did," Papa John said.

"How long ago was that?" asked Jake.

"Oh, when you was a little fellow," Papa John said.
70　"Been years ago."

"Well, I sure woulda liked to tasted that turnip, Papa," Jake said.

"Well, you had your chance," Papa John said. "You et the last piece of it for your dinner today."

IDENTIFY

Pause at line 66. Notice Jake's reaction to the wild story he's just heard—as if all that were nothing out of the ordinary. What exaggeration did he just hear?

_____
_____
_____
_____
_____
_____
_____
_____

IDENTIFY

What's the final joke?

_____
_____
_____
_____
_____
_____
_____
_____
_____
_____

OWN THE STORY

Forms of Fiction   List three features of a tall tale. Next to each feature, write a sentence explaining how this characteristic is reflected in "Papa John's Tall Tale."

Feature	Sentence
_____	_____
	_____
_____	_____
	_____
_____	_____
	_____

KEEPING TRACK

Personal Word List   Record the words you learned from this tall tale in your Personal Word List.

Personal Reading Log   Add this tall tale to your Personal Reading Log, and describe how you feel about tall tales. Give yourself 1 point on the Reading Meter for reading "Papa John's Tall Tale."

Checklist for Standards Mastery   Use the Checklist for Standards Mastery to see how well you have mastered the standards.

Papa John's Tall Tale ▪ *Interactive Reading,* page 173

Go Beyond a Literary Text

Outline a Tall Tale   America is known as a country that specializes in tall tales. You might know the tall tales about the lumberjack Paul Bunyan and his blue ox, Babe. They dug a canal so big it turned out to be the Mississippi River. Maybe you've heard about the frontiersman Davy Crockett. He cooked himself bear steaks with a piece of the sunrise that he carried in his pocket.

Write yourself a tall tale. Before you write, think about your hero or heroine and the challenges he or she faces. Then brainstorm some exaggerated feats, and write them on the outline below.

Tall-Tale Features	My Ideas
Hero or heroine	
Setting	
Challenges	
Feats (this is where the exaggeration comes in)	
Features of the country or world (explained by the hero's/heroine's feats)	

Chapter Preview In this chapter you will—

Strategy Launch:
"Say Something"

LITERARY FOCUS: BIOGRAPHY AND AUTOBIOGRAPHY

Autobiography and **biography** are literary forms that tell the story of a person's life. The events, places, and people in biography and auto-biography are real.

An **autobiography** is the story of a person's life written by that same person. In an autobiography, the subject's own experiences, thoughts, and feelings are revealed.

A **biography** is the story of a person's life written by another person. Biographers research the lives of the subjects they write about. In general this research is presented **objectively**—it sticks closely to the facts. Sometimes, though, a biographer chooses to take a more **subjective** approach—that is, to include his or her opinions and emotional reactions to the story's subject.

A STRATEGY THAT WORKS: "SAY SOMETHING"

The "Say Something" strategy can be particularly helpful when reading a biography or an autobiography. Here's how the strategy works: As you read, you pause regularly and say something—make a comment or ask a question—about what you've just read. You can:

- make a prediction
- ask a question
- make a comment
- make a connection

POINTERS FOR USING "SAY SOMETHING"

)))➡ Read a text, pausing from time to time to "Say Something" about what you've read. What you say should be in the form of a prediction, question, comment, or connection, and it should relate to what you've just read.

)))➡ When you've finished reading the story, pause to reflect on your "Say Something" questions and comments. Sum up your reading experience with a final comment.

Reading Standard 1.4
Monitor expository text for unknown words or words with novel meanings by using word, sentence, and paragraph clues to determine meaning.

Reading Standard 2.3
Connect and clarify main ideas by identifying their relationship to other sources and related topics.

Reading Standard 3.5
Identify the speaker, and recognize the difference between first- and third-person narration (for example, autobiography compared with biography).

BEFORE YOU READ

"The Picture" is an excerpt from an autobiography. The writer, Helene Leconte, recounts an incident from her life that set her on the way to a successful career. This selection is a good example of how an autobiography can be informative and provide exciting and suspenseful reading.

The Picture

Helene Leconte

IDENTIFY

What clues in the second paragraph tell you that you are reading an autobiography?

_____

_____

_____

_____

_____

_____

VOCABULARY DEVELOPMENT

shelf (shelf) *n.:* sand bar or reef.

The meaning of the word *shelf* in this passage is a specialized one. The common meaning of *shelf* is "thin, flat length of material that is used for holding something."

"Helene Leconte was born in Paris, France, in such-and-such a year and studied photography in such-and-such a school. She is best known for her vivid color images of undersea life."

This is what the encyclopedia says about me, more or less, now that I am known around the world. But it wasn't easy becoming a legendary undersea photographer. In fact, my career almost ended on its first day.

It happened off the coast of North Africa. I had signed
10   aboard a small diving ship with a group of scientists who were studying the life forms of the ocean **shelf.** My job was to keep a visual record of the scientists' explorations. That meant following them as they swam under the water in their wet suits and scuba gear. It also meant taking pictures of whatever school of fish or growth of coral or forest of underwater plants they might come across.

My private task, though, was different. It was to get The Picture. What was The Picture? I wouldn't know before

I took it. After I took it, I would know it as well as I knew
anything. It would be the important, famous, beautiful
photo that would make my name in the field. It would be
reprinted in articles and books. It would be my ticket to
future assignments—high-paying, glamorous ones.

And it would involve some danger in the taking. I
knew that ahead of time. Most people who have taken
spectacular photos have had to stretch for them. They have
climbed mountains or crawled on skyscraper ledges or
stood on battlefields in the midst of bullets. To be great in
this profession, you must go places and do things that you
otherwise wouldn't.

I had done a bit of skin diving before, but when I
joined the scientists' party I didn't yet plan to specialize
in undersea pictures. It was just an assignment I'd
happened to get. It sounded fun. So there I was, zipping
my wet suit and buckling my air tank and checking my
underwater camera.

Dr. Dumas and Professor Simon dove in ahead of
me. I watched as they went into a tuck position and
dropped head-down through the waves. With ease they
swam away from the boat. I took a deep breath, clamped
my teeth onto the mouthpiece of the air hose, shut my
eyes, and followed suit.

Splash! Opening my eyes, I found myself in a slower,
more beautiful world. The green-gray water seemed to melt
around me. It was patched with sunlight from above. It was
flecked with tiny plants and shreds of seaweed. Sluggishly
kicking my rubber fins, I swam through a curtain of my
own upward-floating air bubbles. Except that the water was
freezing—it felt as if I was moving through liquid glass.

SAY SOMETHING

Pause at line 23. What have
you learned about the storyteller so far?

_____

_____

_____

_____

_____

SAY SOMETHING

Pause at line 36. What do
you predict will happen next?

_____

_____

_____

_____

_____

FLUENCY

Read the boxed text aloud
as if you were the author
telling this story to an audience. Bring the experience
alive by varying your speaking rate and the tone of
your voice.

IDENTIFY

In an autobiography the writer can tell us his or her private thoughts and feelings. Underline some of the writer's thoughts and feelings revealed in lines 50–69.

SAY SOMETHING

Pause at line 75. If you had the opportunity to talk to the narrator, what question might you want to ask her?

_____

_____

_____

_____

_____

_____

_____

_____

_____

VOCABULARY DEVELOPMENT

gloss (glôs) *n.:* brightness or luster of a smooth, polished surface; sheen.

The word *gloss* has a number of other meanings. As a verb, it means "give a smooth surface to something." As a noun, *gloss* can mean "note or comment on a text." In that sense this very note you're reading is a gloss!

50　　　I tried to keep up with the others, but they were much more experienced divers than I. Plus, they knew where they were going, and I did not. In addition, I kept pausing to gaze through my camera. I was in a wonderland and didn't want to miss a single sight.

　　　I was so entranced by this strange new world that I got separated from my companions. Mere seconds into my dive, I had broken the first rule of safe diving!

　　　When I finally located Dr. Dumas and Professor Simon after a frantic scan of my surroundings, they were

60　only some thirty meters ahead. But under the sea, thirty meters can be the distance between life and death. I got scared and began to flounder. I wanted to call out, but if I opened my mouth I would lose my air hose. Anyway, humans can't hear under water.

　　　Then I did something stupid. I kicked as fast as I could, trying to catch up with them. One reason it was stupid was because I was wasting energy and air and not getting far. A more important reason: my frantic motion drew the attention of the surrounding creatures.

70　　　Scarcely knowing where I was, I looked for the sunlit part of the water, which would be the part nearest to the surface. Then, to check my bearings, I looked back into the deeper darkness—and saw something round and gray, like a small, slightly bent, gray log. But this log had an eye at each end. And it was staring at me.

　　　It was a hammerhead shark, lurking about three meters away. For one of the weirdest fish in the sea, it was a beauty. Its skin had a high **gloss.** Its fins were broad, its gill slits big. In its mouth were several rows of the sharpest

80　teeth I have ever seen. They looked like triangular razor blades.

Hammerheads have been known to attack humans for no reason at all. I'm very grateful I didn't know that then. But I did realize that I was looking at something alien. I knew it *might* decide to eat me, and if it decided to, it could.

Although I was terrified, a small, forward part of my brain remained calm. It tested ideas and visualized outcomes. It tried to remember the best way to react to a shark. Were you supposed to flee, or stay still? Surely, the best advice was to stay calm and not panic.

I flicked my flippers up and down as mildly, as gently as I could. But the shark was not persuaded to leave me alone. Perhaps it did not believe I was no threat. Perhaps it was hungry. At any rate, it glided toward me, slowly at first. I had enough presence of mind to glide slowly upward, out of its way.

Then its tail gave a flick. I was sure I was going to be its meal in a matter of seconds. But as the shark approached, a miracle happened. The shark got distracted. It looked to its right, into the darkness. I looked, too.

From that dark corner of the waters, a fierce activity burst suddenly upon us. Sleek, torpedo-shaped bodies rushed at us, slicing cleanly through the water. At first I assumed more sharks were coming to fight over me. I was wrong, thankfully. These creatures surged at the hammerhead, and with their large, bulbous heads they smacked into its middle.

My saviors were bottlenose dolphins. They were dark gray on top and white underneath, and about two and a half meters long. They came at the shark from every direction, hitting it with their "melon," the large, round, front part of their heads. The dolphins' blows drove the shark back.

IDENTIFY

Underline more of the writer's thoughts and feelings revealed on this page.

· · · · · · · Notes · · · · · · ·

_____

_____

_____

_____

_____

_____

_____

IDENTIFY

A good writer always tries to help the reader share an experience. Circle details that help you visualize the dolphins.

· · · · · · · Notes · · · · · · ·

_____

_____

_____

_____

_____

pod (pod) *n.:* small group of animals, especially seals, whales, dolphins, and so on.

Can you name any other words that mean "a group of a certain kind of animal"? You've probably heard of a *school* of fish, but what about a *pride* of lions?

SAY SOMETHING

Pause at line 130. What comment can you make about what you've just read? Do you have any questions about what will be described next?

_____

_____

_____

_____

_____

_____

_____

_____

_____

IDENTIFY

Circle the descriptive words in lines 134–150 that help you visualize this unusual scene. What do you visualize as "dolphin braids" (line 146)?

The shark didn't know where to turn. With their wonderful brains and their ability to act in concert, these seagoing mammals could kill a shark despite its fearsome teeth. I almost felt sorry for the shark. Not too sorry, though.

When I realized that I was being saved, I began clicking
120 the shutter as fast as I could. I took thirty-one photos of the dolphins mauling the shark. Did I get The Picture? I got a good handful of them. They were the most dramatic, close-up photos anyone had ever taken of a **pod** of dolphins attacking a shark. If you have ever seen photos of that subject in a book or magazine, you have probably seen my photos. And many other pictures of underwater life that have gained notice over the years have been mine as well.

As I watched the maimed hammerhead drift down and away, I reminded myself to get back to the boat. But where
130 *was* the boat? I looked around and couldn't locate it.

I needn't have worried. One of the dolphins—their leader, I think, the one that had attacked first—turned to me. She swam smoothly in my direction. Then she dipped her head and dove below me, and then rose underneath me. Soon I was riding her as if she were a horse. Thrillingly fast, we swam to the surface. I broke through into fresh, warm air and saw the boat floating nearby.

The crew were leaning excitedly over the bow. They stretched their hands for me and pulled me up. I was
140 surrounded by hugs and cheers and anxious questions. I pulled off my diving mask and tried to answer.

But then we all stopped to look at the carnival in the water. The dolphin rescuers were swimming joyfully alongside our boat. They jumped above the water and plunged in again. Crossing one another's paths, they wove dolphin braids in the water. Some of them swam behind the boat like water skiers for the excitement of riding across its wake.

The dolphins whistled their **signature** tunes, calling
150   to one another. Were they happy for me? Were they proud of their heroism? Who knows? I would like to believe that they were.

A couple of minutes later, Dr. Dumas and Professor Simon climbed up the side of our boat. They had missed all the action. Removing his mask, Dr. Dumas glared at me disapprovingly as his wet suit dripped water onto the deck of the boat. He asked, "And where were you all this time, expert photographer?"

"Out getting pictures," I said casually.

160   The good professors actually wanted to fire me until the crew told them of my adventure. From then on they were a little in awe of me. They asked me to suggest places to swim in search of interesting finds. The truth was, I still had no idea what I was doing. The shark attack had been an accident—one that turned out to be very, very fortunate.

Dumas and Simon were right to put their trust in me for one reason, though. I could lead them to dolphins. For the remainder of our two-week cruise, the dolphins reap-peared whenever I dove down into their liquid **realm.** As I
170   swam, they would keep me company and offer me rides to the surface. They seemed to love to poke their heads above the water and look around at an airy world they were made to breathe in, but could not live in. I owe those dolphins so much—they not only helped save my life, they gave birth to my new career as an undersea photographer.

signature (sig′nə·chər) *adj.*: typical of or identified with a person, place, or thing.

Signature is more often used as a noun, meaning "a person's name written by that person."

realm (relm) *n.*: region; sphere; area.

The phrase "liquid realm" would be very strange with-out knowing the context—here it obviously refers to the underwater world in which this story mostly takes place. The word *realm* can also refer to a kingdom, as in "the realm of Queen Elizabeth." *Realm* can also refer to something abstract, as in the sentence "Passing the test is in the realm of possibility."

SAY SOMETHING

What comments would you make about this story?

_____

_____

_____

_____

_____

IDENTIFY

Underline the words in this last paragraph that state the writer's main point in writing this part of her life story.

OWN THE STORY

Autobiography   Identify this story's speaker, and trace your questions and comments by filling out the "Say Something" Summary on the following page. Then, on the lines below, write down your final comment on "The Picture."

_____

_____

_____

Main Idea   What is the narrator's main point in telling this part of her life story? Write two or three sentences in which you sum up her main point in telling this incredible story. Quote one passage from the article to support what you say. Be sure to use quotation marks for a direct quotation.

_____

_____

_____

_____

_____

KEEPING TRACK

Personal Word List   Record the words you learned in this selection in your Personal Word List. Put a star next to any words that have novel or unusual meanings.

Personal Reading Log   As you record "The Picture" in your Personal Reading Log, explain why you liked or disliked this story. Award yourself 4 points on the Reading Meter for reading it.

Checklist for Standards Mastery   Check your progress in achieving the reading standards. Turn to the Checklist for Standards Mastery, and place a checkmark next to standards you have mastered.

The Picture ■ *Interactive Reading,* page 180

Interact with a Literary Text

"Say Something" Summary   As you read "The Picture," you should have paused at several stopping points to "say something"— to ask yourself a question about what you'd read or to make a comment. Use the boxes below to record your "Say Somethings."

Line Number	Prediction	Question	Comment	Connection

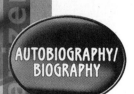

Storm

AUTOBIOGRAPHY/ BIOGRAPHY

Interact with a Literary Text

Point-of-View Questionnaire   Understanding the characteristics of an autobiography or a biography helps you to focus on what you read. Use the following questionnaire to help you analyze "Storm."

Who is the narrator of this story?

_____

_____

What does the narrator tell you about the main characters?

_____

_____

_____

Does the narrator tell you what the characters think and feel?

_____

_____

_____

_____

From which point of view is this story told?

_____

_____

Which pronoun is used by the narrator to tell the story?

_____

_____

What do you think is the relationship between the narrator and the writer of this story?

_____

_____

This story is an example of _____ **writing.**
(circle one)   biographical   autobiographical

Bringing Tang Home; Where the Heart Is

Interact with Informational Texts

Main-Idea Web Sometimes you are asked to connect the main ideas in one reading selection to those in another. Here is a Main-Idea Web that will help you connect "Bringing Tang Home" with "Where the Heart Is."

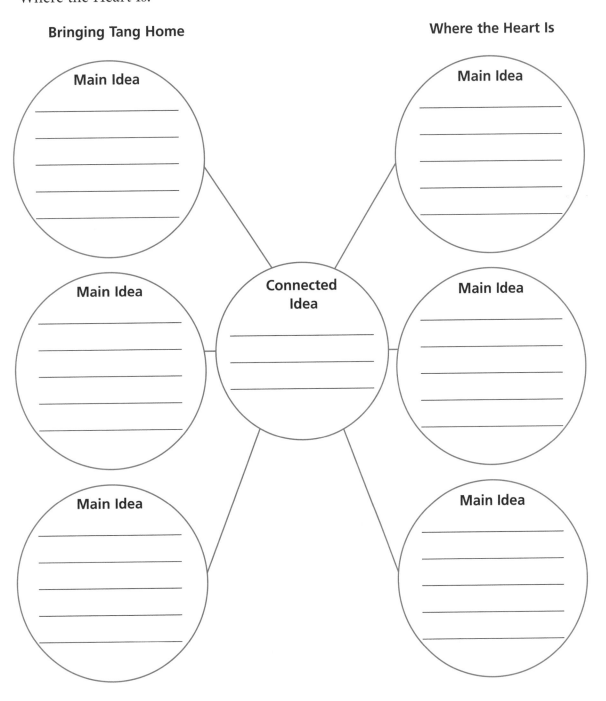

Bringing Tang Home

Main Idea

Main Idea

Main Idea

Where the Heart Is

Main Idea

Main Idea

Main Idea

Connected
Idea

Brother

AUTOBIOGRAPHY/ BIOGRAPHY

Interact with a Literary Text

Description Chart   Biography and autobiography use description to make subjects and events come alive for us. Fill out this Description Chart as you read "Brother," to see how Maya Angelou uses words to appeal to your senses.

You should write down the descriptive passage in the left-hand column. Then check off the sense or senses that the words appeal to. The first one is done for you. Be sure to put quotation marks around the direct quotes.

Description Chart

Title: Brother   Author: Maya Angelou

Passage	Sight	Touch	Smell	Taste	Hearing
"I was big, elbowy, grating"	✔				

The Brother I Never Had

Interact with a Literary Text

Main-Idea Chart   Fill out this Main-Idea Chart after you read "The Brother I Never Had." The main ideas in the essay are listed at the left. You should find a detail that supports each idea and write it in the box to the right.

Main Idea	Detail from "The Brother I Never Had"
Young people can have strong relationships.	
Love and respect are important in strong relationships.	
Relationships from youth teach life lessons.	

NARRATION

from **The Land I Lost**

Interact with a Literary Text

Narration-Example Chart   The writer of *The Land I Lost* begins by telling his own story; then he tells the stories of others. When he tells his own story, he uses first-person narration (he uses the first-person pronouns "I," "me," "we," and "us"). When he tells the stories of other people, he uses the third person ("he," "she," "they," and so on). After you read the excerpt from *The Land I Lost,* fill out the following with examples of each type of narration. The first one is done for you.

First-Person Narration	Third-Person Narration
"I was born on the central highlands of Vietnam . . ."	"Trung was happiest when Lan was helping his mother."

A Glory over Everything

for use with
Holt Literature and Language Arts,
page 288

Interact with a Literary Text

Biography Chart   Some biographies are written by people who know their subjects well. Others are written hundreds, even thousands, of years after the subject has died. All biographies require careful research. Almost all biographies will contain some details that cannot be proved true—or false. Such material is based on inferences the biographer makes, and those are based on facts in the historical record.

After you read this biography of Harriet Tubman, identify details that can be proved true and details that are based on the biographer's educated guesswork.

The first examples are done for you.

Objective Facts Based on Research	Probable Details Provided by Author
In 1849, Harriet Tubman meets a woman who offers to give help.	The woman "nodded her head, clucked to the horse, and drove off murmuring."

MAIN IDEA

All Aboard with Thomas Garrett; Harriet Tubman: The Moses of Her People; The Harriet Tubman Series

Interact with Informational Texts

"Making Connections" Chart   After you read and view these three selections about Harriet Tubman, fill out a "Making Connections" Chart. Three of the main ideas that the selections have in common are provided at the left.

Main Idea	Detail from *All Aboard with Thomas Garrett*	Detail from *Harriet Tubman: The Moses of Her People*	Detail from *The Harriet Tubman Series*
People risked their lives to escape slavery. They also risked never seeing their families again.			
Those who were not slaves also helped in the Underground Railroad.			
Tubman's life was often lonely. She was driven by her mission.			

Literature

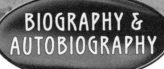
AUTHOR STUDY

In *Holt Literature and Language Arts,* you read "Brother," from **Maya Angelou's** autobiography *I Know Why the Caged Bird Sings.* In the selections you are about to read, you will learn more about the experiences that made Maya Angelou the extraordinary individual she is today.

In the biographical essay "Maya Angelou," Joyce Hansen gives us a sense of the events that shaped Angelou's life.

Angelou's poem "Life Doesn't Frighten Me" presents a more subjective viewpoint. "Life Doesn't Frighten Me" exists as a personal statement in which Angelou herself tells us how she's managed to overcome the fears that otherwise might have beaten her down.

Marguerite Johnson, who became known as Maya Angelou, was born on April 4, 1928, in St. Louis, Missouri. She and her brother, Bailey, were raised by their grandmother, the owner of a country store in Stamps, Arkansas.

During her lifetime, Angelou struggled to overcome many difficult circumstances, a process she believes made her strong. The events of her life became known to millions through the 1970 publication of her autobiography *I Know Why the Caged Bird Sings,* which was nominated for a National Book Award and later used as the basis for a TV movie.

Reading Standard 3.5
Identify the speaker, and recognize the difference between first- and third-person narration (for example, autobiography compared with biography).

BEFORE YOU READ

How did you become *you*? What are the circumstances that helped shape you? Who are the individuals who changed your life? This biographical essay provides a sketch of the experiences that formed Maya Angelou.

from Women of Hope: African Americans Who Made a Difference

Maya Angelou

Joyce Hansen

SAY SOMETHING

As you begin to read the essay, circle the pronouns *I* and *she*. Ask yourself: Whom do these pronouns refer to? What is this person's relationship to the subject of the essay?

_____

_____

_____

_____

_____

_____

_____

_____

_____

_____

VOCABULARY DEVELOPMENT

perceptive (pər·sep′tiv) *adj.:* able to comprehend through insight or intuition.

segregated (seg′rə·gāt′id) *adj.:* set apart or separated according to race.

"I was mute for five years," Maya Angelou has said. "I wasn't cute and I didn't speak. . . . But my grandma told me all the time, 'Sister, Mama don't care what these people say about you being a moron, being a idiot. Mama don't care. Mama know, Sister, when you and the good Lord get ready, you're gonna be a preacher.' "

In *I Know Why the Caged Bird Sings,* the first of her five autobiographies, Maya Angelou begins to chronicle her life. She was a little girl with a poet's heart. But when she

10 was seven, her song was silenced by a terrible experience and she stopped speaking. With the help of her grandmother who raised her in Stamps, Arkansas, the close-knit black community there, and a **perceptive** teacher who recognized her literary gifts and introduced her to literature, Maya found her voice again. She graduated from her **segregated** school at the top of her eighth-grade class.

She left Arkansas at thirteen to go to California to live with her mother. By sixteen, she had a child of her own to raise. "The greatest gift I've ever had was the birth of my

20 son. . . . When he was small, I knew more than he did, I expected to be his teacher. So because of him I educated myself. When he was four . . . I taught him to read. But then he'd ask questions, and I didn't have the answers, so I started my lifelong love affair with libraries. . . ."

She also refused to be controlled by a society that defined her as inferior because she was black and female.

"I decided many years ago to invent myself. I had obviously been invented by someone else—by a whole society—and I didn't like their invention." Maya Angelou
30 **redefined** herself. When she was in her twenties, she studied dance and was in a musical that toured Europe and Africa. Angelou also used her talents to try to help make the world a better place. In 1960, she and another performer wrote, produced, and appeared in the revue *Cabaret for Freedom* to raise money for the civil rights movement. She also spent time in Ghana, West Africa, working as a journalist in the 1960s. She has written, produced, directed, and acted in theater, movie, and television productions. She was nominated for an Emmy Award for her performance in the
40 television miniseries *Roots* and was nominated for the Pulitzer Prize in poetry. Maya Angelou also has twelve honorary doctorates.

Millions of Americans saw and heard her recite her poem "On the Pulse of Morning" for President Clinton's **inauguration** in 1993.

The message she brings through the example of her life and her art is clear. "All of my work is meant to say, you may encounter many defeats, but you must not be defeated."
50 Maya Angelou continues to rise, and we soar with her.

VOCABULARY DEVELOPMENT

redefined (rē′dē·fīnd′) v.: changed the nature of; reinvented.

Redefined is used in an unusual way here. Draw a box around the context clue in line 29 that helps you figure out the sense in which the word *redefined* is used.

inauguration (in·ôg′yə·rā′shən) n.: ceremony that signifies the formal or official beginning of the president's term.

IDENTIFY

Underline the activities Angelou has participated in, as well as the jobs or careers she has had. These details convey some important life decisions that Angelou has made. What do these details reveal about Angelou?

_____
_____
_____
_____
_____
_____
_____
_____
_____
_____

Life Doesn't Frighten Me

Maya Angelou

FLUENCY

Read the boxed stanza silently at first, circling words you think are most important. Then, read the stanza aloud. Where will you pause?

INFER

Why do you think the speaker calls Mother Goose "mean" (line 7)?

_____

_____

_____

_____

WORD KNOWLEDGE

The word *counterpane* in line 11 means "bedspread." This word is rarely used anymore.

• • • • • • Notes • • • • • •

_____

_____

_____

_____

_____

Shadows on the wall
Noises down the hall
Life doesn't frighten me at all
Bad dogs barking loud
5 Big ghosts in a cloud
Life doesn't frighten me at all.

Mean old Mother Goose
Lions on the loose
They don't frighten me at all
10 Dragons breathing flame
On my counterpane
That doesn't frighten me at all.

I go boo
Make them shoo
15 I make fun
Way they run
I won't cry
So they fly
I just smile
20 They go wild
Life doesn't frighten me at all.

Tough guys in a fight

All alone at night

Life doesn't frighten me at all.

25 Panthers in the park

Strangers in the dark

No, they don't frighten me at all.

That new classroom where

Boys pull all my hair

30 (Kissy little girls

With their hair in curls)

They don't frighten me at all.

Don't show me frogs and snakes

And listen for my scream.

35 If I'm afraid at all

It's only in my dreams.

I've got a magic charm

That I keep up my sleeve,

I can walk the ocean floor

40 And never have to breathe.

Life doesn't frighten me at all

Not at all

Not at all

Life doesn't frighten me at all.

INFER

How old do you think the narrator of this poem is? Do you think this speaker is the poet or someone else?

_____

_____

_____

_____

INFER

What do you think the speaker means by "kissy little girls" (line 30)?

_____

_____

_____

_____

INFER

Do you think that, despite all her brave remarks, this little girl is not really so brave?

_____

_____

_____

_____

OWN THE SELECTIONS

Biography/Poem   Write a few sentences telling how the biographical essay and the poem work together to provide you with a sense of who Maya Angelou is.

_____

_____

_____

_____

_____

_____

KEEPING TRACK

Personal Word List   Record the words you learned from the essay in your Personal Word List.

Personal Reading Log   As you record this selection in your Personal Reading Log, write a few sentences explaining which of the pieces you liked better. Award yourself 1 point on the Reading Meter for reading these selections.

Checklist for Standards Mastery   Check your progress in recognizing first-person and third-person narration. Use the Checklist for Standards Mastery in the back of this book to track your progress in mastering the standards.

Maya Angelou;
Life Doesn't Frighten Me ■ *Interactive Reading,* page 196

Go Beyond Literary Texts

Author "Interview"   Think about what you know of Maya Angelou and what you'd like to find out. Then write a list of interview questions that you would prepare if you had the opportunity to meet her.

A good interview contains a mix of question types. Avoid asking questions that can be answered by a simple "yes" or "no" or by simple research.

Interview Questions

1. _____

_____

_____

2. _____

_____

_____

3. _____

_____

_____

4. _____

_____

_____

5. _____

_____

_____

Information

ARTICLE

Does life sometimes frighten you? Does it stress you out? If your mind ever goes blank before a big exam, if you've ever experienced stage fright, if you sometimes get cold feet when all you want is to be *cool*, you'll want to read this next selection. It's about that ordinary but less-than-pleasant problem called stress.

Reading Standard 2.3 Connect and clarify main ideas by identifying their relationship to other sources and related topics.

What Is Stress?

by Jerrold Greenberg, Ed.D., and Robert Gold, Ph.D.

Racquel had no idea how she was going to do it—the idea of getting up in front of her English class terrified her. What if she went totally blank and forgot everything she was going to say?

She could pretend to be sick and stay home the day she was supposed to give her speech, but she knew she would have to give it anyway when she went back to school. There wasn't any way out of it, and it was making Racquel a nervous wreck.

If you, like Racquel, have had physical reactions to a change in your life situation, you have experienced stress. All of us do. The key is learning how to manage stress so that it doesn't make you miserable or sick.

Before you can cope with stress, you have to know how it develops. First, a situation arises that is new or **potentially** unpleasant. This situation is called a stressor. In Racquel's case, the stressor was the speech that she had to give in her English class. Racquel felt anxious, her heart raced, and her hands started sweating when she thought about the speech. What she was experiencing was a stress response, the body's reaction to a stressor.

It is important to remember that stressors only have the *potential* to cause a stress response. For some people, giving a speech would not cause a stress response. It's only when a stressor does cause a stress response that stress results. Therefore, stress is the combination of the presence of a stressor and the occurrence of a stress response.

Stressors

Stressors can occur in almost every area of life. At school, you may experience stress when you try out for a sport or the school play or if you have trouble becoming part of a certain social group. You may feel stress if you don't have the money to buy the clothes you want for a school dance or if other students pick on you.

A stressor can be something as simple as trying to get paper clips untangled, getting stuck at a red light when you're in a hurry, or getting a busy signal when you really need to talk with someone. If you let them, these kinds of "daily hassles" can add up and cause a tremendous amount of stress.

TEXT STRUCTURE

Skim this article. Circle its subheadings. What other feature do you find?

_____

_____

VOCABULARY DEVELOPMENT

potentially (pō·ten′shəl·lē) *adv.*: possibly.

· · · · · · Notes · · · · · ·

_____

_____

_____

_____

_____

TEXT STRUCTURE

The main topic of this section is stressors. What examples of stressors do the writers provide? Number them. You should find eight.

· · · · · · Notes · · · · · ·

_____

_____

_____

_____

motivate (mōt′ə·vāt) *v.*: move
to take action.

· · · · · · **Notes** · · · · · ·

_____

_____

_____

_____

_____

_____

_____

TEXT STRUCTURE

The writer poses two
questions in this paragraph.
Underline the questions and
the answer.

· · · · · · **Notes** · · · · · ·

_____

_____

_____

_____

_____

_____

_____

_____

_____

Even positive situations can be stressors. Making the
all-star basketball team is an example of a positive life-
changing event that can cause stress.

Having some stressors is perfectly normal and healthy.
They **motivate** us to confront challenges and accomplish
things. The ideal balance is to be able to deal with stressors
effectively so we don't become ill from too much stress.

The Stress Response

40 The stress response occurs because of the relationship
between your brain and the rest of your body. Your brain
recognizes a stressor and evaluates it. If your brain decides
that the stressor isn't anything to worry about, nothing
happens to your body. But if the stressor is seen as a threat,
your brain tells your body to produce certain chemicals
that contribute to the stress response.

Why does the brain tell the rest of the body to respond
this way? It doesn't seem as though the stress response
would help us at all. It certainly didn't help Racquel prepare
50 for her speech. When could the stress response possibly be
helpful to us?

Well, imagine that you are walking down the street
and a huge dog suddenly leaps at you from behind a
garbage truck, snarling, teeth bared, and ready to bite you.
What do you do? Do you try to defend yourself against the
dog, or do you run away as fast as you can? Whichever you
do—fight the dog or run away—will require you to act
immediately and with great physical effort.

60　　The stress response makes it possible for you to protect yourself. Your body produces the hormone called adrenaline, which gives you the rush of extra energy you need. Your breathing speeds up, which helps get more oxygen throughout your body. Your heart beats faster, which increases the flow of blood to your muscles. And your muscles tense up, which prepares you to move quickly.

　　At the same time these changes are occurring, other changes are also taking place throughout your body. Because all your physical resources are **mobilized** to help you respond to danger, other body functions take a back 70　seat. The digestive system may begin to function strangely. Less saliva is produced, because it is a low priority to your body during times of physical danger. As a result, your mouth becomes dry.

　　The stress response is sometimes called the "fight-or-flight" response because it prepares you to either "fight" or "take flight." It prepares you to do something *physical.* So when you are physically threatened and need to respond physically, the stress response is helpful.

　　However, your body also responds the same way to a 80　*nonphysical* threat. Giving a speech can cause the same stress response as being attacked by an animal. But giving a speech, unlike defending yourself against an animal attack, does not require you to release stress in any physical way. The stress that is not released can make you physically ill.

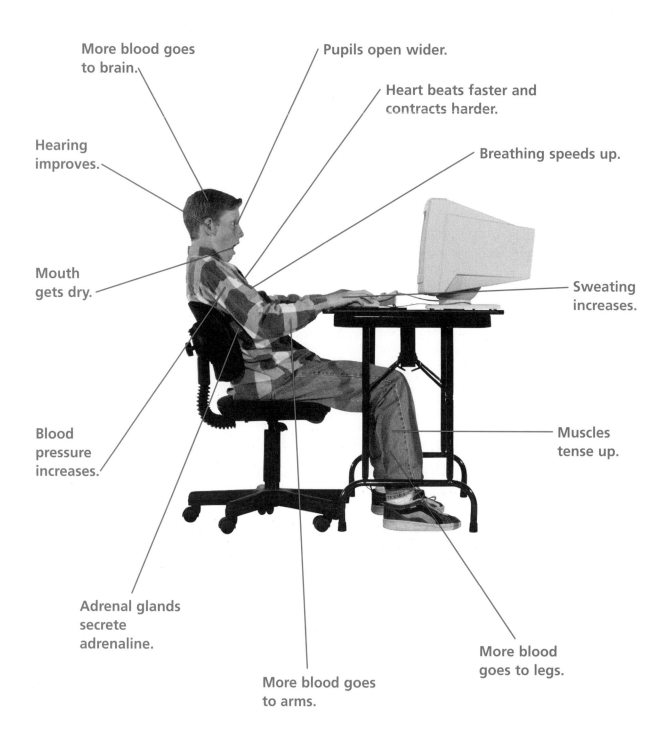

More blood goes to brain.

Pupils open wider.

Heart beats faster and contracts harder.

Hearing improves.

Breathing speeds up.

Mouth gets dry.

Sweating increases.

Blood pressure increases.

Muscles tense up.

Adrenal glands secrete adrenaline.

More blood goes to arms.

More blood goes to legs.

The physical changes of the stress response prepare the body to run away or to stay and fight.

Selective Awareness

Though you can **eliminate** some stressors from your life, you cannot get rid of all of them. You can, however, use selective awareness to make your stressors less disturbing. Selective awareness is choosing to focus on the aspects of a
90 situation that make you feel better. For example, if your stressor is having to make a speech in one of your classes, you could choose to focus on the positive aspect of the situation—having a chance to present your ideas to others.

Make a list of five stressors in your life, and then write the positive aspects of each one. It may also be helpful to take time just before you go to sleep each night to recall all the *good* things about the day. Pat yourself on the back for what you accomplished and the problems you handled successfully.

TEXT STRUCTURE

Skim the text included under this heading. What is the main idea? How do you know?

_____

_____

_____

VOCABULARY DEVELOPMENT

eliminate (ē·lim′in·āt) *v.*: get rid of; remove.

· · · · · · **Notes** · · · · · ·

_____

_____

_____

_____

_____

_____

_____

_____

_____

_____

_____

_____

OWN THE TEXT

PRACTICING THE STANDARDS

Main Idea   Re-read "What Is Stress?" and summarize the main ideas below.

_____

_____

_____

_____

_____

_____

_____

_____

KEEPING TRACK

Personal Word List   Choose one of the words you've added to your Personal Word List. Try to use it during a class discussion today.

Personal Reading Log   As you record this article in your Personal Reading Log, jot down your responses to the advice it offers. Give yourself 2 points on the Reading Meter for reading this article.

Checklist for Standards Mastery   Turn to the back of the book, and use the Checklist for Standards Mastery to track your progress in mastering the reading standards.

What Is Stress? ▪ *Interactive Reading, page 202*

Go Beyond an Informational Text

Letter Outline   Suppose you are the writer of a monthly health column called "Ask the Health Expert" for your school newspaper. You have received a letter from a student who wants information about stress. Fill out this outline to help you plan your letter of information. Refer to "What Is Stress?" for your factual information.

Response to Letter Writer:

I. What Is Stress?

    A. Definition of Stress _____

    B. What Is a Stressor? _____

II. Examples of Stressors:

    A. Negative Stressor Example _____

    _____

    B. Positive Stressor Example _____

    _____

III. What Is Happening When I'm Stressed?

    A. Causes of Responses _____

    _____

    _____

    B. What Happens to the Body When It Is Stressed?

    _____

    _____

    _____

    C. What Can I Do About Stress?

    _____

    _____

    _____

Look for more ways to deal with stress in the next issue.

Literature

BIOGRAPHY/ LETTERS

The biggest successes often result from the most difficult battles. This can be said about Maya Angelou and also about Rosa Parks. Rosa Parks became widely known in 1955 when, after a long, hard day at work, she refused to give up her seat on the bus to a white man.

Parks's actions resulted in a widespread protest led by Martin Luther King, Jr. Protests like it inspired other protests and ultimately led to the civil rights legislation that would change life for millions of people in the United States—both black and white. People from around the world now honor Rosa Parks as a hero.

This selection contains two parts: a preface, which contains a brief biographical sketch of Parks, and a group of letters that children have written to Rosa Parks, along with Parks's responses.

Reading Standard 3.5 Identify the speaker, and recognize the difference between first- and third-person narration (for example, autobiography compared with biography).

Civil rights pioneer Rosa Parks smiles as she arrives at the twenty-eighth annual NAACP Image Awards ceremony, February 8, 1997, in Pasadena, California.

from DEAR MRS. PARKS

Rosa Parks with Gregory J. Reed

Preface

Rosa Parks was born Rosa Louise McCauley on February 4, 1913, in Tuskegee, Alabama. Named after her maternal grandmother, Rosa was the first child of James and Leona (Edwards) McCauley. James was a carpenter and a builder. Leona was a teacher. When Rosa was still a toddler, James decided to go north in search of work. Leona, who was pregnant with Rosa's brother by then, wanted a stable home life for her children. She and Rosa moved in with her par-
10 ents, Sylvester and Rose, in Pine Level, Alabama. Rosa saw her father again briefly when she was five years old, and after that did not see him until she was grown and married.

Though Rosa longed to go to school, **chronic** illnesses kept her from attending regularly in her early years. Her mother taught her at home, and nurtured Rosa's love of books and learning. The schools for black children in Pine Level didn't go beyond the sixth grade, so when Rosa completed her education in Pine Level at age eleven, her mother enrolled her in the Montgomery Industrial School
20 for Girls (also known as Miss White's School for Girls), a private school for African American girls. Several years later Rosa went on to Alabama State Teachers' College for Negroes, which had a program for black high school students in training to be teachers. When Rosa was sixteen, her grandmother became ill. Rosa left school to help care for her. Her grandmother Rose died about a month later.

IDENTIFY

Is the information about Parks's life being given by Parks herself or by someone else? How do you know?

_____

_____

_____

_____

_____

_____

VOCABULARY DEVELOPMENT

chronic (krä′nik) *adj.*: occurring often; repeated.

· · · · · Notes · · · · ·

_____

_____

_____

_____

_____

_____

_____

_____

VOCABULARY DEVELOPMENT

domestic (dō·mes′tik) *adj.:* having to do with one's country.

The adjective *domestic* can also refer to things associated with one's own home.

IDENTIFY

What evidence in lines 45–49 supports the idea that Rosa Parks was involved in the civil rights struggle early in the 1940s? Underline the facts you find.

• • • • • • **Notes** • • • • • •

_____

_____

_____

_____

_____

_____

_____

_____

_____

_____

_____

_____

_____

_____

_____

As Rosa prepared to return to Alabama State, her mother also became ill. Rosa decided to stay home and care for her mother, while her brother, Sylvester, worked to help
30 support the family.

Rosa married Raymond Parks in December 1932. Raymond was born in Wedowee, Alabama, in 1903. Like Rosa's mother, Leona McCauley, Geri Parks encouraged her son's love of education. Even though he received little formal education, Raymond overcame the confines of racial segregation and educated himself. His thorough knowledge of **domestic** affairs and current events led most people to believe he had gone to college.

Raymond supported Rosa's dream of completing her
40 formal education, and in 1934 Rosa received her high school diploma. She was twenty-one years old. After she received her diploma, she worked in a hospital and took in sewing before getting a job at Maxwell Field, Montgomery's army air force base.

In their early married years, Raymond and Rosa worked together in the National Association for the Advancement of Colored People (NAACP). In 1943 Rosa became secretary of the NAACP, and later served as a youth leader.

50 It was also in 1943 that Rosa tried to register to vote. She tried twice before being told that she didn't pass the required test. That year Rosa was put off a Montgomery city bus for boarding in the front rather than in the back, as was the rule for African American riders.

She tried again in 1945 to register to vote. This time she copied the questions and her answers by hand so she could prove later she had passed. But this time she received her voter's certificate in the mail.

In August of 1955, Rosa met the Reverend Martin
60 Luther King, Jr., at an NAACP meeting, where he was a guest speaker. Some months later, Rosa was busy organizing a workshop for an NAACP youth conference. On the evening of December 1, 1955, Rosa finished work and boarded the bus to go home. She noticed that the driver was the same man who had put her off the bus twelve years earlier. Black people were supposed to ride in the back of the bus. Rosa took a seat in the middle.

Soon the bus became crowded with passengers. The "white" seats filled up. A white man was left standing. Tired
70 of giving in to injustice, Rosa refused to surrender her seat on the bus. Two policemen came and arrested her.

Rosa's act of quiet courage changed the course of history.

Four days later, the black people of Montgomery and sympathizers of other races organized and announced a **boycott** of the city bus line. Known as the Montgomery Bus Boycott, this protest lasted for 381 days. During this time, African Americans walked or arranged for rides rather than take the bus. Reverend King, the spokesperson
80 for the boycott, urged participants to protest nonviolently. Soon the protest against racial injustice spread beyond Montgomery and throughout the country. The modern-day civil rights movement in America was born.

The bus boycott ended on December 21, 1956, after the U.S. Supreme Court declared bus segregation in Montgomery unconstitutional on November 13. Not long afterward, Rosa and Raymond, who had endured threatening telephone calls and other **harassments** during the boycott, moved to Detroit.

· · · · · · Notes · · · · · ·

_____

_____

_____

_____

_____

VOCABULARY DEVELOPMENT

boycott (boi′kät′) *v.:* join together to refuse to buy, sell, or use a product or service.

Have you ever come across this word before? Were you able to figure out its meaning from the context of the paragraph? The word derives from a man named Boycott, who was the target of a protest by his neighbors in Ireland in the late 1800s.

IDENTIFY

Underline the key sentence that states the result of Rosa Parks's action.

IDENTIFY

Underline the sentence that states the result of the Montgomery bus boycott.

VOCABULARY DEVELOPMENT

harassments (hə·ras′məntz) *n.:* actions that cause someone trouble or torment.

This biographical essay contains information about the subject that you probably would not find in an auto-biography. Underline a sentence in the paragraph beginning on line 97 that reflects a sentiment Parks herself would probably not have written. Why not?

90 Rosa remained active in the civil rights movement. She traveled, spoke, and participated in peaceful demonstrations. From 1965 to 1988, she worked in the office of Congressman John Conyers of Michigan. During those years, Rosa endured the assassination of Dr. Martin Luther King, Jr., in 1968, and she suffered the deaths of her husband and brother in 1977 and her mother in 1979.

Rosa's interest in working with young people stayed strong, and in 1987 she co-founded the Rosa and Raymond Parks Institute for Self-Development for the purpose of
100 motivating young people to achieve their highest potential. In the years since her arrest, Rosa Parks has been recognized throughout America as the mother of the modern-day civil rights movement. For children and adults, Mrs. Parks is a role model for courage, an example of dignity and determination. She is a symbol of freedom for the world.

In 1995 Mrs. Parks joined children and adults all over the world to mark the fortieth anniversary of the Montgomery Bus Boycott, through marches, lectures,
110 exhibits, and many other events. She co-founded a new organization, The Parks Legacy. A movement among legislators was launched to establish February 4, Mrs. Parks's birthday, as a national legal holiday.

—Gregory J. Reed

Letters of Hope and Courage

Dear Mrs. Parks,

I am sorry that you went to jail because you did not give in to the system. Mrs. Parks, please try and stop the violence and the killing, because where I live lots of people get taken out (killed).

120

Juan Hua,
Oakland, California

My own experiences and the changes I have lived to see in this world have taught me that we must do what is right and not harm one another. I am deeply disturbed to see so many young people who are not being taught that every person's life is meaningful. Life should not be taken for granted.

It takes courage to grow up and reach your highest potential, not violence. We must respect and care for one

130

another so that we all can live and be free. I hope I have set an example for you to follow through the life that I have lived. If I can save one life by writing to you, I believe I have done something worthwhile.

Dear Mrs. Parks,

What is hope? I have read that you hope for this world to be a better place to live in, and you haven't given up. I'm still figuring out what is "hope," and then maybe I can help "hope" out to make this a better world and be like you.

Elizabeth,
Grosse Point, Michigan

140

IDENTIFY

Who has written the first letter? Who has written the letter in response? How can you tell?

_____

_____

_____

_____

_____

_____

_____

INTERPRET

Re-read lines 134–155, and circle the word *hope* each time it appears. How many times did you circle the word? Why do you think it is repeated so often?

_____

_____

_____

_____

_____

_____

_____

TEXT STRUCTURE

Underline the direct quotation in the letter from Parks to Elizabeth. Whose words are these?

_____

_____

_____

_____

_____

_____

FLUENCY

Decide with a partner who will read the letter from Sierra and who will read Parks's response. Use the tone of your voice to portray the age, experience, and personal style of each letter writer. Speak slowly and clearly so that others may follow along.

VOCABULARY DEVELOPMENT

race (rās) *n.:* major group into which people are categorized. Some experts say the term is scientifically inexact and should be replaced with *ethnic stock* or *group.*

Race can also be a verb meaning "compete against in a contest of speed."

Elizabeth, many times we as adults seek to teach students like you without giving you examples of what the true meanings of words are so that you can learn from them.

Hope is wanting something that means a lot to you. It is like wanting something that you do not have. Hope is something we feel with our hearts. When we hope for something with our hearts, it becomes an expectation.

Hope is also something we believe in. Many people I have known believed in ending racial segregation in this
150 country, and their hope that it could happen influenced their actions and brought about change. A friend of mine, the Reverend Jesse Jackson, says, "We must keep hope alive." I agree. You can help keep hope alive by believing in yourself. Your hope for yourself and for the future can make this world a better place to live.

Dear Mrs. Parks,
My mother is always saying, "I hope you will be like Rosa Parks." What shall I do? I love my mother and you.

Sierra,
160   Toledo, Ohio

It is nice to hear that someone wants her child to be like you. However, this is not always good. A statement like this can be too heavy to bear. I always want all children to reach their highest potential. I want you and all children to be the best people you can be—and hopefully better than me. If we place our hope in becoming the best we can be, then we as a human **race** will always be advancing. I believe all of us—young people and adults—should have people we look up to as examples. I hope you will be like your mother and
170 even more if you desire.

Your mother takes time to nurture and care for you. A person can have more than one role model, and that is good, and OK. There is not one person who knows everything. You can be like your mother, me, and anyone who sets a good example. I had several role models who helped me earlier in my life. I list my husband, Raymond Parks, among the persons I admired the most. He was good, full of courage and quiet strength. My mother, Leona McCauley, helped me to grow up feeling proud of myself and black people. She taught me not to judge people by what they have. My Grandma Rose helped me to be a strong woman by setting an example with her own strong will and love for her children and grandchildren. Dr. Martin Luther King, Jr., set a profound example for me in living day to day with determination and dignity. People who are younger than I am set examples as role models for me, too.

You can learn something from everyone. Remember, no one is perfect. Keep this in mind as you set examples for others.

★ ★ ★ ★ ★ ★ ★ ★

Dear Mrs. Parks,
The sixth-graders are doing a history project. We chose you. The theme is "Taking a **stand** in history." We have some questions. Can you answer them? How did you feel when you were on the bus? Have you had any experiences with the Ku Klux Klan?

Jennifer and Jamie,
La Puente, California

Your theme is a good one. A person should not take a stand to make history. Taking a stand for what is right is most

AUTOBIOGRAPHY

Circle the names of the people that Parks mentions in her letter to Sierra. Why does Parks mention them? What do they help you learn about her life?

_____
_____
_____
_____
_____
_____
_____
_____
_____
_____
_____

VOCABULARY DEVELOPMENT

stand (stand) *n.:* strong opinion or position on an issue.

What are some other meanings of *stand* as a verb?

_____
_____
_____
_____

important. You may take a stand to make history, and it can be the wrong one. So many people did this during the civil rights movement, and many are still doing it today.

The custom of getting on the bus for black people in Montgomery in the 1950s was to pay at the front door, get off the bus, and then reenter through the back door to find a seat. Black people could not sit in the same rows with the white people. This custom was humiliating and **intolerable.**

210 When I sat down on the bus the day I was arrested, I decided I must do what was right to do. People have said over the years that the reason I did not give up my seat was because I was tired. I did not think of being physically tired. My feet were not hurting. I was tired in a different way. I was tired of seeing so many men treated as boys and not called by their proper names or titles. I was tired of seeing children and women mistreated and disrespected because of the color of their skin. I was tired of Jim Crow laws, of legally enforced racial segregation.

I thought of the pain and the years of oppression and
220 mistreatment that my people had suffered. I felt that way every day. December 1, 1955, was no different. Fear was the last thing I thought of that day. I put my trust in the Lord for guidance and help to endure whatever I had to face. I knew I was sitting in the right seat.

I did experience the Ku Klux Klan when I was young. I remember being about six years old and hearing about how the KKK terrorized African Americans by burning down their churches and beating up or even killing people. My
230 family talked about wearing our clothes to bed so we would be ready to escape our house if we had to.

My grandfather never seemed afraid. He was a proud man who believed in protecting his home. When the hate crimes **escalated,** he sat up many nights with his shotgun. He said if the KKK broke into our house, he was going to get the first one who came through the door. The Klansmen never did try to break into our house, but their violence continued. After these experiences, I learned that I must not be afraid and must always trust in God.

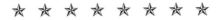

Dear Mrs. Parks,

240   What gave you the courage to say no and not move to the back of the bus and then get arrested?

Ashley,

Detroit, Michigan

God has always given me the strength to say what is right. I did not get on the bus to get arrested; I got on the bus to go home. Getting arrested was one of the worst days in my life. It was not a happy experience. Since I have always been a strong believer in God, I knew that He was with me, and only He could get me through the next step.

250   I had no idea that history was being made. I was just tired of giving in. Somehow, I felt that what I did was right by standing up to that bus driver. I did not think about the consequences. I knew that I could have been lynched, manhandled, or beaten when the police came. I chose not to move, because I was right. When I made that decision, I knew that I had the strength of God and my ancestors with me.

WORD KNOWLEDGE

escalated (es′kə·lāt′id) *v.*: expanded, increased, or grew rapidly.

A related word is *escalator,* which refers to the moving stairs you find in department stores and elsewhere.

INFER

How do you think Rosa Parks kept herself strong in the face of all her difficulties? What do you learn here that was not as evident in the essay?

_____

_____

_____

_____

_____

_____

_____

_____

SAY SOMETHING

What question might you have for Rosa Parks about her life?

_____

_____

_____

_____

OWN THE SELECTION

Biography/Autobiography The first part of this selection is a biographical sketch. The second part of the selection consists of letters to Rosa Parks and her answers. Which form of writing tells you the most about Rosa Parks? Write an answer to this question in two or three sentences. Cite at least one passage from the text in your response. Be sure to put quotation marks around direct quotes from the text. Use the Biography and Autobiography Chart on the next page as you formulate your answer.

_____

_____

_____

_____

_____

_____

_____

_____

KEEPING TRACK

Personal Word List Record the words you learned from this story in your Personal Word List. Put a star next to the words that have multiple meanings.

Personal Reading Log Record this selection in your Personal Reading Log. Then, write the two questions you would most like to ask Rosa Parks. Give yourself 5 points on the Reading Meter for completing this selection.

Checklist for Standards Mastery Use the Checklist for Standards Mastery in the back of this book to track your progress in mastering the standards.

from **Dear Mrs. Parks** ■ *Interactive Reading,* page 211

AUTOBIOGRAPHY/ BIOGRAPHY

Interact with a Literary Text

Biography and Autobiography Chart Fill out this chart after you read the two excerpts from *Dear Mrs. Parks.*

	Preface to Book	**Replies to Children's Letters**
Author		
Point of View		
Information: Objective or Subjective		
What did you learn from each text?		

Chapter **6**

Looking at Texts
Uses of the Imagination

Chapter Preview In this chapter you will—

Strategy Launch:
"What and Why?"

LITERARY FOCUS: LITERARY DEVICES

Writers use all kinds of literary devices to create meaning and to engage our emotions and imaginations. Writers use **images** to help us form mental pictures. Images may even help us to use our other senses to share an experience. Writers use **metaphors** and **similes,** imaginative comparisons between unlike things, to help us see surprising connections. Writers also use **symbols**—objects, places, or even people—that function as themselves in a text and as something much broader as well. Symbols deepen a text and add ripples and ripples of meaning to it.

A STRATEGY THAT WORKS: "WHAT AND WHY?"

As good readers, we automatically note these "literary devices." When we come upon a literary device in a story or poem, or in any text, we ask, "What literary device is this?" "Why does the writer use it?" (What is the writer trying to make me see, feel, or understand?)

POINTERS FOR USING THE "WHAT AND WHY?" STRATEGY

⟫➡ Read the text. Use sticky notes to mark the literary devices.

⟫➡ Ask yourself **what** literary device the writer is using.

⟫➡ Once you've identified the type of literary device, ask yourself **why** the writer chose to use it. **Ask:** "What effect does this have on me, the reader?"

Reading Standard 1.5
Understand and explain "shades of meaning" in related words.

Reading Standard 2.7
Make reasonable assertions about a text through accurate supporting citations.

Reading Standard 3.7
Explain the effects of common literary devices (for example, symbolism, imagery, metaphor) in a variety of fictional and nonfictional texts.

Practice Read

BEFORE YOU READ

Some people live lives full of adventure, suspense, romance, intrigue, and mystery. Cleopatra was one of them. Although Cleopatra lived two thousand years ago, she has never been forgotten.

WHO WAS CLEOPATRA?

Richard Cohen

WHAT & WHY?

Underline the **images** in the Shakespeare quotation that help you see and even smell Cleopatra's barge.

WORD KNOWLEDGE

A *poop* (line 10) is an enclosure or small building on a ship's deck.

WHAT & WHY?

Re-read the third paragraph to find the **analogy,** or comparison. Underline the analogy. Why does the writer use this analogy here?

_____

_____

_____

_____

_____

Her name is one of the most well known in all of history. But how much do you really know about Cleopatra? How fully can anyone today understand this great and brilliant queen?

She was so famous that William Shakespeare wrote a play about her and her love affair with Marc Antony. Here is how Shakespeare described Cleopatra's arrival in Tarsus, in Asia Minor (she is on her way to meet Antony):

"The barge she sat in, like a burnished throne,
10   Burned on the water: the poop was beaten gold;
Purple the sails, and so perfumed that
The winds were lovesick with them; the oars were silver,
Which to the tune of flutes kept stroke. . ."

(Act II, Scene 2)

All the information we have about Cleopatra comes from her enemies, the Romans. Can you imagine if we knew about George Washington only from British sources? Or Robert E. Lee from the generals who fought against him?

To most people Cleopatra was a seducer who stole the
20   hearts of men. Maybe this is because so many glamorous movie stars have portrayed her onscreen.

What most people don't understand, however, is that Cleopatra was a brilliant and clever ruler. She was famous for her personality rather than for her beauty. (She probably had a large chin and a large nose.) Her famous thickly braided hair was almost certainly a wig. But she had beautiful liquid eyes, and when she spoke, the greatest rulers of her time listened. A Greek writer said her voice was like an instrument of many strings. Her charm was

30 rooted in her intelligence, and she used her intelligence as a weapon. Cleopatra was highly educated, for she had all the advantages of a member of the royal Ptolemy (täl′ə·mē) family.

The Ptolemies ruled Egypt for more than 300 years. They lived in the capital city of Alexandria, which was built by Alexander the Great. Situated on the banks of the Nile River delta, Alexandria was one of the most beautiful urban centers in the world. It was like a jewel in a beautiful setting. Its vast library contained 400,000 scrolls of papyrus. Its

40 Pharos lighthouse was the world's tallest building—a soaring structure that commanded the skyline. The museum was a magnet for scholars, thinkers, poets, and students from many lands. Those people from many different nations—Egyptians, Greeks, Jews, and Arabs— lived there in harmony. They enjoyed a public theater, a huge gym, and even a zoo.

Born in 69 B.C., Cleopatra learned Greek and Egyptian myths as a child. Later she studied philosophy, literature, art, science, and languages. She was the first Ptolemy who

50 could actually speak Egyptian—the language of the local people. She also knew Arabic and Hebrew. She loved to discuss serious subjects with the most famous philosophers, scientists, doctors, and writers of the time.

WHAT & WHY?

Underline the **images** in lines 25–29 that help you imagine what Cleopatra looked like.

DECODING TIP

Some words and names in this text may be difficult to pronounce. Underline the words *Ptolemies* (line 32) and *Pharos* (line 40). *Ptolemies* is pronounced (täl′ə·mēz), and the *ph* in *Pharos* is pronounced as an *f* (far′ōz). As you read the next paragraph, look for another word where the *ph* makes the /f/ sound. Circle it.

WHAT & WHY?

Underline the **simile** in line 38 that helps you imagine the city of Alexandria.

· · · · · · Notes · · · · · ·

A **metaphor** is a figure of speech that compares two unrelated things. Find and underline the metaphor in the paragraph that begins on line 69. What does the metaphor help you *see*?

_____

_____

_____

jeered (jird) *v.*: made fun of; mocked.

Which word shows more disrespect—*laughed* or *jeered*?

_____

feuds (fyo͞odz) *n.*: long-running quarrels, usually between families or clans. How would a fight differ from a feud?

_____

_____

deposed (dē·pōzd′) *v.*: removed from office or power; forced from the throne.

· · · · · · Notes · · · · · ·

_____

_____

_____

_____

Cleopatra had five siblings and half-siblings. Each was raised separately, with his or her own guardians and servants. From a very early age, the six children knew that they were competing for the leadership of Egypt. They **jeered** each other rather than played with each other. **Feuds** among them were common. For example, once

60 when their father was away in Rome, the eldest sister seized the throne. She was immediately killed by the second-eldest, who had the backing of the people. When Ptolemy returned, he retook the throne. How? Easy. He had his upstart daughter executed.

Cleopatra, the third-eldest sibling, became queen at age eighteen when her father died. She ruled jointly with her ten-year-old half-brother, Ptolemy VIII. (By the way, Cleopatra was officially Cleopatra VII.)

Cleopatra wished to return Egypt to its former

70 greatness as a world power, but her path to the throne was a minefield of obstacles. Ptolemy's advisers wanted to destroy Cleopatra and grabbed every opportunity to do so. Their chance to overthrow Cleopatra came when she took a long journey up the Nile to learn more about her kingdom. When she returned to Alexandria, she found that Ptolemy had turned many of the people against her. Learning of a plot to have her **deposed,** Cleopatra fled to Syria, a nearby country. There she formed an army to try to retake command of Egypt. She joined forces with Julius Caesar, a

80 Roman general, a war hero who was famous for his leadership and battle skills.

Caesar, fighting on the side of Cleopatra, defeated young Ptolemy in battle. The young king of Egypt, fifteen years old, drowned in the Nile while trying to escape. He was weighed down by his gold armor.

Caesar and Cleopatra were a powerful couple, reigning over the region for years. Caesar, however, was assassinated by Roman generals who feared his **ambitious** nature and thirst for power.

90 Following Caesar's death, Cleopatra joined forces with Marc Antony, a Roman leader who rose to power following Caesar's death. Although they were a powerful and **dynamic** team, Antony and Cleopatra angered other Romans with their leadership. Their forces came under attack by those of Octavius, Antony's former ally. Cleopatra and Antony lost everything in battle. Soon after the defeat, Marc Antony killed himself, mistakenly believing that Cleopatra was dead.

Cleopatra died soon after, in 30 B.C., while a captive of Octavius. She was only thirty-nine years old.

VOCABULARY DEVELOPMENT

ambitious (am·bish′əs) *adj.:* full of desire to gain power, fame, or wealth.

How might an ambitious person differ from a greedy person?

_____

_____

dynamic (dī·nam′ik) *adj.:* full of energy; forceful.

Which word, *dynamic* or *forceful,* has a more positive meaning?

_____

OWN THE SELECTION

PRACTICING THE STANDARDS

Literary Devices   Fill out the Literary-Devices Chart on the next page to survey the literary devices used in "Who Was Cleopatra?"

KEEPING TRACK

Personal Word List   Record new words from this selection, with their definitions, in your Personal Word List.

Personal Reading Log   Record this selection in your Personal Reading Log, and explain why you would or wouldn't want to read a novel about Cleopatra. Give yourself 2 points on the Reading Meter for reading "Who Was Cleopatra?"

Checklist for Standards Mastery   Record your progress in understanding writers' use of literary devices on the Checklist for Standards Mastery.

LITERARY DEVICES

Who Was Cleopatra? — *Interactive Reading,* page 224

Interact with a Literary Text

Literary-Devices Chart   Fill out the following chart with examples of literary devices you found in "Who Was Cleopatra?" Then, describe how these devices affected your reading experience.

Imagery	Simile	Metaphor	Analogy
_____	_____	_____	_____
_____	_____	_____	_____
_____	_____	_____	_____
_____	_____	_____	_____
_____	_____	_____	_____
_____	_____	_____	_____
_____	_____	_____	_____
_____	_____	_____	_____
_____	_____	_____	_____
_____	_____	_____	_____
_____	_____	_____	_____
_____	_____	_____	_____
_____	_____	_____	_____

Overall Effect on My Reading:

_____

_____

_____

_____

The Mysterious Mr. Lincoln

Interact with a Literary Text

Metaphor-Matching Map   A **metaphor** compares two things without using a comparison word such as *like* or *as.* As you read "The Mysterious Mr. Lincoln," look for metaphors. (You will find that many expressions we use every day are metaphors.) In each box on the left, write each metaphor, and explain what the metaphor means or symbolizes.

Metaphor		Meaning
	→	
	→	
	→	
	→	

Lincoln's Humor

for use with
Holt Literature and Language Arts,
page 339

Interact with an Informational Text

Assertion Chart   An **assertion** is a statement or claim. Assertions can be supported by citations or supporting evidence, such as examples, facts, statistics, and quotations from experts. Complete the assertion chart below after you read "Lincoln's Humor." Record each assertion you find in the text. Then, list **citations** that prove or support each assertion.

Assertion (Claim)	Citation (Support or Proof)

A Civil War Thanksgiving

Interact with an Informational Text

Text/Graphic Features Chart   Informational materials have text features that help you get the information you need. To understand text and graphic features and how they work, fill in the chart below with an example of each text feature in "A Civil War Thanksgiving." Then write the purpose of each text feature.

Type of Feature	Example	Purpose
Main Heading		
Subheading		
Boldface Type		
Art		
Caption		

SYMBOLISM

What Do Fish Have to Do with Anything?

for use with
Holt Literature and Language Arts,
page 348

Interact with a Literary Text

Symbol Chart   A **symbol** is a person, place, or thing that functions as itself in a piece of literature and as something broader than itself at the same time. Symbols are found in ordinary life too. A *dove,* for example, is a bird, and it is also a symbol of peace. A *heart* is a muscle in the body, and it is also a symbol of love. Complete the symbol chart below for "What Do Fish Have to Do with Anything?" In the first column, write the main symbol you find in the story. In the second column, write the passage in the story that alerts you to the significance of the symbol. In the third column, explain what each symbol means. In the fourth column, explain *why* you feel that the symbol means what it does.

Symbol	Key Passage	What Symbol Means	Why You Feel That Way

Getting Leftovers Back on the Table

for use with
Holt Literature and Language Arts,
page 360

ASSERTIONS

Interact with an Informational Text

Assertion Web   After you finish reading the essay "Getting Leftovers Back on the Table," you can make assertions about it. To make an assertion, think about what you learned from the essay. Ask yourself, *What statement or claim can I make about the information I read? Is there evidence in the essay to support this assertion?* Then, complete the graphic organizer below. Make an assertion, and support it with citations or evidence from the essay.

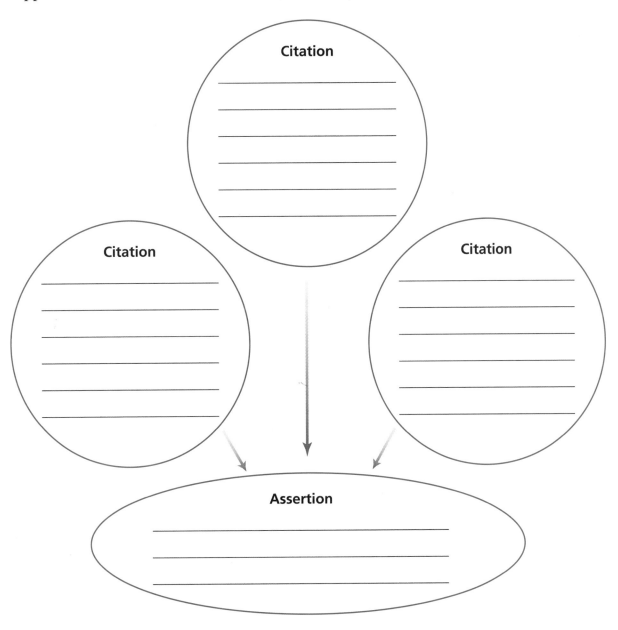

Citation

Citation

Citation

Assertion

Eleven

for use with
Holt Literature and Language Arts,
page 364

Interact with a Literary Text

Imagery Grid   **Imagery** is language that appeals to the senses. Images describe sights, smells, tastes, sounds, and the way things feel when you touch them. Writers use imagery to help us share an experience. Fill in the imagery chart below with images that Sandra Cisneros uses throughout "Eleven." Then answer the questions.

Sight	Touch

Sound	Taste	Smell

Questions

1. Which sense from the diagram had the most images?

   _____

2. Which had the least?

   _____

3. Which image from the story do you like the most? Why?

   _____

Literature

AUTHOR STUDY

In *Holt Literature and Language Arts,* you read Sandra Cisneros's "Eleven," about a girl named Rachel and her awful experience in school on her eleventh birthday. Although Rachel is a fictional character, she is similar to Cisneros as a young girl. Like Rachel, Cisneros was shy and awkward and sometimes had a hard time in school. Cisneros's childhood experiences are very much a part of her writing.

In "Three Wise Guys," you read about a family waiting for the day they'll get to open a mysterious present and what happens to them once they discover what's inside.

BEFORE YOU READ

Did you ever receive a present you weren't allowed to open right away? Did you think about it *all the time?* So do the Gonzaleses, the family in "Three Wise Guys." As you read this story, try to guess what the present is. Then, at the end of the story, think about the effect of the present on each family member.

Here's what you need to know before you read this story:

- This story is based on the Spanish tradition of exchanging gifts on Three Kings' Day, January sixth.
- The story includes some Spanish words, which are defined by the footnotes at the bottom of each page.

Reading Standard 3.7
Explain the effects of common literary devices (for example, symbolism, imagery, metaphor) in a variety of fictional and nonfictional texts.

Three Wise Guys

Sandra Cisneros

WORD KNOWLEDGE

Actually, *Dia de los Reyes* means "Day of the Kings." The kings were Magi, or wise men.

TEXT STRUCTURE

Notice the superscript numbers (the raised numbers) next to Spanish words. These numbers are references to the footnotes at the bottom of the pages. Why are these footnotes important in this story?

_____

_____

_____

WHAT & WHY?

Find and underline three examples of **imagery** in this paragraph. What does this imagery add to the story?

_____

_____

_____

_____

_____

_____

The big box came marked "Do Not Open till Xmas," but the mama said not until the Day of the Three Kings. Not until Dia de los Reyes, the sixth of January, do you hear? That is what the mama said exactly, only she said it all in Spanish. Because in Mexico where she was raised, it is the custom for boys and girls to receive their presents on January sixth, and not Christmas, even though they were living on the Texas side of the river[1] now. Not until the sixth day of January.

10 Yesterday the mama had risen in the dark same as always to reheat the coffee in a tin saucepan and warm the breakfast tortillas.[2] The papa had gotten up coughing and spitting up the night, complaining how the evening before the buzzing of the *chicharras*[3] had kept him from sleeping. By the time the mama had the house smelling of oatmeal and cinnamon, the papa would be gone to the fields, the sun already tangled in the trees and the *urracas*[4] screeching their rubber-screech cry. The boy Ruben and the girl Rosalinda would have to be shaken awake for school. The 20 mama would give the baby Gilberto his bottle and then she would go back to sleep before getting up again to the chores that were always waiting. That is how the world had been.

---

1. **river** *n.:* Rio Grande, which separates Mexico and Texas.
2. **tortillas** (tôr·tē′yəs) *n.:* thin, flat cakes of cornmeal or flour.
3. **chicharras** (chē·chä′räs) *n.:* cicadas, insects that make a loud, high-pitched sound.
4. **urracas** (oō·rä′käs) *n.:* magpies, black and white birds belonging to the crow family, known for their chattering.

But today the big box had arrived. When the boy Ruben and the girl Rosalinda came home from school, it was already sitting in the living room in front of the television set that no longer worked. Who had put it there? Where had it come from? A box covered with red paper with green Christmas trees and a card on top that said "Merry Christmas to the Gonzales Family. Frank, Earl, and Dwight Travis. P.S. Do Not Open till Xmas." That's all.

Two times the mama was made to come into the living room, first to explain to the children and later to their father how the brothers Travis had arrived in the blue pickup, and how it had taken all three of those big men to lift the box off the back of the truck and bring it inside, and how she had had to nod and say thank-you thank-you thank-you over and over because those were the only words she knew in English. Then the brothers Travis had nodded as well, the way they always did when they came and brought the boxes of clothes, or the turkey each November, or the canned ham on Easter, ever since the children had begun to earn high grades at the school where Dwight Travis was the principal.

But this year the Christmas box was bigger than usual. What could be in a box so big? The boy Ruben and the girl Rosalinda begged all afternoon to be allowed to open it, and that is when the mama had said the sixth of January, the Day of the Three Kings. Not a day sooner.

It seemed the weeks stretched themselves wider and wider since the arrival of the big box. The mama got used to sweeping around it because it was too heavy for her to push in a corner. But since the television no longer worked ever since the afternoon the children had poured iced tea through the little grates in the back, it really didn't matter if

INFER

Why do the brothers bring clothes and food on holidays? What can you infer about the family's financial status?

FLUENCY

Some sentences within the boxed passage are long. Practice reading the passage aloud, and pay special attention to the long sentences. Notice where the commas are, and use them as a signal to pause. Practice reading at a rate that is not too fast and not too slow.

Sandra Cisneros   **237**

obstructed (əb·struk′tid) *v.:* blocked.

distract (di·strakt′) *v.:* draw attention away from; sidetrack.

simplicity (sim·plis′ə·tē) *n.:* absence of complexity; plainness.

Replace the word *simplicity* with the word *plainness* in the sentence. Is the sentence as effective? Why or why not?

_____

_____

_____

_____

_____

_____

_____

_____

_____

_____

_____

_____

_____

_____

_____

_____

_____

the box **obstructed** the view. Visitors that came inside the house were told and told again the story of how the box had arrived, and then each was made to guess what was inside.

60   It was the comadre[5] Elodia who suggested over coffee one afternoon that the big box held a portable washing machine that could be rolled away when not in use, the kind she had seen in her Sears Roebuck catalog. The mama said she hoped so because the wringer washer she had used for the last ten years had finally gotten tired and quit. These past few weeks she had had to boil all the clothes in the big pot she used for cooking the Christmas tamales.[6] Yes. She hoped the big box was a portable washing machine. A washing machine, even a portable one, would be good.

70   But the neighbor man Cayetano said, what foolishness, comadre. Can't you see the box is too small to hold a washing machine, even a portable one. Most likely God has heard your prayers and sent a new color TV. With a good antenna you could catch all the Mexican soap operas, the neighbor man said. You could **distract** yourself with the complicated troubles of the rich and then give thanks to God for the blessed **simplicity** of your poverty. A new TV would surely be the end to all your miseries.

Each night when the papa came home from the fields,
80   he would spread newspapers on the cot in the living room, where the boy Ruben and the girl Rosalinda slept, and sit facing the big box in the center of the room. Each night he imagined the box held something different. The day before yesterday he guessed a new record player. Yesterday an ice chest filled with beer. Today the papa sat with his bottle of

---

5. **comadre** (ko·mä′drä) *n.:* woman who is a relative or close friend of the family (the "co-mother").

6. **tamales** (tə·mä′lēz) *n.:* meat and peppers cooked in a corn husk.

beer, fanning himself with a magazine, and said in a voice as much a plea as a prophecy: air conditioner.

But the boy Ruben and the girl Rosalinda were sure the big box was filled with toys. They had even punctured it in one corner with a pencil when their mother was busy cooking, but they could see nothing inside but blackness.

Only the baby Gilberto remained uninterested in the contents of the big box and seemed each day more fascinated with the exterior of the box rather that the interior. One afternoon he tore off a fistful of paper, which he was chewing when his mother swooped him up with one arm, rushed him to the kitchen sink, and forced him to swallow handfuls of lukewarm water in case the red dye of the wrapping paper might be poisonous.

When Christmas Eve finally came, the family Gonzalez put on their good clothes and went to Midnight Mass. They came home to a house that smelled of tamales and atole,[7] and everyone was allowed to open one present before going to sleep. But the big box was to remain untouched until the sixth of January.

On New Year's Eve the house was filled with people, some related, some not, coming in and out. The friends of the papa came with bottles, and the mama set out a bowl of grapes to count off the New Year. That night the children did not sleep in the living-room cot as they usually did, because the living room was crowded with big-fannied ladies and fat-stomached men sashaying to the accordion music of the midget twins from McAllen.[8] Instead the children fell asleep on a lump of handbags and crumpled suit jackets on top of the mama and the papa's bed, dreaming of the contents of the big box.

7. **atole** (ä·tō′lä) *n.*: broth made from corn flour.
8. **McAllen:** Texas city near the Mexican border.

INTERPRET

What do you learn in lines 60–89 about each person based on what he or she hopes is inside the box?

_____
_____
_____
_____
_____
_____
_____
_____
_____
_____
_____
_____
_____
_____
_____
_____
_____
_____
_____

WHAT & WHY?

Underline the **images** in lines 100–116 that help you imagine what the house was like on the holidays.

Finally, the fifth of January. And the boy Ruben and the girl Rosalinda could hardly sleep. All night they whispered last-minute wishes. The boy thought perhaps if
120 the big box held a bicycle, he would be the first to ride it, since he was the oldest. This made his sister cry until the mama had to yell from her bedroom on the other side of the plastic curtains, Be quiet or I'm going to give you each the stick, which sounds worse in Spanish than it does in English. Then no one said anything. After a very long time, long after they heard the mama's wheezed breathing and the papa's piped snoring, the children closed their eyes and remembered nothing.

The papa was already in the bathroom coughing up
130 the night before from his throat when the urracas began their clownish chirping. The boy Ruben awoke and shook his sister. The mama, frying the potatoes and beans for breakfast, nodded permission for the box to be opened.

With a kitchen knife the boy Ruben cut a careful edge along the top. The girl Rosalinda tore the Christmas wrapping with her fingernails. The papa and the mama lifted the cardboard flaps and everyone peered inside to see what it was the brothers Travis had brought them on the Day of the Three Kings.

140 There were layers of balled newspaper packed on top. When these had been cleared away the boy Ruben looked inside. The girl Rosalinda looked inside. The papa and the mama looked.

This is what they saw: the complete Britannica Junior Encyclopaedia, twenty-four volumes in red imitation leather with gold-embossed letters, beginning with Volume 1, Aar–Bel and ending with Volume XXIV, Yel–Zyn. The girl Rosalinda let out a sad cry, as if her hair was going to be cut again. The boy Ruben pulled out

150 Volume IV, Ded–Fem. There were many pictures and many
words, but there were more words than pictures. The papa
flipped through Volume XXII, but because he could not
read English words, simply put the book back and grunted,
What can we do with this? No one said anything, and
shortly after, the screen door slammed.

Only mama knew what to do with the contents of the
big box. She withdrew Volumes VI, VII, and VIII, marched
off to the dinette set in the kitchen, placed two on
Rosalinda's chair so she could better reach the table, and

160 put one underneath the plant stand that danced.

When the boy and girl returned from school that
day, they found the books stacked into squat pillars against
one living-room wall and a board placed on top. On this
were arranged several plastic doilies and framed family
photographs. The rest of the volumes the baby Gilberto
was playing with, and he was already rubbing his sore gums
along the corners of Volume XIV.

The girl Rosalinda also grew interested in the books.
She took out her colored pencils and painted blue on the

170 eyelids of all the illustrations of women and with a red
pencil dipped in spit she painted their lips and fingernails
red-red. After a couple of days, when all the pictures of
women had been colored in this manner, she began to cut
out some of the prettier pictures and paste them on loose-
leaf paper.

One volume suffered from being exposed to the rain
when the papa improvised a hat during a sudden shower.
He forgot it on the hood of the car when he drove off.
When the children came home from school they set it on

IDENTIFY

What does each person do with the gift? See lines 156–177.

WHAT & WHY?

The plant stand in line 160 is **personified**—that is, it is spoken of as if it were human. What is the plant stand doing that only humans can do?

Sandra Cisneros **241**

WHAT & WHY?

What could the colors in the final lines of the story symbolize?

_____

_____

_____

_____

_____

_____

_____

INFER

What do you think the story's title means? Could it have more than one meaning?

_____

_____

_____

_____

_____

_____

_____

180 the porch to dry. But the pages puffed up and became so fat, the book was impossible to close.

Only the boy Ruben refused to touch the books. For several days he avoided the principal because he didn't know what to say in case Mr. Travis were to ask how they were enjoying the Christmas present.

On the Saturday after New Year's the mama and the papa went into town for groceries and left the boy in charge of watching his sister and baby brother. The girl Rosalinda was stacking books into spiral staircases and
190 making her paper dolls descend them in a fancy manner.

Perhaps the boy Ruben would not have bothered to open the volume left on the kitchen table if he had not seen his mother wedge her name-day corsage[9] in its pages. On the page where the mama's carnation lay pressed between two pieces of Kleenex was a picture of a dog in a space ship. "First dog in space" the caption said. The boy turned to another page and read where cashews came from. And then about the man who invented the guillotine. And then about Bengal tigers. And about clouds. All afternoon the boy read,
200 even after the mama and the papa came home. Even after the sun set, until the mama said time to sleep and put the light out.

In their bed on the other side of the plastic curtain the mama and the papa slept. Across from them in the crib slept the baby Gilberto. The girl Rosalinda slept on her end of the cot. But the boy Ruben watched the night sky turn from violet. To blue. To gray. And then from gray. To blue. To violet once again.

---

9. **name-day corsage** (kôr·säzh') *n.:* flower or a bunch of flowers that are worn to celebrate the feast day of the saint for whom a person is named.

OWN THE STORY

PRACTICING THE STANDARDS

Symbolism   A **symbol** is a thing that represents something besides itself. What do you think the encyclopedias are symbolic of? Write your answer in two or three sentences.

_____

_____

_____

_____

KEEPING TRACK

Personal Word List   You probably came across some new words in this story. They may have been Spanish words or English words you were unfamiliar with. Choose five words, and add them to your Personal Word List. Write an English word that means the same thing as each Spanish word.

Personal Reading Log   Did you enjoy this story? Explain why or why not in your Personal Reading Log. Give yourself 4 points on the Reading Meter for completing it.

Checklist for Standards Mastery   You've finished reading and responding to another selection. Use the Checklist for Standards Mastery to determine how far you've come in mastering the standards.

Three Wise Guys ▪ *Interactive Reading,* page 236

Go Beyond a Literary Text

Author Profile   Use your library and the Internet to find out more about Sandra Cisneros. As you find information, enter it on the author-profile chart below.

Profile of: Sandra Cisneros _____

Date of Birth: _____

Place of Birth: _____

Parents: _____

Other Family Members: _____

Description of Her Childhood and Childhood Interests: _____

_____

_____

_____

_____

_____

Education: _____

Famous Books or Other Works: _____

_____

_____

_____

_____

Author Quotation: _____

_____

_____

_____

_____

_____

_____

Information

BEFORE YOU READ

How did the first library begin? What was it like? Why were some people determined to get rid of it? Find out the answers to these questions as you read all about the ancient library of Alexandria, how it came to be, and how it was eventually destroyed.

Here's what you need to know before you begin reading:

- Ancient books were written on papyrus and rolled into scrolls.
- The library of Alexandria, in Egypt, was the first universal library. This means that it was the first library where scrolls from different countries were collected.
- The library was not only a place to read. It was also a great center where people came to do research, debate, discuss, study, teach, and share ideas. In many ways the library was like an educational resort, because people who came from distant lands lived and ate at the library.

Reading Standard 2.7
Make reasonable assertions about a text through accurate supporting citations.

from Cricket, May 2000

The Ancient Library of Alexandria

Anne Nolting

About 2,300 years ago, a great king ruled the country of Egypt. His name was Ptolemy I Soter, and he was a wise and inquisitive monarch with a deep longing for knowledge. His wish was for Egypt to become the most powerful nation in the world.

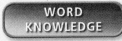

WORD KNOWLEDGE

Underline *inquisitive* (in·kwiz'ə·tiv) in line 3. What words in this first paragraph help you guess what it means? Circle the clues.

Inquisitive means "eager to learn."

_____

_____

_____

_____

_____

_____

_____

IDENTIFY

The author makes a statement that Alexandria became the greatest center of trade in the world (line 19). Circle this assertion. Then, read on, and underline facts and examples that support this assertion.

· · · · · · **Notes** · · · · · ·

_____

_____

_____

_____

_____

_____

_____

"You must read, great Ptolemy," his friend Demetrius urged. "This is the way to understand how to use power wisely."

Demetrius supplied Ptolemy with every document in Egypt. The books were written on thin, dried papyrus sheets and rolled into large scrolls.

As Ptolemy studied the Egyptian scrolls, he became more and more curious about the world outside his country. He realized that wealthy empires would trade their goods with Egypt if his country welcomed them with a safe port. In 300 B.C., the ruler ordered the building of a mighty fleet of ships to patrol in the Mediterranean Sea. Within a few years, the beautiful capital city of Alexandria became the greatest center of trade in the world. From his magnificent white-marble palace, Ptolemy watched the ships from distant countries sail into port. The docks at Alexandria were covered with fabulous products from far-off lands. Tin came from the British Isles, silk from China, cotton from India. But it was in the captain's quarters of these great boats that Ptolemy discovered the most precious cargo of all. The ships carried scrolls describing life in remote lands.

Ptolemy addressed a letter to be carried from Alexandria on every departing ship. "To all the Sovereignties and Governors on Earth," he wrote. "Send me every kind of written work your country has to offer. I would like to read the words of your poets and historians, your doctors and inventors. I would like to study the works of your astrologers, mathematicians, and geniuses. Do not hesitate to send all of these!"

Ptolemy appointed Demetrius the first librarian for his collection of books. Demetrius organized the translations

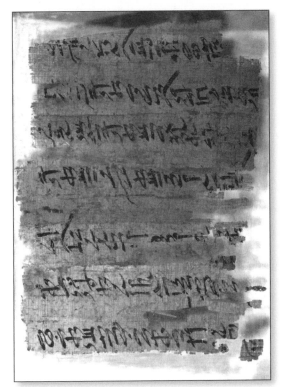

Papyrus from the Middle Kingdom of Egypt, c. 1900 B.C.

WORD KNOWLEDGE

Circle the word *colossal* (line 39). The dictionary meaning is "stupendous; so great in size or force or extent as to inspire awe." The dictionary gives this example of its use: "the colossal crumbling ruins of an ancient temple." Why do you think it's a good word choice here?

_____

_____

_____

_____

_____

_____

WORD KNOWLEDGE

A few words in this selection are in italicized type. Circle *Mouseion* (line 40). Then, skip three paragraphs in the text to find and circle the italicized word *bibliothekai* (line 72). These are Greek words. Right after each word, you'll find its definition.

VOCABULARY DEVELOPMENT

universal (yoō′nə·vʉr′səl) *adj.:* regarded as complete; whole.

deposited (dē·päs′it·id) *v.:* entrusted for safekeeping; put.

of the "ships' collection," and the number of scrolls grew rapidly. Ptolemy erected a colossal building next to his
40   palace in Alexandria. He called it *Mouseion,* or Shrine of the Muses, and dreamed it would become a treasury that would store every document in the world. A branch was established at the temple of Serapis. Thus the first **universal** library was born.

   After Ptolemy I died, his successors continued to collect scrolls, and the great library of Alexandria flourished. The priest Manetho wrote a three-scroll work on Egypt's history and religion under Ptolemy II, who also authorized seventy Jewish scholars to translate the Old Testament from
50   Hebrew into Greek. All these works were **deposited** in the great library. Scholars from distant lands traveled to Egypt.

They came to study, to teach, and to share their inventions. Poets, astronomers, physicists, mathematicians, zoologists, and doctors of many different races lived together at the library. They ate their meals in one gigantic dining hall, and the high ceiling reverberated with echoes from the lively debates.

60 The chambers of the great library were spacious and bright. Visitors sat on luxurious couches to enjoy the lilting voices of the poets and to listen to the melodies played by musicians. Across the hall, doctors carried out research in vast laboratories and dissecting rooms. In still another chamber, inventors gathered to assemble their new contraptions. Day and night the library pulsed with activity. At dusk, astronomers met on the rooftop observatory to map the constellations. At dawn, botanists could be seen ambling through terraced gardens where they observed new varieties of fruit trees and crops. Behind the library walls, animal keepers tended the world's first-known zoo.

70 Open walkways, bordered by lovely fountains and lotus flowers, divided the courtyards from the library chambers. Along these walks stood the *bibliothekai,* the name given to the niches, or cubbyholes, filled with scrolls. The library stored 500,000 scrolls, and none of them ever left the library. Scholars sat on small stools near the niches to read, unrolling the papyrus sheets on their laps to view the columns of writing. Some of the scrolls were twenty feet long!

The most knowledgeable people in the world traveled 80 to Egypt to study and lecture at the great Library of Alexandria. The names of many geniuses have been lost, but the few men and women who have been remembered offer us a glimpse into the exciting life of research at this great library.

A painting on papyrus of a tomb painting from ancient Egypt. Lotus flowers are shown at the right.

CONNECT

In ancient times, books were written on papyrus scrolls. Today, books are written on paper, and the pages are bound together. What do you think made reading from scrolls difficult?

_____

_____

_____

_____

FLUENCY

Read this boxed passage aloud. Concentrate on reading at a steady, even pace. Break difficult names and long words, such as *Eratosthenes* and *Elephantine*, into syllables to help you pronounce them. Before you read the numbers aloud, think about how to say them.

VOCABULARY DEVELOPMENT

stationary (stā′shə·ner′ē) *adj.:* unmoving; fixed or still.

If you wanted to describe how the leaves of a tree look when the air is calm, would you choose the word *stationary* or *unmoving* to describe the leaves? Explain.

_____

_____

_____

_____

The geographer Eratosthenes served as the director of the Library of Alexandria for forty years, beginning in 245 B.C. He was a brilliant mathematician and astronomer whose geometric calculations proved that the earth was a sphere. Eratosthenes calculated the size of the earth by
90 measuring the lengths of shadows cast by sticks placed in the Egyptian cities of Alexandria and Elephantine. From measurements taken at noon on the summer solstice, he estimated earth's diameter to be 7,850 miles (12,630 kilometers). This is very close to the measurement of 7,900 miles (12,700 kilometers) we use today. Building upon Eratosthenes' research, geographers began to map possible trade routes to India eastward across the Indian Ocean.

Another brilliant scholar who worked at the library was Aristarchus, a Greek astronomer. The earth, he
100 claimed, is not **stationary.** He concluded that the world is one of many planets that revolve around a sun. He wrote

IDENTIFY

The author asserts that an exciting life of research took place at this great library in Alexandria. Circle the names of four great scholars mentioned in lines 107–115.

WORD KNOWLEDGE

Hypatia (hī·pā′shə) invented the astrolabe, which measures the angle of a star on the horizon (line 118). What other words come from the root astro-, meaning "star"?

_____

_____

_____

_____

_____

_____

IDENTIFY

In line 124, the writer poses a question. What facts does she go on to cite to answer the question?

_____

_____

_____

_____

_____

treatises, or theories, proving his ideas. Democritus, a philosopher, added his thoughts. "The Milky Way is not the spilled milk of the goddess," Democritus explained. "It is composed of stars, millions of stars."

The great inventors used the library courtyards to test their designs. Archimedes constructed many machines, including the lever. "Give me a place to stand on," Archimedes declared, "and I will move the earth." Heron,

110 another inventor of Alexandria, added his works to the library. He wrote *Automata,* the first book on robots. Callimachus produced a 120-scroll catalog of authors and their works in the library.

Not all scholars who worked in the library were men. Hypatia was a gifted mathematician and astronomer whose fame spread to many countries. She taught at the library, wrote manuscripts, and worked on many of her own inventions, including an astrolabe, an instrument to measure the angle of a star from the horizon.

120 For seven centuries, the most brilliant minds in the world contributed their ideas to the storehouse of knowledge in Alexandria. Then, during one brief, chaotic time in history, the scrolls that told the stories of the world disappeared. What tragedies occurred to destroy this first great universal library?

First, in 47 B.C., a fire broke out in the great library's warehouses during Julius Caesar's Alexandrine War. Then, around A.D. 270, the Palace Quarter was destroyed and the library seriously damaged. Later, in A.D. 391, the branch

130 library and the temple of Serapis were destroyed. The main library survived but in a much diminished state.

At that time Emperor Theodosius ruled the Roman Empire. His beliefs differed from those of the scholars who

taught at the Library of Alexandria. Most of the scholars based their studies on the Greek tradition of mathematics and philosophy. The Christian emperor believed that ancient Greek scholars were pagans. He published **edicts** that closed the temples and destroyed written documents that did not agree with his doctrines.

140 Theodosius died in A.D. 395, and antipagan feelings grew stronger. In A.D. 415, Hypatia was set upon by a mob of religious fanatics in the streets and brutally murdered. Many scrolls, so faithfully collected for centuries, were burned as fuel for the public baths.

About A.D. 640, the Arabs invaded the city of Alexandria. The library was in ruins when the Arabs arrived, but they salvaged some of the remaining documents. As the Roman Empire fell to barbaric tribes and Europe entered the Dark Ages, the Arabs preserved the world's rich culture 150 of mathematics, astronomy, and science.

Today there are libraries in every town, and books of every kind are available to everyone. The words of ancient and present-day writers are standing on open shelves, waiting for any reader to encounter them.

Gold coin showing Theodosius the Great, 4th century (A.D. 379–395)

VOCABULARY DEVELOPMENT

edicts (ē'dikts) *n.:* orders; decrees.

INFER

In these times a pagan was any person who worshipped the gods of ancient Greece or Rome or the gods of the so-called barbarians. The prefix *anti-* means "against." What would *antipagan* feelings be?

The Ancient Library of Alexandria 251

OWN THE TEXT

Outline/Summary   Write a summary of this article on the ancient library at Alexandria. Before you write your summary, outline the article to be sure you include its key ideas and supporting details. The graphic organizer on the next page will help.

Research/Making Assertions   Not every informational article that appears in print is accurate. A good reader asks questions and evaluates the assertions a writer makes. At the end of your summary, note the assertions that this writer makes about the library and about its destruction. Look for details she uses to support her assertions. Does she use facts, quotations from experts, or scholarly sources? Does she cite any sources she used in researching this article? To support your own assertions, you will have to do research in an encyclopedia or in a reliable source on the Internet. Remember, if you cite anything based on your own research, you have to credit your sources.

Description   Describe your own public library. Try to use **images** that will help your readers see your library (inside and outside), perhaps even smell it, and hear the sounds (if any) you hear when you go there. Open your description with a sentence that tells where your library is located and how often you visit it.

KEEPING TRACK

Personal Word List   In your Personal Word List, record the words you learned while reading this selection.

Personal Reading Log   Do you think people value libraries today? Explain your response in your Personal Reading Log. Then, give yourself 3 points on the Reading Meter for reading this article.

Checklist for Standards Mastery   By reading this text, you've probably mastered reading standard 2.7. Track your progress on the Checklist for Standards Mastery.

The Ancient Library
of Alexandria ▪ *Interactive Reading,* page 245

Interact with an Informational Text

Outline Form   A simple formal outline is set up this way:

1. Main idea
   A. Supporting detail
   B. Supporting detail
2. Main idea
   A. Supporting detail
   B. Supporting detail

Usually you can get help in making an outline of an informational article by referring to its subheads. This article, however, does not have subheads. Therefore, you will have to read carefully and note when the main topic changes.

You can use the following outline form to show the structure of this article. This outline divides the article into four main sections.

1. The founding of the library at Alexandria
   A. _____
   B. _____
2. Scholars at the library
   A. _____
   B. _____
   C. _____
   D. _____
   E. _____
   F. _____
3. Destruction of the library
   A. _____
   B. _____
   C. _____
   D. _____
4. Arab invasion A.D. 640
   A. _____
   B. _____

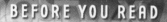

PROSE

BEFORE YOU READ

Jerry Spinelli is famous for his funny, true-to-life books. His most famous book, *Maniac McGee,* received several top awards, including the Newbery Medal. Spinelli's wife, Eileen, is also a children's-book writer. The Spinellis have seven children.

The following story is from Spinelli's *Knots in My Yo-yo String: The Autobiography of a Kid.* Read on to see just why Spinelli's works are treasured by so many readers.

Reading Standard 3.7 Explain the effects of common literary devices (for example, symbolism, imagery, metaphor) in a variety of fictional and nonfictional texts.

from The Autobiography of a Kid

Jerry Spinelli

IDENTIFY

Circle the words that tell you what Spinelli is going to talk about.

VOCABULARY DEVELOPMENT

subscription (səb·skrip′shən) *n.:* agreement to pay for a magazine or newspaper for a certain period of time.

FLUENCY

Read the boxed passage aloud twice. Experiment with your tone and speed to produce a comic effect.

I did not read. Not books, anyway. Now, cereal boxes—that was another story. Every morning I pored over boxes of Wheaties and Cheerios at the breakfast table. I looked forward to new cereals as much for a change in reading material as for a change in breakfast fare.

And comics. I read them by the hundreds.

Mostly I read cowboy and war comics. I bought them at corner stores and newsstands. Then when I was twelve, I got serious. I decided the comic should come to me. I got

10 my first **subscription:** *Bugs Bunny.* Once a month, accompanied by the metallic flapping of the front door mail slot, the postman delivered Bugs's latest adventures to me.

My favorite comic character of all, however, was neither man nor rabbit. In fact, I'm still not sure what it was. All I know is that it was called the Heap, and it looked something like a haystack. The Heap never spoke, and the reader never saw it move, but the Heap appeared on the scene when people were having problems. Somehow or other the Heap managed to solve the problem, though it never got credit. As far as most of the people knew, it was just another haystack in the field.

Of course, I read the newspaper comics too. While I never missed "Dick Tracy," "Little Lulu," and "Mandrake the Magician," my favorite of all was "Alley Oop."

Another part of the newspaper got my attention as well: sports.

Mostly I read the sports pages of the *Times Herald*. I especially liked the clever writing of sports editor Red McCarthy in his daily column. Until then I had thought there was only one English language—the language I spoke and heard in the West End of Norristown. I was happily surprised to discover that there was more than one way to say something, that the words and their arrangement could be as interesting as the thing they said.

From April to September in the Sunday *Philadelphia Inquirer,* I read the major league baseball batting statistics. They were printed in small type in a long box, row after row of numbers and names, hundreds of them—every player in the majors. To the non-baseball fan, they were as boring as a page in a phone book. I loved it. I wallowed in the numbers. What was Ted Williams's batting average this week? Stan Musial's? Richie Ashburn's? Was Ralph Kiner still the leader in home runs? Who had the most RBIs? Did Mantle have a shot at the Triple Crown? Or Mays? It was like peeking at a race once every seven days, watching the lead change places from week to week.

IDENTIFY

Stop at line 24. Sum up what Spinelli has told you so far about his reading.

_____

_____

_____

_____

IDENTIFY

Based on lines 25–26, what is Spinelli going to talk about next?

_____

_____

_____

_____

WHAT & WHY?

The sentence "I wallowed in the numbers" (lines 40–41) cannot be taken literally. What might this figurative expression mean? What is its effect?

_____

_____

_____

_____

_____

_____

_____

VOCABULARY DEVELOPMENT

curriculum (kə·rik′yo͞o·ləm) *n.:* courses offered at a school.

INTERPRET

Repetition of sentence length and structure, and even the words within a sentence, is a literary device called **parallel structure.** Re-read the last paragraph on this page, and explain the effect of parallel structure on the reader.

_____

_____

_____

_____

_____

_____

_____

_____

_____

_____

Cereal boxes, comics, baseball stats—that was my reading. As for books, I read maybe ten of them, fifteen tops, from the day I entered first grade until graduation

50 from high school. I remember reading a few Bobbsey Twins adventures, and in junior high, sports stories about Chip Hilton, a fictional high school hotshot athlete. I read *The Adventures of Robin Hood,* a Sherlock Holmes mystery, and *Kon-Tiki,* the true story of a man who crossed the Pacific in a raft. That's about it.

Why didn't I read more?

I could blame it on my grade school, which had no library. I could blame it on the **curriculum,** which limited my classroom reading to "See Dick run. See Jane run.

60 See Spot do something on the rug." I could blame it on history, for enrolling me in life and school before the time of book fairs and author visits. I could blame it on my friends, because like me, the only books they read were comic books.

But I can't do that.

It's always handy to blame things on one's parents, but I can't do that either. My father had his books on display in the dining room. Thirty times a day I passed his collection of histories and Ellery Queen mysteries. Some of my earliest memories are of my mother reading to me, stories like *Babar* and *The Little Engine That Could.* My parents steered me in the right direction.

And the fact is, on those few occasions when I actually did read a book, I enjoyed it. Yet for some reason I would not admit this to myself. Instead of saying, Hey, that was good, that was fun, I think I'll read another—I would dump my baseball glove into my bike basket and head out the path to the Little League field, and months would go by before I picked up a book again. Reading a book was for times when I was totally bored and lacking anything else to do.

And what about words, which, packed together, made up a book as cells made up my body? I liked them. Yet this was such a naturally occurring, unachieved sort of thing that if someone had asked me in those days, "Do you like words?" I probably would have shrugged and **blithely** answered, "No."

Still, whether I knew it or not, words were claiming me. When I visited Hartenstine Printing, where my father worked as a typesetter, I saw words being created letter by letter, one thin slug of lead at a time.

Once, in a comic book, someone with a bad heart was described as having a bum ticker. That tickled me to no end. I kept whispering "bum ticker" to myself for days.

WHAT & WHY?

What **simile** can you find in lines 82–83? Underline it.

IDENTIFY

How does the writer support his statement that words were claiming him (lines 88–89)?

_____

_____

_____

_____

_____

_____

_____

VOCABULARY DEVELOPMENT

blithely (blī*th*′lē) *adv.:* in a carefree way; casually.

How would you describe the difference between *blithe* and *careless*?

_____

_____

_____

_____

A *gossoon* (gä·so͞on′) (line 106) is a young boy. It comes from the Irish.

INFER

What does Spinelli mean in lines 112–115, beginning with "The tickle . . ."?

_____

_____

_____

_____

_____

_____

PREDICT

Pause at line 123. What do you predict happened when he wrote a poem?

_____

_____

_____

_____

_____

_____

_____

_____

Except for the Heap, my favorite comic book characters were Bugs Bunny and Daffy Duck. I liked them as much for their words as their ways. For me, the highlight of a scene was not what happened, but what Bugs or Daffy said about what happened. This is probably why Mickey

100 Mouse never much appealed to me. His speech was too bland for my taste.

Occasionally I had to look up a word in the dictionary. Sometimes my eye would stray to the surrounding words. Invariably it stopped at an interesting one, and I read the definition. In one such instance I discovered that I was a gossoon. I clearly remember two feelings attached to these moments: (1) surprise that a dictionary could be so interesting, and (2) a notion to sit down and look through more pages. I never did.

110 And then of course there was my success in spelling.

All of these items were indicators of an early leaning toward language, but I failed to see them as such. The tickle of a rabbit's wit, the rattle of alphabet in a compositor's drawer—they simply took their place among the Popsicles and penknives and bike tires of my days.

With one exception.

In sixth grade our teacher assigned us a project: Make a scrapbook of Mexico. I found pictures of Mexico in *National Geographic* and other magazines and pasted them

120 in my scrapbook, for which my father made a professional-looking cover at the print shop. Then I did something extra. It wasn't part of the assignment. I just did it.

I wrote a poem.

Three stanzas about Mexico, ending with a touristy come-on: "Now, isn't that where you would like to be?" I wrote it in pencil, longhand, my best penmanship, on a piece of lined classroom paper. I pasted it neatly on the last page of my scrapbook and turned in my project.

130 Several days later my mother walked the three blocks to my school. She met with my teacher, who told her she did not believe that my poem about Mexico was my own work. She thought I copied it from a book. (Hah! If she only knew how few books I read, and never one with poetry.) I was suspected of plagiarism.

I don't know what my mother said to her, but by the time she walked out I was in the clear, legally at least. Five years would pass before I wrote another poem.

WORD KNOWLEDGE

Plagiarism (plā'jə·riz'əm) means "taking someone else's ideas and passing them off as if they are your own." For example, a plagiarist might steal a plot or a passage from another writer. *Plagiarize* comes from a Latin word for "kidnapper."

Which verb has a more negative meaning: *copy* or *plagiarize*?

_____

_____

_____

_____

_____

_____

_____

_____

INFER

Why do you suppose the teacher thought Spinelli had plagiarized the poem?

_____

_____

_____

_____

_____

_____

_____

OWN THE STORY

Literary Devices   Jot down three short phrases from the story that contain literary devices. Then, explain how the story might differ if those devices had not been used.

_____

_____

_____

_____

Autobiography   This is a chapter from the autobiography of a famous writer of novels for young adults. In this chapter, Spinelli focuses on the reading he did as a boy (what there was of it). Write a brief account about what *you* have read so far in your life. Cite titles and characters, even if they are titles of comic books and characters in movies. Open with a general statement about how you feel about reading. Be honest. That is what readers look for in autobiographies.

_____

_____

_____

_____

_____

KEEPING TRACK

Personal Word List   Record the words you learned in your Personal Word List.

Personal Reading Log   Record this selection in your Personal Reading Log, and write a brief response to it. Give yourself 3 points on the Reading Meter for completing this selection.

Checklist for Standards Mastery   Use the Checklist for Standards Mastery to track your progress in mastering the standards.

from The Autobiography of a Kid ▪ *Interactive Reading, page 254*

Interact with a Literary Text

Story-Image Frames   Summarize the main events in this part of Spinelli's autobiography in a series of "frames." Use drawings (you can use stick figures if you wish) to show what is happening in Jerry's "life as a reader." Give each frame a title, perhaps a title taken from the text.

Frame 1:

Frame 2:

Frame 3:

Chapter 7

Rhyme and Reason

Strategy Launch: "Text Reformulation"

LITERARY FOCUS: POETRY

Poetry creates music with rhythms, rhymes, and other kinds of repetition. Poets help us see the world in fresh, new ways by using images and figures of speech, such as similes, metaphors, and personification.

Like all pieces of literature, poetry also conveys a tone. **Tone** refers to the writer's attitude toward a subject. Tone can be light and funny, serious and sad, cynical, cruel, or nostalgic. Poets convey tone through word choice and through their use of sounds.

A STRATEGY THAT WORKS: "TEXT REFORMULATION"

To think critically about a poem and its tone, use a strategy called "Text Reformulation." When you reformulate a poem, you restate the content of the poem in another format. Text reformulation helps you think critically about a poem, but it is also fun, because it puts your imagination to work. You can reformulate a poem by recasting it as a story, a letter, a play, a newspaper article, or even a comic book.

POINTERS FOR USING "TEXT REFORMULATION"

When you reformulate a poem or any other text, you have to be sure you understand the structure of the new form. For example, if you want to turn a narrative poem into a news article, you have to be sure you know what the structure of a news article is. You will find information on various text structures in *Holt Literature and Language Arts*.

Reading Standard 1.2 Identify and interpret figurative language.

Reading Standard 2.8 Note instances of unsupported inferences, fallacious reasoning, persuasion, and propaganda in text.

Reading Standard 3.4 Define how tone or meaning is conveyed in poetry through word choice, figurative language, sentence structure, line length, punctuation, rhythm, repetition, and rhyme.

Practice Read

Find out what happens when a group of friends start the Just Us Club. "The Just Us Club" is a narrative poem written in a pattern of six-line stanzas. Each stanza has rhyming lines.

Think about the name the Just Us Club. What does it mean? How would you expect other kids to react to this club and its members?

Read the poem aloud. Listen for its tone.

The Just Us Club

Richard Cohen

IDENTIFY

Circle the words that rhyme in the first stanza. Use a letter of the alphabet to indicate each rhyme. Check to see if both stanzas on this page rhyme *aabaab*.

• • • • • • Notes • • • • • •

When I was small—say ten or so—
I formed a club with Mike and Jo.
"Let's invite all the kids we know," said Mike.
But guess what? When we turned to Jo,
5   she said, "I totally don't know.
I only want to ask the kids I like."

Well, that was fine with all of us,
So we invited Kim and Gus.
Asked Kim, "What will we call our brand-new club?"
10 "And where will we sit on the bus?"
Said I, "We'll call ourselves Just Us.
And all those lowly other kids we'll snub."

"Great idea!" Jo said in a rush,

"Most excellent!" trumpeted Gush—

15   I mean Gus. (That didn't come out just right.)

Well, anyway, we all were thrilled,

And all that day we sat and chilled

Until the sun said, "It is night."

"This club," I said, "what will it do?

20   And how will the club turn me and you

Into the most popular kids in sight?"

Gus answered, "We'll associate

Just with ourselves, and stay up late,

For as a group we'll be very tight.

25   "And all of those who want to join

Will have to pay us in big time coin,

But even then they won't get in.

We'll give them tests, and if they fail,

We'll jeer them, with a nasty hail

30   of insults and a mocking grin.

"And then we'll make up secret games

And give ourselves new, secret names

And we'll invent a code no one can break.

We'll talk in code all through the day

35   And they'll all whine, 'Please, can we play?'

But we'll just say, '*No!* Go jump in the lake.'"

INTERPRET

The poet chose an unusual verb to describe Gus's manner of speaking. Circle that verb, and describe how Gus talked.

_____

_____

_____

_____

IDENTIFY

What is the purpose of the club?

_____

_____

EVALUATE

How does this speaker make you feel? What is his **tone**?

_____

_____

_____

_____

FLUENCY

Read the boxed stanzas aloud twice. The second time you read, try to improve your speech and the smoothness of your delivery. In a third reading, work on conveying the speaker's **tone**.

EVALUATE

What details reveal the
values of the club members?
(See lines 37–49.)

_____

_____

_____

_____

_____

INFER

Underline the verbs the
speaker uses in line 50. What
do you think of using these
methods to be popular?

_____

_____

_____

INTERPRET

What **tone** does the punctuation in lines 49–53 suggest?
How does the tone change in
the last line?

_____

_____

_____

_____

_____

_____

_____

_____

Then Kim said, "And, like, when we're grown,

We'll still be friends, all on our own,

Doing anything we want.

40   We'll own ten houses, twenty cars,

We'll fly to Venus and to Mars,

They'll name computers for us, and a font!

"Planets we'll discover, and

Gold treasures we'll uncover, and

45   Over the whole wide world we'll cast our spell.

Even our fathers and mothers,

Sisters, brothers, and all others

Will kneel—and give us credit cards, as well."

What dreams! We went to school next day

50   All set to push and shove our way

Right to the top of popularity!

We had it all so neatly planned!

Our club was going to be so grand!

But we had planned without much clarity.

55   We went to school fully prepared

To take command, but no one cared

Or even wondered what we were about.

"You can't join us!" we said, but they

Had never asked to anyway.

60   And when they played kickball they kicked us out.

"Hey, want to join our club?" I begged
One kid. He sneered, "We've got you pegged
As snobs. If we were like you we would say
You can't play with *us*. We'd shun you.
65 You'd have no friends. Your fate you'd rue.
But, see, you're lucky, that's just not our way.

"Forget this dumb old clubby pose
And join the class, and join with those
Who play with everyone and don't exclude.
70 'Just Us' is wrong. *Justice* is right.
Yes, count on that by day or night.
'Be fair to all' is what you might conclude."

The kid left then, but his words took.
I know them better than a book.
75 He spoke so truly that he left no doubt.
He was twelve and we were ten,
But now we're twelve ourselves, and when
We play we keep nobody out.

WORD KNOWLEDGE

Rue (rōō) (line 65) is a verb that means "regret." This word is not used very often in modern speech.

IDENTIFY

Why doesn't anyone want to join the club?

_____

_____

_____

_____

_____

_____

INTERPRET

What is the relationship between the club name *Just Us* and the word *justice*?

_____

_____

_____

_____

_____

_____

_____

_____

OWN THE POEM

PRACTICING THE STANDARDS

Text Reformulation   Write the account of "The Just Us Club" as a journal entry. Let the same speaker tell the story as "I." When you finish, compare your reformulations in class. Does the new format change the speaker's tone? The graphic on the next page will help you with your reformulation.

_____

_____

_____

_____

Tone and Meaning   Write a brief paragraph analyzing the tone in "The Just Us Club." Focus on these questions: What is the tone for half the poem? Where does the tone change? How do the sounds of the poem—its bouncy rhythms and rhymes—affect the tone? Quote at least one passage from the poem to support your response. Be sure to put quotation marks around the poet's exact words.

_____

_____

_____

_____

KEEPING TRACK

Personal Word List   Record the words you learned from the poem in your Personal Word List.

Personal Reading Log   As you record this poem in your Personal Reading Log, think about how the Just Us Club is like the Sneetches in Dr. Seuss's poem. Award yourself 1 point on the Reading Meter for reading "The Just Us Club."

Checklist for Standards Mastery   Track your mastery of the reading standards by using the Checklist for Standards Mastery.

The Just Us Club ▪ *Interactive Reading,* page 264

Interact with a Literary Text

"Text Reformulation" Chart Work with a partner. Take turns reformulating key passages from "The Just Us Club" into sentences that might appear in a diary or personal journal entry.

Lines from "The Just Us Club"	Text Reformulation
Said I, "We'll call ourselves Just Us. And all those lowly other kids we'll snub."	
"Our club was going to be so grand! But we had planned without much clarity."	
"You'd have no friends. Your fate you'd rue."	
" 'Be fair to all' is what you might conclude."	

TONE

The Sneetches

Interact with a Literary Text

Rhyme-Alliance Chart   The words that rhyme in a poem contribute to the poem's tone and meaning. Fill out the Rhyme-Alliance Chart below after you read the first nine stanzas of "The Sneetches." Circle any rhyming words that are made-up. They also provide clues to the speaker's tone. In the bottom box, comment on how the sounds of the poem affect its tone.

End-Rhyme Alliances:
Sneetches with _____
small with _____
snort with _____
walking with _____
roasts with _____
near with _____
stars with _____
keen with _____
unhappy with _____
need with _____

Internal-Rhyme Alliances:
Line 40: _____
_____
_____

Tone Reflected in Rhymes:
_____
_____
_____

Ode to Mi Gato; In a Neighborhood in Los Angeles; Hard on the Gas

Interact with Literary Texts

Comparative-Elements Chart   When you compare poems, you look at their subjects, their use of figurative language, and their form or structure.

Use this Comparative-Elements Chart to compare "Ode to Mi Gato," "In a Neighborhood in Los Angeles," and "Hard on the Gas."

Poem Title	Subject	Examples of Figurative Language	Form or Structure

Words That Describe Tone:

"Ode to Mi Gato" _____

_____

"In a Neighborhood in Los Angeles" _____

_____

"Hard on the Gas" _____

_____

Haiku

Interact with Literary Texts

Balance-Scale Diagrams   Japanese haiku often create a balance between two opposing ideas, images, or feelings. See if you can find balanced ideas, images, or feelings in these haiku.

Try filling out this graphic with a partner. You might disagree on what should be in the balanced squares. That is all right—disagreement will force you to look more closely at the poems. The first scale has been filled in.

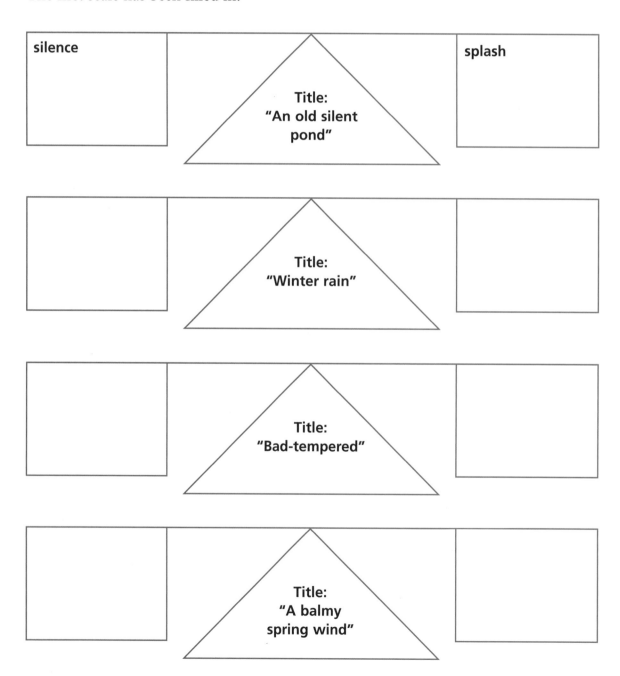

| silence | Title: "An old silent pond" | splash |

| | Title: "Winter rain" | |

| | Title: "Bad-tempered" | |

| | Title: "A balmy spring wind" | |

Poem *and* Motto

Interact with Literary Texts

Tone Webs   Word choice, figurative language, rhyme, rhythm, and other forms of repetition work together to convey tone. As you re-read "Poem" and "Motto," fill out the Tone Webs below.

Examples of Rhyme

_____

_____

_____

_____

**Title:
Poem**

tone:

_____

_____

_____

**Description of Rhythm or
Other Forms of Repetition**

_____

_____

_____

**Examples of Figurative
Language**

_____

_____

_____

**Examples of Unusual
Word Choice**

_____

_____

_____

Examples of Rhyme

_____

_____

_____

**Title:
Motto**

tone:

_____

_____

_____

**Description of Rhythm or
Other Forms of Repetition**

_____

_____

_____

**Examples of Figurative
Language**

_____

_____

_____

**Examples of Unusual
Word Choice**

_____

_____

_____

John Henry

Interact with a Literary Text

Text Reformulation Pyramid   "John Henry" is a ballad, a song that tells a story using refrains. Rewrite the story of John Henry as if it were a newspaper report. The format of a news report is like an inverted pyramid. The key details of the story come first; more specific details and perhaps some eyewitness accounts or human interest stories come later.

The headline tries to grab the reader's attention. "Dateline" refers to the date and place from which the story is filed. For this story, you will have to get dateline information from information in the text.

Before you write your news story about John Henry, fill in the details in the following graphic.

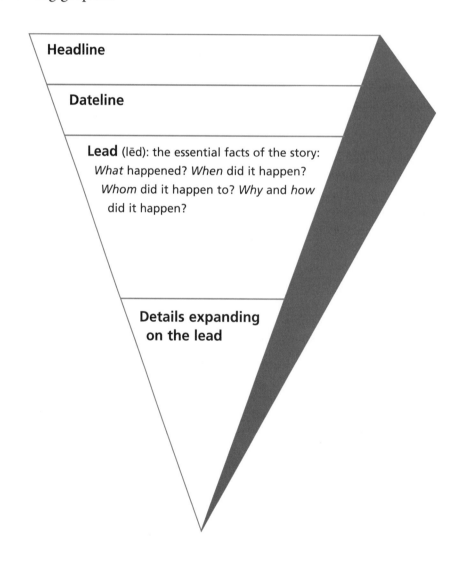

Headline

Dateline

Lead (lēd): the essential facts of the story: *What* happened? *When* did it happen? *Whom* did it happen to? *Why* and *how* did it happen?

Details expanding on the lead

Literature

AUTHOR STUDY

In this chapter you read a poem by **Dr. Seuss** (Theodor Geisel) about imaginary creatures called *Sneetches.* Dr. Seuss has been known to readers of many generations for the memorable characters he has written about and drawn. Theodor Seuss Geisel, born in 1904, was the son of a curator at the Forest Park Zoo in Springfield, Massachusetts. His father hoped that young Theodor would become a doctor. To honor that wish, Theodor decided to add *Dr.* to his middle name and use that new name, *Dr. Seuss,* as a pen name for his children's books.

BEFORE YOU READ

Imagine this situation from the perspective of Dr. Seuss: You are not a peculiar creature like a *Sneetch,* but a human child. Like all humans, there is a day on which you were born. You might have siblings, and you definitely have a guardian, who calls out your name from time to time for any number of reasons, including asking you to come to breakfast. How can these situations be funny or strange or even outrageous? You're about to find out when you read "If We Didn't Have Birthdays," "Too Many Daves," and "Vrooms"—all by Dr. Seuss.

Before you begin, it might interest you to know that the books in which these poems appeared were *Happy Birthday to You* ("If We Didn't Have Birthdays"), *The Sneetches and Other Stories by Dr. Seuss* ("Too Many Daves"), and *On Beyond Zebra!* ("Vrooms").

Reading Standard 3.4 Define how tone or meaning is conveyed in poetry through word choice, figurative language, sentence structure, line length, punctuation, rhythm, repetition, and rhyme.

If We Didn't Have Birthdays

Dr. Seuss

TONE

Read the poem aloud, and mark the syllables that are stressed with an accent mark (´). Circle end words that rhyme. How does the poem's sound affect its tone?

If we didn't have birthdays, you wouldn't be you.

If you'd never been born, well then what would you do?

If you'd never been born, well then what would you be?

You *might* be a fish! Or a toad in a tree!

5   You might be a doorknob! Or three baked potatoes!

You might be a bag full of hard green tomatoes.

Or worse than all that . . . Why, you might be a WASN'T!

A Wasn't has no fun at all. No, he doesn't.

A Wasn't just isn't. He just isn't present.

10   But you . . . You ARE YOU! And, now isn't that pleasant!

Dr. Seuss shakes hands with the Cat in the Hat, one of the famous characters he created. This photo was taken in 1988.

Too Many Daves

Dr. Seuss

Did I ever tell you that Mrs. McCave

Had twenty-three sons and she named them all Dave?

Well, she did. And that wasn't a smart thing to do.

You see, when she wants one and calls out, "Yoo-Hoo!

5   Come into the house, Dave!" she doesn't get *one*.

All twenty-three Daves of hers come on the run!

This makes things quite difficult at the McCaves'

As you can imagine, with so many Daves.

And often she wishes that, when they were born,

10 She had named one of them Bodkin Van Horn

And one of them Hoos-Foos. And one of them Snimm.

And one of them Hot-Shot. And one Sunny Jim.

And one of them Shadrack. And one of them Blinkey.

And one of them Stuffy. And one of them Stinkey.

15 Another one Putt-Putt. Another one Moon Face.

Another one Marvin O'Gravel Balloon Face.

And one of them Ziggy. And one Soggy Muff.

One Buffalo Bill. And one Biffalo Buff.

And one of them Sneepy. And one Weepy Weed.

20 And one Paris Garters. And one Harris Tweed.

And one of them Sir Michael Carmichael Zutt

And one of them Oliver Boliver Butt

And one of them Zanzibar Buck-Buck McFate . . .

But she didn't do it. And now it's too late.

TONE

Read the poem aloud. Circle the name options that Dr. Seuss suggests for all twenty-three Daves. What effect does this list of names have on the **tone** of the poem?

_____

_____

_____

_____

_____

_____

_____

_____

_____

_____

_____

_____

_____

_____

_____

_____

_____

_____

Vrooms

Dr. Seuss

On a world near the sun live two brothers called VROOMS
Who, strangely enough, are built sort of like brooms
And they're stuck all alone up there high in the blue
And so, to kill time, just for something to do
5 Each one of these fellows takes turns with the other
In sweeping the dust off his world with his brother.

Dr. Seuss and some "friends."

OWN THE POEMS

PRACTICING THE STANDARDS

Tone and Meaning   Choose one of the three Dr. Seuss poems, and prepare it for an oral presentation. As you practice, be aware of the tone of the poem. In your presentation, be sure to get that tone across.

KEEPING TRACK

Personal Word List   Record some of your favorite rhyming words in your Personal Word List.

Personal Reading Log   As you record this group of poems in your Personal Reading Log, describe the tone of the poems as a group. Give yourself 1 point on the Reading Meter for completing the poems.

Checklist for Standards Mastery   Use the Checklist for Standards Mastery to track your progress with the reading standards.

If We Didn't Have Birthdays; Too Many Daves; Vrooms ▪ *Interactive Reading,* page 276

Go Beyond Literary Texts

Author Profile   Use your library and the Internet to find out more about Dr. Seuss (Theodor Geisel). Fill out the author profile below.

When and where was the author born?
What kind of education did he receive?
What were some of the author's first jobs?
What was his first book?
What was a turning point in the author's career?
What are some interesting facts about the author?

Reading Standard 2.8
Note instances of unsupported inferences, fallacious reasoning, persuasion, and propaganda in text.

BEFORE YOU READ

As the Vrooms look down from high in the blue, what do you think they see? Possibly, they might observe areas of Earth where the climate has changed, where plentiful water resources have dried up, where forests that used to thrive no longer exist. Get ready to read how the actions of humans affect Earth and its most precious resources.

from The World Almanac for Kids 2001

Save Our Earth

Protecting Our Water

Every living thing needs water to live. Many animals also depend on water as a home. People not only drink water, but also use it to cook, clean, cool machinery in factories, produce power, and irrigate farmland.

Where Does Water Come From?

Although about two thirds of the Earth's surface is water, we are able to use only a tiny fraction of it. Seawater makes up 97% of Earth's water, and 2% is frozen in glaciers and 10 ice around the north and south poles. Freshwater makes up only 1% of our water, and only part of that is close enough to Earth's surface for us to use.

The water we can use comes from lakes, rivers, reservoirs, and groundwater. Groundwater is melted snow or rain that seeps deep below the surface of the Earth and collects in pools called aquifers.

TEXT STRUCTURE

Skim this article. What two parts is it divided into? What do its headings tell you about its coverage?

_____

_____

_____

_____

_____

_____

IDENTIFY

Circle the statistics in the second paragraph. How does the writer answer the question in the heading?

_____

_____

Overall, the world has enough freshwater, but sometimes it is not available exactly where it is needed. Extreme water shortages, or droughts, can occur when an area gets

20   too little rain or has very hot weather over a long period of time, causing water supplies to dry up.

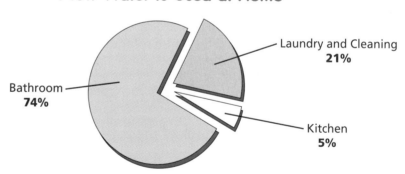

HOW MUCH WATER DO WE USE?

◆ Average American's daily cooking, washing, flushing, and lawn care: 183 gallons

◆ An average load of wash in a washing machine: 50 gallons

◆ 10-minute shower or a bath: 25–50 gallons

◆ One load of dishes in a dishwasher: 12–20 gallons

◆ One person's daily drinking and eating: 2 quarts

30   ## How Water Is Used at Home

Bathroom **74%**

Laundry and Cleaning **21%**

Kitchen **5%**

What Is Threatening Our Water?

Water is polluted when it is not fit for its intended uses, such as drinking, swimming, watering crops, or serving as a habitat. Polluted water can cause disease and kill fish and other animals. Some major water pollutants include sewage, chemicals from factories, fertilizers and weed killers, and leakage from landfills. Water pollution is

being reduced in some areas, such as Lake Erie, the
Willamette River in Oregon, Boston Harbor, and the
40   Hudson River in New York State. Companies continue to
look for better ways to get rid of wastes, and many farmers
are trying new ways to grow crops without using polluting
fertilizers or chemicals.

The Importance of Forests

Trees and forests are very important to the environment. In
addition to holding water, trees hold the soil in place. Trees
use carbon dioxide and give off oxygen, which animals and
plants need for survival. And they provide homes and food
for millions of types of animals.

50   Cutting down trees—usually to use the land for something besides a forest—is called deforestation. Although
people often have good reasons for cutting down trees,
deforestation can have serious effects. In the Amazon rain
forest in South America, for example, thousands of plants
and animal species are being lost before scientists can even
learn about them. In the Pacific Northwest, there is a
conflict between logging companies that want to cut down
trees for lumber and people who want to preserve the
ancient forests.

TEXT STRUCTURE

What is the next topic in this article?

_____

_____

_____

_____

TEXT STRUCTURE

How does the writer support the assertion in line 45?

_____

_____

_____

_____

_____

_____

_____

_____

_____

_____

WORD KNOWLEDGE

The word *deforestation* (line 51) is defined in context. Underline the definition.

TEXT STRUCTURE

To answer the question in line 66, the writer cites a series of causes and effects. What happens when trees are cut down?

_____

_____

_____

_____

_____

_____

_____

_____

_____

_____

_____

_____

_____

_____

_____

_____

TEXT STRUCTURE

How does the writer answer the question in line 77? Put a number in front of each answer.

60   **Why Do We Cut Down Trees?** People cut down trees for many reasons. When the population grows, people cut down trees to clear space to build houses, schools, factories, and other buildings. People may clear land to plant crops and graze livestock. Sometimes all the trees in an area are cut and sold for lumber and paper.

What Happens When Trees Are Cut Down? Cutting down trees can affect the climate. After rain falls on a forest, mist rises and new rain clouds form. When forests are cut down, this cycle is disrupted, and the area eventu-

70   ally grows drier, causing a change in the local climate.

     If huge areas of trees are cut down, the carbon dioxide they would have used builds up in the atmosphere and contributes to the greenhouse effect. And without trees to hold the soil and absorb water, rain washes topsoil away, a process called soil erosion. Farming on the poorer soil that is left can be very hard.

What Are We Doing to Save Forests? In many countries trees are being planted faster than they are being cut down. Foresting companies are working on

80   more efficient methods of replacing and growing forests. In addition, communities and individuals are helping to save forests by recycling paper.

OWN THE TEXT

Supporting Assertions An **assertion** is a position you take on a topic. The writer of this article has asserted that we must save our water resources and our forests. Various facts support that assertion. Make an assertion of your own about the environment. You could focus on oil drilling, preserving endangered species, the danger of fuel emissions, and so on. Your assertion can be stated negatively or positively. Whichever way you state your position, you have to give at least two facts to support your assertion.

_____

_____

_____

_____

_____

KEEPING TRACK

Personal Word List Record the words or terms you learned from this article in your Personal Word List. Tell a partner an opinion you hold about the environment, using one word or term from your list.

Personal Reading Log As you record this article in your Personal Reading Log, identify a problem in the environment you most care about. Give yourself 2 points on the Reading Meter for reading the article.

Checklist for Standards Mastery Track your progress in identifying arguments and how they are supported, using the Checklist for Standards Mastery.

Save Our Earth

Interactive Reading, **page 281**

Interact with an Informational Text

Argument-Evaluation Chart   Evaluate the arguments in "Save Our Earth" by filling in the Argument-Evaluation Chart. Then, rate the writer's argument based on your findings.

Statement: _____

_____

Support: _____

_____

Statement: _____

_____

Support: _____

_____

Statement: _____

_____

Support: _____

_____

Evaluation of argument:

_____

_____

_____

_____

_____

_____

Literature

POETRY

BEFORE YOU READ

If young people do not act responsibly toward the environment, wild or crazy things might happen—or so this poet claims. What could those wild and crazy things be? Get ready to find out as you read "Sarah Cynthia Sylvia Stout Would Not Take the Garbage Out" and "Turning Off the Faucet."

Sarah Cynthia Sylvia Stout Would Not Take the Garbage Out

Shel Silverstein

Sarah Cynthia Sylvia Stout
Would not take the garbage out!
She'd scour the pots and scrape the pans,
Candy the yams and spice the hams,

5   And though her daddy would scream and shout,
She simply would not take the garbage out.
And so it piled up to the ceilings:
Coffee grounds, potato peelings,
Brown bananas, rotten peas,

10 Chunks of sour cottage cheese.
It filled the can, it covered the floor,
It cracked the window and blocked the door
With bacon rinds and chicken bones,
Drippy ends of ice cream cones,

WORD KNOWLEDGE

In lines 1–10 circle the **alliteration**—repetition of the same beginning consonant sound. What effect does the use of alliteration have on you, the reader?

_____

_____

_____

_____

_____

_____

_____

_____

_____

_____

_____

_____

_____

_____

_____

_____

_____

_____

INFER

What do you think happened to Sarah Cynthia Sylvia Stout (line 43)?

_____

_____

_____

_____

_____

_____

_____

15 Prune pits, peach pits, orange peel,

Gloppy glumps of cold oatmeal,

Pizza crusts and withered greens,

Soggy beans and tangerines,

Crusts of black burned butter toast,

20 Gristly bits of beefy roasts . . .

The garbage rolled on down the hall,

It raised the roof, it broke the wall . . .

Greasy napkins, cookie crumbs,

Globs of gooey bubble gum,

25 Cellophane from green baloney,

Rubbery blubbery macaroni,

Peanut butter, caked and dry,

Curdled milk and crusts of pie,

Moldy melons, dried-up mustard,

30 Eggshells mixed with lemon custard,

Cold french fries and rancid meat,

Yellow lumps of Cream of Wheat.

At last the garbage reached so high

That finally it touched the sky.

35 And all the neighbors moved away,

And none of her friends would come to play.

And finally Sarah Cynthia Stout said,

"OK, I'll take the garbage out!"

But then, of course, it was too late . . .

40 The garbage reached across the state,

From New York to the Golden Gate.

And there, in the garbage she did hate,

Poor Sarah met an awful fate,

That I cannot right now relate

45 Because the hour is much too late.

But children, remember Sarah Stout

And always take the garbage out!

Turning Off the Faucet

Jeff Moss

If you don't turn the faucet off tight
When you're done in the bathroom,
You'll be wasting water.
Also, the sink might fill up
5   And overflow and flood the bathroom,
And then the bathroom would fill up
And overflow and flood the bedroom,
And all your clothes would get soaking wet,
And when you wore them, you'd catch a horrible cold
10   And have to stay home from school
And you couldn't learn anything
Or see your friends.

And after you'd missed school long enough,
All your friends would forget you
15   And you would be so sad and wet
You'd probably just stay in bed
Wearing your sad, wet clothes
With your sad, wet head
On your sad, wet pillow
20   Until you just shriveled up and wasted away.
And nobody would care.
Except your parents
And they'd be all sad and wet
And shriveling and wasting away, too,
25   Because you didn't turn the faucet off.

TEXT STRUCTURE

This poem is a series of comical **causes and effects**. The first event, the original cause, is cited in line 1. The final event occurs in line 20. Underline all the events that happen in between. You should be able to find ten events.

• • • • • • Notes • • • • • •

OWN THE POEMS

PRACTICING THE STANDARDS

Tone and Meaning Fill in the Tone Cards on the following page to analyze the tone of each poem. Share your completed cards with a partner, noting similarities and differences in your choices.

Tone Prepare one of these poems for reading aloud. The Silverstein poem is longer and more difficult. You might want to present that poem in a group reading. If you select a group reading, you will have to determine which lines will be spoken by which reader. In your reading, focus on pronunciation and fluency, but you will also have to think about tone. What tone do you want to convey in your poem?

KEEPING TRACK

Personal Word List Record the words you learned from the poems in your Personal Word List.

Personal Reading Log Record these poems in your Personal Reading Log. Write a few sentences telling how the poems might be the subject of a poster you find in a hallway or classroom of your school. Give yourself 1 point on the Reading Meter.

Checklist for Standards Mastery Each time you read, you learn more. Check your progress in mastering the standards using the Checklist for Standards Mastery.

Sarah Cynthia Sylvia Stout Would Not Take the Garbage Out; Turning Off the Faucet

Interactive Reading, page 287

TONE

Interact with Literary Texts

Tone Cards   Use the following cards to analyze the poems you have just read. When you finish, write a brief description of the tone of each poem.

Title: "Sarah Cynthia Sylvia Stout Would Not Take the Garbage Out"

Word Choice: _____

_____

Rhyme and Other Sound Effects: _____

_____

_____

Rhythm: _____

_____

Description of Tone: _____

_____

Title: "Turning Off the Faucet"

Word Choice: _____

_____

Rhyme and Other Sound Effects: _____

_____

_____

Rhythm: _____

_____

Description of Tone: _____

_____

Chapter 8

You the Critic

Chapter Preview In this chapter you will—

Strategy Launch: "Save the Last Word for Me"

LITERARY FOCUS: CHARACTER AND PLOT

A **character** is a person or an animal who takes part in the action of a story, play, or other literary work. The process of revealing the personality of a character in a story is called characterization. A **credible character** is a character who is believable—one who says and does things an actual person might say and do.

    Plot is a series of related events that make up a story. Plot is "what happens" in a short story, novel, play, or narrative poem. A **realistic plot** is one in which the events make sense—one event causes another to happen, and the story events as a whole are understandable. A **contrived plot** is one in which the events are connected by unbelievable causes and effects.

A STRATEGY THAT WORKS: "SAVE THE LAST WORD FOR ME"

Now it's your turn to be the judge of how well a writer creates credible, or realistic, characters and events. A strategy that gives you a chance to do this is "Save the Last Word for Me."

POINTERS FOR USING THE "SAVE THE LAST WORD FOR ME" STRATEGY:

⟫⟶ Find a passage in the text that you have an opinion about. Is the detail believable, or is it unbelievable?

⟫⟶ Copy the passage word for word. Then, write your comments about it. Why did you choose it?

⟫⟶ Read the passage to your classmates, and ask for their responses.

⟫⟶ After listening to your classmates' comments, read the comments you wrote. Make a final comment.

⟫⟶ No one can change what you say. You have the last word!

Reading Standard 1.4 (Grade 4 Review) Know common affixes, and use this knowledge to analyze the meaning of words.

Reading Standard 2.5 Follow multiple-step instructions for preparing applications (for example, for a public library card, bank savings account, sports club, league membership).

Reading Standard 3.8 Critique the credibility of characterization and the degree to which plot is contrived or realistic (for example, compare use of fact and fantasy in historical fiction).

BEFORE YOU READ

How would you feel if you could visit the past? Could it be more complicated than you think? The story you're about to read will take you back about two thousand years to a place of danger and mystery.

My Field Trip to Pompeii

Richard Cohen

IDENTIFY

Circle the dates that tell you when the field trip starts, where it is going, and what its purpose is.

PREDICT

Re-read lines 9–10. What do you think this comment could mean?

_____

_____

IDENTIFY

How would time travelers be able to talk to ancient people?

_____

_____

_____

This is my report about the time travel field trip Mr. Aybrams's class took to ancient Pompeii to see the eruption of Mt. Vesuvius. We handed in our signed consent forms and left on Monday morning, March 13, 4001, and returned a nanosecond later. In between, we visited Pompeii on August 21–24, A.D. 79. We saw many sights in the ancient Roman seaport and talked with the Roman people. Finally, we witnessed the spectacle of Mt. Vesuvius erupting! We saw other things too, which to be honest, I

10 wish I hadn't seen.

Our class was well prepared for the trip. The week before, we got language implants, downloading ancient Latin into our brains. Some of us got headaches during the week while the language data was downloading. Learning a foreign language is never easy. However, it worked okay in the end for all the kids in the class. Of course, Mr. Aybrams already knew ancient Latin because he had that program implanted way back in college when he was a student teacher.

20   We got shots to **vaccinate** us against any ancient
Roman diseases. We wore "ancient" Roman tunics that
the school supplied for us. Promptly at nine o'clock in
the morning, we lined up and went to the school's time
travel lab.

The machine whirred out of the time stream and back
into three-dimensional space in a grove of elm trees above
Pompeii, with a view of the bay. It was a beautiful curved
bay, and we would see a little city a few miles away. We
stepped out, stretching our legs, and Mr. Aybrams pressed

30   the remote to **compress** the time machine. He tucked the
time machine in a belt strapped under his toga for the rest
of the field trip. Boy, am I glad he didn't lose it! That happened to my older sister's class once, during the French
Revolution, and they had all kinds of trouble getting back.

We walked downhill to the city on a trail Mr. Aybrams
knew about. It was fun wearing Roman sandals and wearing clothes made out of loose, white cotton. Mr. Aybrams
reminded us to scuff our sandals a little and to throw dirt
at one another so our clothes wouldn't look too new. That

40   was one of the most fun parts of the field trip. After that,
we all looked like we'd been hanging around on the streets
of Pompeii all our lives so we didn't attract any suspicion
when we walked into town. Nobody ever guessed that we
were visitors from the future.

The first day was a getting-acquainted day in Pompeii.
We walked around the city in small groups. We talked Latin
to everyone. There was this one old man, a chestnut
vendor, who sold me chestnuts with the Roman coins the
school gave us to spend. I guess I spoke pretty good Latin

50   because he thought I was a Roman kid studying rhetoric

vaccinate (vak′sə·nāt) *v.:*
make immune to disease;
immunize.

compress (kəm·pres′) *v.:*
make more compact.

IDENTIFY

Pause at line 34. What detail
tells you that time travel is as
common in this future classroom as class trips are today?
Does this seem believable?

_____

_____

_____

_____

_____

_____

EVALUATE

Pause at line 44. How do the
time travelers fit in? Is this
believable?

_____

_____

_____

_____

_____

_____

_____

_____

_____

_____

_____

_____

_____

_____

FLUENCY

Read aloud the boxed passage twice. Bring the scene to life by varying your tone and speed of delivery.

VOCABULARY DEVELOPMENT

arena (ə·rē′nə) *n.:* center of an ancient Roman amphitheater where contests and other spectacles were held.

WORD KNOWLEDGE

Circle the word *forum* (line 77). Underline the context clues that tell you what the *forum* was.

and logic, whatever they are. He teased me about whether I was going to be another great orator like Cicero. Cicero must have been some famous politician back in ancient Rome. But this chestnut vendor was nice and I liked to ask him questions about his life as I stood there peeling roasted chestnuts. I began to feel a little uncomfortable because I knew what was going to happen to his town—and I thought maybe he would die when the volcano erupted. This trip was more complicated than I thought it would be.

60   That evening we strolled through the market and saw all the foods the ancient Pompeiians had for sale. It was mostly strange stuff like water-buffalo steaks, or worse, actual dead rabbits hanging from hooks, with their fur and little fuzzy tails still on.

The next day we visited the gymnasium. It wasn't a big room with a high ceiling like at school. It was an open-air exercise **arena** with columned walls. We saw gladiators practicing with real swords and shields. It was strange to think that they were training for a sport where most of
70   them would get killed. But it was even worse to think that they were all going to get killed anyway because of the volcano, so it didn't matter if they won their gladiatorial contests or not. I was disliking knowing all that was going to happen to these people.

On the third day, the column of smoke rising from Mt. Vesuvius was higher. We spent that day walking around in the forum, the public square and marketplace, listening to what people said about the smoke. They argued about whether it was dangerous, whether it was a sign from the

80 gods, and stuff like that. It was hard not to break into their conversation and scream "Get out of here fast! Run!" We recorded their comments on our audiochip implants.

Finally, Eruption Day came. We just had time to eat a little breakfast (raisin cakes, figs, and walnuts) before the air started to get thick from the gas. Of course, the people didn't notice it yet, but we did because we'd learned about it in class. Quickly but quietly we hiked out of town toward the sea. Mr. Aybrams re-enlarged the time machine in a protected cove where it couldn't be seen. We watched the

90 volcano erupt from a distance. Vesuvius was incredible. There were panicked people running all over the place, getting hit with rocks and ash that were falling from the thick clouds. We heard their screams, and we smelled the lava and gas. Charli G. got scraped pretty bad with a hot cinder on her arm, but she was okay. It was so minor compared with what most of the people of Pompeii were suffering. Then we saw crowds of people starting to stream down to the shore to escape in boats. We watched them for awhile, then Mr. Aybrams said, "All right, everyone, I think we've

100 seen all we can. Now let's get back to class and discuss our observations."

Was I the only one who was upset?

Back in class we formed small groups to do research. My self-assessment is that I learned a lot about ancient Pompeii and volcanoes. I also learned something about these field trips: I don't think we should continue them. I think watching tragedies in a time warp is sort of bad because we have no power to help. Well, I tried to help. There is this rule for field trips that you can't warn any of

WORD KNOWLEDGE

The Latin root *aud* means "hear." What do you guess an *audiochip* is (line 82)?

_____

_____

_____

_____

_____

_____

_____

_____

INFER

Why is the narrator feeling upset in line 102? Do his feelings seem believable?

_____

_____

_____

_____

_____

_____

_____

_____

_____

SAVE THE LAST
WORD FOR ME

Go back through the story, and underline any passage that you think is especially believable. Circle any passage that you think is not believable.

110 the people about what is about to happen. On eruption morning I advised the chestnut man to get himself and his family out of town fast. I hope they did.

Next year I heard we might go to the American Civil War. I'm going to lobby to visit the United States in the early 2000s. It's not a time when a lot of big wars or anything were happening, but they were inventing a lot of things back then. I always think that was the time when everything started to get good.

A nighttime infrared photo of Mount Vesuvius in 1943.

OWN THE STORY

"Save the Last Word for Me" Evaluation   Did you believe the story? Remember that even a fantasy story has to be believable. The plot must be a series of believable causes and effects. The characters must behave the way actual people behave, even if they are totally imaginary. Evaluate the credibility of this fantasy story by completing the first two cards on page 300. Then, share your cards with a small group of classmates. After your discussion, fill out the third card. This is your last word!

Express Your Evaluation   Review the notes you took on the cards on the next page. Then, write a paragraph telling whether you found the story credible or contrived. Express your opinion in your opening sentence. Then, support your opinion with at least two specific details from the story.

_____

_____

_____

_____

_____

KEEPING TRACK

Personal Word List   List the vocabulary words for this story in order of difficulty in your Personal Word List.

Personal Reading Log   Jot down your general responses to fantasy stories in your Personal Reading Log. Give yourself 2 points on the Reading Meter for this selection.

Checklist for Standards Mastery   Use the Checklist for Standards Mastery to see how confident you feel about your mastery of the standards. Note areas in which you want to improve.

My Field Trip to Pompeii ▪ *Interactive Reading,* page 294

Interact with a Literary Text

"Save the Last Word for Me" Cards   Is this story credible or contrived? Choose a passage that best supports your opinion. Copy down the passage word for word. Then write your comments about the passage. State one good reason telling why you chose it. Share your passages and comments with a group of classmates. After your discussion, revise your comments, if you like.

Chosen Passage:

Comments About the Passage:

Revised Comments About the Passage (if any):

The Dog of Pompeii

Interact with a Literary Text

Chain-of-Events Chart   Trace the plot events in "The Dog of Pompeii" by filling in the chain-of-events chart below. You can summarize plot events or choose actual lines from the story for your chart entries. Did you find the plot credible? Contrived? Put a question mark beside events you did *not* find credible. Then, fill in the notes at the bottom of the chart with your reasons.

Event	Event	Event	Event

Event	Event	Event	Event

☐ **Credible?** ☐ **Not Credible? Why?** _____

_____

Pompeii

for use with
Holt Literature and Language Arts,
page 442

Interact with an Informational Text

Parallel-Events Chart   In "Pompeii," Robert Silverberg re-creates the eruption of Mount Vesuvius. His re-creation is based on scientific information. Silverberg weaves a human story into this scientific happening, showing what one particular group of people did during the crisis. Fill out the first column of the chart below with events describing the eruption of the volcano. Then, fill out the second column, showing the actions and reactions of the people.

Events Caused by Erupting Volcano	Human Reactions

Zlateh the Goat

Interact with a Literary Text

Plot Map   The plot events in "Zlateh the Goat" work together to build suspense. Re-create the plot events by filling in the plot map below. Then, use a star to mark the point at which your interest in the story began to increase. Use a question mark to indicate any plot event you thought was contrived, or not believable.

					Event 6
				Event 5	
			Event 4		
		Event 3			
	Event 2				
Event 1					

☐ **Credible?** ☐ **Not Credible? Why?** _____

_____

Trial by Fire

for use with
Holt Literature and Language Arts,
page 457

Interact with Informational and Literary Texts

Venn Diagram   Even animals have characteristics, or personalities. Use the following diagram to compare Scarlett the cat with Zlateh the goat from Isaac Bashevis Singer's story. Give examples from the text that describe each animal's qualities.

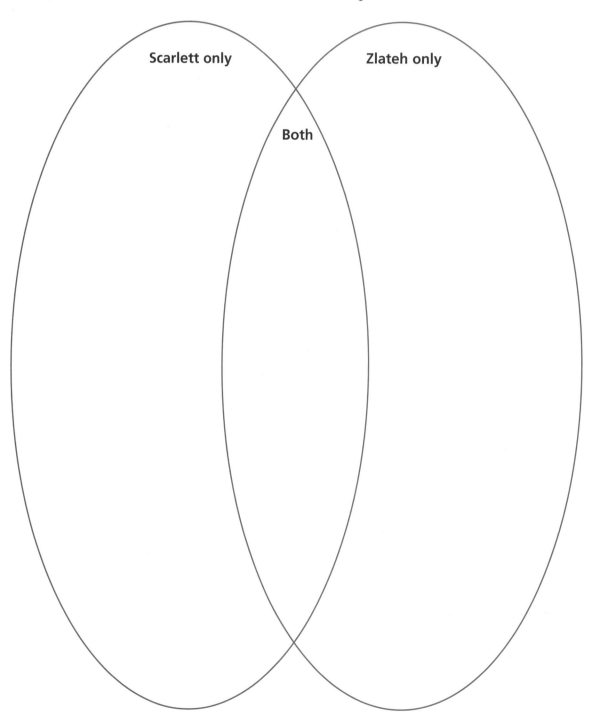

Scarlett only

Zlateh only

Both

Literature

AUTHOR STUDY

Isaac Bashevis Singer was born in 1904 in Poland. He wrote mostly in Yiddish, a language spoken by Eastern European Jews. He came to the United States in 1935 and at first earned his living writing for Yiddish news-papers. He eventually became famous for his stories about Jewish life in Eastern Europe. He won the Nobel Prize for literature in 1978. In his Nobel award speech he said, "The storyteller and poet of our time, as in any other time, must be an entertainer of the spirit. . . ."

Reading Standard 3.8 Critique the credibility of characterization and the degree to which plot is contrived or realistic (for example, compare use of fact and fantasy in historical fiction).

Utzel and His Daughter, Poverty

Isaac Bashevis Singer

Once there was a man named Utzel. He was very poor and even more lazy. Whenever anyone wanted to give him a job to do, his answer was always the same: "Not today."

"Why not today?" he was asked. And he always replied, "Why not tomorrow?"

Utzel lived in a cottage that had been built by his great-grandfather. The thatched roof needed mending, and although the holes let the rain in, they did not let the smoke from the stove out. Toadstools grew on the crooked walls and the floor had rotted away. There had been a time when mice lived there, but now there weren't any because there was nothing for them to eat. Utzel's wife had starved to death, but before she died she had given birth to a baby girl. The name Utzel gave his daughter was very fitting. He called her Poverty.

10

IDENTIFY

Underline the words that most strongly show the hopelessness of Utzel's way of life.

WORD KNOWLEDGE

Toadstools (tōd′stoolz) is another word for "mush-rooms."

· · · · · · Notes · · · · · ·

_____

_____

_____

INTERPRET

What is significant about the fact that the lazier Utzel got, the more Poverty grew (lines 27–28)?

_____

_____

_____

_____

_____

VOCABULARY DEVELOPMENT

maintained (mān·tānd′) *v.*: declared; asserted.

charitable (char′i·tə·bəl) *adj.*: kind and generous in giving money or other help to those in need.

EVALUATE

Do you find Utzel's love for Poverty believable (line 32)? Explain.

_____

_____

_____

WORD KNOWLEDGE

A *gulden* is a gold coin once used in European countries. Circle the word *gulden,* and underline the context clues that help you figure out what a *gulden* is.

Utzel loved to sleep and each night he went to bed with the chickens. In the morning he would complain that he was tired from so much sleeping and so he went to sleep again. When he was not sleeping, he lay on his broken-
20 down cot, yawning and complaining. He would say to his daughter, "Other people are lucky. They have money without working. I am cursed."

Utzel was a small man, but as his daughter, Poverty, grew, she spread out in all directions. She was tall, broad, and heavy. At fifteen she had to lower her head to get through the doorway. Her feet were the size of a man's and puffy with fat. The villagers **maintained** that the lazier Utzel got, the more Poverty grew.

Utzel loved nobody, was jealous of everybody. He even
30 spoke with envy of cats, dogs, rabbits, and all creatures who didn't have to work for a living. Yes, Utzel hated everybody and everything, but he adored his daughter. He day-dreamed that a rich young man would fall in love with her, marry her, and provide for his wife and his father-in-law. But not a young man in the village showed the slightest interest in Poverty. When her father reproached the girl for not making friends and not going out with young men, Poverty would say, "How can I go out in rags and bare feet?"

40 One day Utzel learned that a certain **charitable** society in the village loaned poor people money, which they could pay back in small sums over a long period. Lazy as he was, he made a great effort—got up, dressed, and went to the office of the society. "I would like to borrow five gulden," he said to the official in charge.

"What do you intend to do with the money?" he was asked. "We lend money only for useful purposes."

"I want to have a pair of shoes made for my daughter,"
Utzel explained. "If Poverty has shoes, she will go out with
the young people of the village and some wealthy young
man will surely fall in love with her. When they get
married, I will be able to pay back the five gulden."

The official thought it over. The chances of anyone
falling in love with Poverty were very small. Utzel, however,
looked so miserable that the official decided to give him the
loan. He asked Utzel to sign a promissory note and gave
him five gulden.

Utzel had tried to order a pair of shoes for his
daughter a few months before. Sandler the shoemaker
had gone so far as to take Poverty's measurements, but the
shoemaker had wanted his money in advance. From the
charitable society Utzel went directly to the shoemaker
and asked whether he still had Poverty's measurements.

"And supposing I do?" Sandler replied. "My price is
five gulden and I still want my money in advance."

Utzel took out the five gulden and handed them to
Sandler. The shoemaker opened a drawer and after some
searching brought out the order for Poverty's shoes. He
promised to deliver the new shoes in a week, on Friday.

Utzel, who wanted to surprise his daughter, did not tell
her about the shoes. The following Friday, as he lay on his
cot yawning and complaining, there was a knock on the
door and Sandler came in carrying the new shoes. When
Poverty saw the shoemaker with a pair of shiny new shoes
in his hand, she cried out in joy. The shoemaker handed
her the shoes and told her to try them on. But, alas, she
could not get them on her puffy feet. In the months since
the measurements had been taken, Poverty's feet had
become even larger than they were before. Now the girl
cried out in grief.

A *promissory* (präm'i·sôr'ē)
note is a written promise to
pay a certain sum of money
to a certain person on
demand or on a specified
date.

PREDICT

Sandler the shoemaker has
had Poverty's foot measurements for several months.
Predict what might happen
when he uses them to make
the new shoes (line 63).

_____

_____

_____

_____

_____

_____

_____

_____

_____

_____

_____

_____

_____

_____

Isaac Bashevis Singer   **307**

Utzel looked on in **consternation.** "How is it possible?" he asked. "I thought her feet stopped growing long ago."

For a while Sandler, too, stood there puzzled. Then he inquired, "Tell me, Utzel, where did you get the five gulden?" Utzel explained that he had borrowed the money from the charitable loan society and had given them a promissory note in return.

"So now you have a debt," exclaimed Sandler. "That makes you even poorer than you were a few months ago. Then you had nothing, but today you have five gulden less than nothing. And since you have grown poorer, Poverty has grown bigger, and naturally her feet have grown with her. That is why the shoes don't fit. It is all clear to me now."

"What are we going to do?" Utzel asked in despair.

"There is only one way out for you," Sandler said. "Go to work. From borrowing one gets poorer and from work one gets richer. When you and your daughter work, she will have shoes that fit."

The idea of working did not appeal to either of them, but it was even worse to have new shoes and go around barefoot. Utzel and Poverty both decided that immediately after the Sabbath they would look for work.

Utzel got a job as a water carrier. Poverty became a maid. For the first time in their lives, they worked diligently. They were kept so busy that they did not even think of the new shoes, until one Sabbath morning Poverty decided she'd try them on again. Lo and behold, her feet slipped easily into them. The new shoes fit.

At last Utzel and Poverty understood that all a man possesses he gains through work, and not by lying in bed and being idle. Even animals were **industrious.** Bees make honey, spiders spin webs, birds build nests, moles dig holes in the earth, squirrels store food for the winter. Before long Utzel got a better job. He rebuilt his house and bought some furniture. Poverty lost more weight. She had new clothes made and dressed prettily like the other girls of the village. Her looks improved, too, and a young man began to court her. His name was Mahir and he was the son of a wealthy merchant. Utzel's dream of a rich son-in-law came true, but by then he no longer needed to be taken care of.

120

Love for his daughter had saved Utzel. In his later years he became so respected he was elected a warden of that same charitable loan society from which he had borrowed five gulden.

On the wall of his office there hung the string with which Sandler had once measured Poverty's feet, and above it the framed motto "Whatever you can do today, don't put off till tomorrow."

INFER

Why do you think Utzel saved the string that Sandler used to measure Poverty's feet?

_____

_____

_____

_____

_____

_____

_____

_____

_____

_____

SAVE THE LAST WORD FOR ME

What did you think of this story? Did the changes in the characters seem believable? Does the story's message seem true to you—do you accept it as true?

_____

_____

_____

_____

_____

OWN THE STORY

Credibility Think about your own experience and what you know about human nature. Circle a sentence or phrase that rings true to you in "Utzel and His Daughter, Poverty." What makes the characters seem believable or unbelievable? Compare and contrast your responses with a classmate's. Discuss similarities and differences in your opinions.

_____

_____

_____

_____

_____

KEEPING TRACK

Personal Word List Add the new words you learned from this story to your Personal Word List.

Personal Reading Log As you record this selection in your Personal Reading Log, make notes about the story's message and whether or not you think it is true. Then, give yourself 3 points on the Reading Meter.

Checklist for Standards Mastery Use the Checklist for Standards Mastery to gauge your progress in mastering the standards. Note your areas of biggest improvement and the areas in which you still have the furthest to go.

Utzel and His Daughter, Poverty

■ *Interactive Reading,* page 305

Go Beyond a Literary Text

Author Profile   Use your library and the Internet to find out more about Isaac Bashevis Singer. Fill out the author profile below.

Personal Data: Date of Birth/Death: _____

Place of Birth: _____

Family Members: _____

_____

Key Events in Life:
(list at least two)

1. _____

_____

2. _____

_____

Books by Author: _____

_____

_____

_____

_____

_____

_____

_____

_____

Quotation of Author: _____

_____

_____

_____

_____

Hundreds and hundreds of articles are published yearly, aimed at people who want tips on how to do something. There are articles on how to choose a new home, how to buy a computer, how to make friends, and so on. Here is an article on how kids use their free time. In the second part of the article, kids tell the audience (other kids) what they can do to use their time more wisely.

This article is based on a survey done by *Zillions* magazine. Watch for facts cited by the writer.

from Zillions magazine

I Never Have Enough Time

Nearly half of all Zillions *readers say they're too busy after school—and 4 out of 10 wish they organized their time better! Is time putting the squeeze on you?*

TEXT STRUCTURE

Preview the text structure of this article. Underline the sentence in the first paragraph that explains the first three headings.

VOCABULARY DEVELOPMENT

measly (mēz′lē) *adj.*: slight or skimpy.

Twenty-four hours. That's all the time you've got in a day. Subtract seven or so hours for school, eight for sleep, and a good hour or so for dressing, bathing, and brushing your teeth (more if you floss—less if you sleep in your clothes). Cross off another two hours for meals, chores, and travel-ing back and forth to school. That leaves you six **measly**
10   hours, at best, to scrunch in the rest of your life. What do kids do with that precious "free" time? We polled 780 *Zillions* readers last spring to find out what they had done after school for the past week.

The activity done by the most kids was—homework!

More than 90 out of every 100 kids we polled had spent some time hitting the books the week of the survey. For many of the kids we interviewed, finding enough time to do that schoolwork—or fit in the rest of life around it—

20 could be tough.

"I have *lots* of homework," Leona griped. "I also play the piano and violin, so I have to practice. With all that, I never have time for my friends." "Last year I had a teacher who gave time-consuming projects on a daily basis," moaned Lauren. "I felt very overworked and couldn't seem to find time for myself."

Reading tied with TV watching for second place.

Amazing but true—some kids *didn't watch TV at all* from

30 Monday to Friday! Eighty-nine out of every 100 kids said they read a book or magazine for fun the week of the survey, and 88 of every 100 watched TV. The numbers are so close, we have to call reading and watching TV a tie.

INTERPRET

How do the students quoted in this section feel about doing homework? Circle verbs that indicate their feelings.

_____

_____

_____

_____

_____

_____

_____

_____

INFER

If students watched TV and read for pleasure from Monday to Friday, what do you think they were doing on weekends? Did they do homework on the weekends?

_____

_____

_____

_____

_____

_____

_____

> **If kids had more time, they'd spend it hanging out with friends.**

Almost one of every three kids surveyed said that if they had more free hours in a week, they'd use that extra time to hang out with friends. Nearly as many kids said they'd use extra time to play sports. Reading more books and
40   magazines came in a distant third.

TIME OUT FOR HELP

In just one week, most kids in our survey juggled at least 8 to 12 different activities after school. But squeezing in so much left many kids like Susannah feeling just plain squeezed. "I'm always busy," she explained. "Every day after school I have different team practices. When I get home, I have a quick snack and then go straight to the piano or homework. I stay up really late. I know it's not the best, but you get things done. Have you ever realized you can add
50   eight or nine hours to your work time if you don't sleep?" We think that's going a bit far. Instead of turning into a sleep-deprived zombie, try these time-management tricks,

---

IDENTIFY

Pause at line 50. Underline the places in this article where the writer uses **statistics**—facts in number form.

IDENTIFY

Turn the page to find out where these "time-management" tricks came from.

---

suggested by our trusty Z-Teamers (kids who found the time to enter—and win—the contest in our April/May issue last year).

Don't put it off.

*"I used to totally **procrastinate.** One time I went shopping, to the movies, and spent the day with friends, when I knew I had this major essay to do for history. I failed history. Now if I* 60 *have a big homework assignment, I'll do it first, then I'll watch TV, talk on the phone, etc., so I won't get stressed at the last minute."*

— Carolyn

Finish one activity before starting another.

"Homework used to take me forever. I was doing chore, home-work, chore, homework, eat. Now I do my homework all at once, then do my chores. I seem to have more time because I don't waste five minutes between activities."

— Stasia

70 ## Schedule a certain time for doing each activity.

"The things I do after school are what I want to do—jazz band, voice lessons, etc. I keep a daily planner so I don't over-schedule myself—it's a hand-held (electronic) calendar that I record everything in. I'd be lost without it."

— Adam

Set **priorities,** then do what's most important.

"With piano, tap, jazz, drama, and tons of homework, I was up until 10 every night and had no free time. Finally I stopped doing jazz, switched piano to Fridays, and dropped 80 *one drama class. Now I put things in order of priority. School*

VOCABULARY DEVELOPMENT

procrastinate (prō·cras′tə·nāt′) *v.:* put off doing something until another time.

priorities (prī·ôr′ə·tēz) *n.:* things that come first or are more important.

· · · · · · Notes · · · · · ·

_____

_____

_____

_____

_____

_____

comes first, and if I can't go to a dance class because of home-work, I don't worry about it. If I don't have time for some-thing, I drop it."

— Jenna

Just say no—you can't do everything.

"I baby-sit about three nights a week and get involved in every sport I enjoy. I had to quit basketball this season. It was a hard choice, but I had to do it. I miss hanging out with my basketball friends."

90

— Laura

OWN THE TEXT

PRACTICING THE STANDARDS

Evaluation Do you think these are realistic tips for time manage-ment? Write three sentences expressing your response to three specific details in the article.

KEEPING TRACK

Personal Word List Add the words you learned to your Personal Word List.

Personal Reading Log Do you think you might use any of the information you have read about? Write your ideas about time management in your Personal Reading Log. Give yourself 2 points on the Reading Meter.

Checklist for Standards Mastery Use the Checklist for Standards Mastery to assess how far you've come in handling the standards.

I Never Have Enough Time ▪ *Interactive Reading,* page 312

Go Beyond an Informational Text

Preparing an Application   A group is looking for people to conduct interviews for a survey on time management. You wish to be one of the interviewers, and you need to apply for the position.

Fill out the application form. Be sure to answer all the questions. If there is a question that does not apply to you, write "Not applicable." If the form requires a signature, be sure to sign it.

Print carefully.

Application for Part-Time Position

1. Date _____   2. Social Security # _____

3. Name _____   4. Age _____

5. Address _____

6. School _____

   Years attended _____

7. Parents' or guardians' names _____

8. Name/phone of one reference _____

9. Have you had any experience interviewing? Please provide dates and names.

   _____

   _____

10. Have you ever had any part-time jobs or summer jobs? Please be specific.

    _____

11. Please write a few sentences telling us why you are interested in this survey project.

    _____

    _____

    _____

You understand that any writing you do for this research project will be the property of the project, and will not be owned by you.
Please sign to show you understand. Your signature will affirm that all the information you have supplied in this application is accurate.

Signature _____

BEFORE YOU READ

You are going to read a folk tale based on a real person, Ole Bull. Ole Bull was born in Norway in 1810 and began playing the violin at age five. He became a world-famous virtuoso violinist. He also founded the Norwegian Theater with the famous playwright Henrik Ibsen in 1850.

Reading Standard 3.8 Critique the credibility of characterization and the degree to which plot is contrived or realistic (for example, compare use of fact and fantasy in historical fiction).

Ola and the Grim

A Norwegian folk tale retold by Eric A. Kimmel

TEXT STRUCTURE

Pause after the first sentence. Circle the words that tell you that this story may not be a folk tale.

· · · · · · Notes · · · · · ·

Once there was—or perhaps there was not—a boy named Ola. He lived on a farm not far from the sea, on the road that leads to the great city of Bergen. Ola loved the fiddle. He would walk for miles to hear a talented fiddler play.

He saved all his money, and one proud day Ola brought home his very own fiddle. His grandfather showed him how to hold the bow and draw it across the strings.

SKREEK! A terrible noise came out. It sounded like two cats fighting. Ola dropped the bow in surprise. His
10   mother picked it up.

"Don't be discouraged, Ola," she said. "Fiddles sound like that when one is learning to play. There will be many sour notes. Keep practicing. The music will come."

Ola practiced and practiced. Whenever he found a spare moment, he took his fiddle and played. He practiced in the barn and in the shade of haystacks until his father asked him to stop. His fiddling frightened the animals. The cows stopped giving milk. The hens stopped laying eggs. The sheep scattered, and the sheepdogs that herded them ran off and were nowhere to be found.

From then on, Ola practiced away from the farm. He sat under trees in the forest and on lonely rocks at the seashore. Crabs scurried into the surf. Seals dived deep. Sea gulls screamed overhead. But Ola **persisted,** even when the seabirds spattered him with their droppings. He kept sawing away at his fiddle. Ola practiced hour after hour, day after day. None of it did any good. He still played as badly as ever. His fiddle sounded like roosters crowing, donkeys braying, oxen bellowing, wagons with axles that needed greasing—everything but what a fiddle should sound like. His family covered their ears. No one wanted to tell Ola to give up. But everyone hoped he would.

One day there was a wedding at a neighboring farm. A fiddler came all the way from Bergen. All the guests agreed he was the finest fiddler they had ever heard. While the man rested between dances, Ola came up and spoke to him.

"Sir, can you give me some advice? I want to be a fiddler like you and make everybody merry. I practice and practice, but I never get any better, no matter how hard I try. Everything sounds like noise. I can't even keep my fiddle in tune. Can you tell me what to do?"

EVALUATE

Pause at line 20. Ola's audience extends beyond his family. Do you think the reactions of the animals are possible?

_____

_____

_____

_____

_____

_____

_____

VOCABULARY DEVELOPMENT

persisted (pər·sist′əd) v.: kept on.

WORD KNOWLEDGE

Pause at line 32. Underline the **similes** the writer uses to let us know what Ola's fiddling sounded like. (Can you add a simile to this list to describe how bad music sounds?)

_____

_____

_____

_____

Ola and the Grim   319

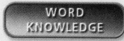

WORD KNOWLEDGE

A *tankard* (line 43) is a large drinking cup with a handle and often a hinged lid.

A *troll* (line 51) is a figure in Scandinavian folklore. Trolls are from a race of imaginary beings, often with special powers or skills.

IDENTIFY

What detail on this page explains the story's **title**?

_____

_____

_____

_____

_____

• • • • • • **Notes** • • • • • •

_____

_____

_____

_____

_____

_____

_____

_____

_____

The fiddler put down his tankard. He leaned over to Ola and whispered in his ear, "How badly do you want to play?"

"Oh, very badly, sir!"

"I was once like you," the fiddler said. "I, too, wanted to play badly. And I did. Very badly! So I went to see the *fosse-grim*."

50   "Who's that?" Ola asked.

"The fosse-grim is a troll. He lives below a waterfall. Sometimes, if you listen closely, you'll hear him playing his harp. The grim is a master musician. He can play any instrument. He can teach you how to play your fiddle. But he won't do it for nothing. You must bring him a gift. The greater the gift, the greater the learning."

"What sort of gift should I bring?" Ola asked.

"The fosse-grim likes meat," the fiddler said. "Bring him something to eat."

60   The next day Ola finished his chores early. He took his fiddle and set out for the mountains. "I'm going to practice awhile," he told his family.

"Come back before dark," his father said. "I don't want the trolls to get you."

"Take something to eat in case you get hungry," his mother added.

No one told Ola not to go. As much as they cared about him, they were grateful not to have to hear him practicing.

70   Ola stopped at the smokehouse. He stuffed a large sausage into his knapsack. Then he set out, following the path that wound along the stream.

    The path took Ola high into the mountains. It led to the foot of a rushing waterfall.

    Ola stood by the falls, listening. He heard music in the tumbling water that sounded like notes played on a harp. The sweet, mysterious music sang to the waterfall. It danced in the silver spray. Ola had never heard anything so beautiful in his life. There is magic in this place, he

80 thought.

    "Grim!" he called. "Fosse-Grim, are you here?"

    A curious creature emerged from the pool beneath the falls. Its skin was **mottled** green, and it cradled a harp in its arms. Strands of green, silky hair, like long threads of algae, hung to its shoulders. It drew its fingers across the harp and spoke in a voice like splashing water.

    "What do you want, boy?"

    "I need your help, Grim," Ola said. "I want to play the fiddle so badly."

90   "Let me hear you."

    Ola took his fiddle from his knapsack. Tuning the strings as best he could, he took up his bow and began to play.

    "Stop! Stop!" cried the grim. "You're hurting my ears! There is nothing I can teach you, boy. You want to play badly. And you do!"

Underline the **simile** in the paragraph beginning at line 107 that helps you imagine how hard it was for Ola to tune his fiddle to the grim's note.

What **simile** is used later on this page to help you imagine what happened inside Ola's head? Underline it.

Pause at the end of the page. What part of Ola's problem has been resolved?

_____

_____

_____

_____

_____

· · · · · · Notes · · · · · ·

_____

_____

_____

_____

_____

_____

_____

_____

_____

"Don't mock me, Grim," Ola said. "You know what I mean. I want to become a good fiddler. Can you help me?"

"I can," the grim said. "But I won't do it for nothing.
100   What did you bring me?"

Ola held out the sausage. The grim snatched it right away. He bit off the end, "Ugh! Tough and stringy! Can't you afford decent sausage, boy? Never mind. I'll give you what it's worth. I can at least teach you how to tune that fiddle. Listen closely. I'll pluck a string on my harp. You match it. Let's begin."

The grim plucked a note. Ola tried to tune his fiddle string to it, but the note slipped away. It was like trying to catch fish barehanded.

110   "No, no, no!" the grim yelled. "That's too high! Now you're too low! What's the matter with you? Are your ears blocked? Can you hear anything?"

The grim stretched out his long, green arm. He pressed the palm of his hand against Ola's ear. Ola felt something inside his head SNAP! It popped and crackled like ice breaking on a pond. Suddenly he heard the sounds around him clearly. It was as if he were listening for the first time.

"Try again," the grim said.

This time Ola tuned his strings effortlessly. And they
120   stayed in tune, no matter how long he played.

"Thank you, Grim," Ola said.

"Keep practicing," the grim snorted as he dived beneath the ripples.

Ola raced home. He tuned his fiddle and sawed away. "Listen to me now!" he cried to everyone. "I can play in tune." And he did, for the first time!

However, there is more to fiddling than playing in tune. Ola still squeaked and scraped. His timing was off; his fingering incorrect. Every song he attempted became a hopeless muddle.

"Keep practicing, Ola. You're getting better," his mother said.

But Ola knew that wasn't true. He could not hope to get anywhere on his own, no matter how hard he practiced. It was time to visit the grim.

Ola packed his knapsack and fiddle. He followed the stream up into the mountains. When he reached the waterfall, he called out, "Grim, come up from the pool! I need you!"

The waters rippled. The fosse-grim appeared, cradling his harp. "What do you want, boy?"

"I want to play the fiddle in the worst way. Help me, please!"

The grim laughed. "You don't need me. You already play in the worst way. You're the worst fiddler I ever heard. You couldn't get any worse if you tried."

"Don't mock me, Grim!" Ola pleaded. "You know what I mean. Playing in tune is not enough. I need to know so much more."

IDENTIFY

Pause at line 130. What further problems does Ola have in his quest to learn to play the fiddle? Underline them.

· · · · · · Notes · · · · · · ·

Ola and the Grim **323**

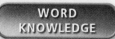

**VOCABULARY
DEVELOPMENT**

adequate (ad′i·kwət) *adj.*:
good enough.

· · · · · · **Notes** · · · · · ·

_____

_____

_____

_____

_____

_____

PREDICT

Pause at the bottom of the
page. Is this what Ola wants?

_____

_____

_____

_____

_____

_____

_____

150   "Nothing buys nothing," the grim replied. "What did
you bring me?"

    "A whole leg of mutton!" Ola took the meat from his
knapsack. He tossed it to the grim, who gnawed it down
to the bone.

    "That's worth something," the grim finally said,
smacking his lips. "Take out your fiddle. We'll play
together."

    The grim came out of the pool. He sat beside Ola,
pressing the boy's fingers down with his left hand and
160   pulling his wrist back and forth with his right.

    "Ow! You're pinching me!" Ola cried.

    "Stop complaining! Open yourself to the music. Feel
its wonder. Let it take you."

    Ola played and played. The grim guided his fingers
from note to note. Ola felt as if he had walked through a
hidden door into a secret realm. He lost himself in the
music that poured from his fiddle like a mountain brook
streaming down a waterfall.

    At last the grim said, "Enough! I've given you a leg of
170   mutton's worth of music. Those tunes are in your fingers
now. Practice every day so you don't forget them.
Otherwise, you'll have to bring me another leg of mutton
to have me teach you again."

    "Will I be a good fiddler?" Ola asked.

    "**Adequate.** Nothing more. What do you expect for a
leg of mutton? You'll earn your living playing at weddings
and festivals. At least people won't run away when you take
out your fiddle. Isn't that what you wanted?"

    "I guess so," said Ola.

180　But it wasn't. Everyone loved Ola's playing now. His family begged him to take out his fiddle in the evening, after the day's work was done. Neighbors invited him to their farms to play for them. Whenever a joyous occasion arose, people sent for Ola to play. "You're a great fiddler, Ola!" everyone said.

It wasn't so, and Ola knew it. A vast gulf lay between what Ola wanted to play and what he could play. He heard music everywhere: in the wind, in trees, rippling fields of wheat and rushing streams, in surging ocean waves and 190　quiet mountain meadows. He tried to capture it with his fiddle, but the notes slipped away. Ola felt like a fisherman carried out to sea by a running tide. He sees the land clearly, but he cannot reach it, no matter how hard he rows.

"I must visit the fosse-grim," Ola said to himself.

Once more Ola followed the stream. He struggled up the path, bent double with the weight of a whole side of beef on his shoulders.

"Grim, come out! I need you!" Ola called to the waterfall.

200　The fosse-grim emerged from the pool. "What do you want, boy?"

"Grim, it is not enough to be a good fiddler. I want to be a great fiddler. I want to be able to play the music I hear, the music I love. I will practice night and day. I will do anything you ask. Look! I have brought you half of a whole steer. If it is not enough, I will go back down the mountain for more. Tell me what I must do, Grim, to become the fiddler I want to be."

"Put down the beef and take out your fiddle," the grim 210　said. He climbed out of the pool to sit beside Ola. "You and

WORD KNOWLEDGE

Pause at line 193. Underline the extended **simile** that the writer uses to help us imagine how Ola feels about his music.

INTERPRET

Pause at line 194. What is it that Ola wants now? What will he do to find it?

_____

_____

_____

_____

_____

_____

_____

_____

IDENTIFY

Have you noticed that the amount of food Ola brings the grim gets larger and larger? What has he brought the grim now?

_____

_____

_____

_____

What does the grim mean when he says, "Did you expect to buy greatness for a side of beef" (lines 222–223)? Do you agree that "Pain is the price of genius"?

_____

_____

_____

_____

_____

_____

_____

_____

_____

_____

_____

_____

_____

IDENTIFY

How has Ola's problem been resolved?

_____

_____

_____

_____

_____

I will play together. Keep playing, no matter what happens. Play until I tell you to stop."

The grim took hold of Ola's wrist and fingers. Together they began to play: songs, scales, exercises. Hour after hour. Ola's wrists began to cramp.

"Let me rest, Grim! My hands ache!"

"Keep playing!" The grim pulled Ola's arm back and forth. He pressed the boy's fingers onto the strings until blisters rose from his fingertips.

220   "Let me go, Grim! You're torturing me! This is more than I can endure!"

"What a fool you are! Did you expect to buy greatness for a side of beef? Pain is the price of genius. The great ones of the world are always disappointed, neglected, misunderstood. And still they keep on. But look at you! A few little blisters and you're ready to quit. Go ahead! What do I care? I have your beef. Dolts like you keep me well fed."

Ola set his jaw. He clamped the fiddle beneath his chin. "No. I will go on."

230   "Then play!"

Ola and the grim played through the night until the sun came up. By then, Ola's hands had tightened into claws, the fiddle's strings had snapped, and the bow hung in pieces.

"But you're a real fiddler now," said the grim. "Go! Make your way in the world. I have nothing more to teach you."

Ola left without a word of thanks. He felt too weary to speak. He stumbled down the mountain, and it was many weeks before he had the strength to take up his

240   fiddle again.

But when he did . . .

Years later, a special performance took place in Bergen's concert hall. People came from all over Scandinavia to hear Ole Bull, Norway's most famous violinist. All the critics agreed, "Ole Bull has no peer. He is the finest musician in Scandinavia. The best in Europe. The greatest in the world."

At the reception afterward a small, odd-looking man with a mottled green complexion was seen heaping his plate at the smorgasbord in back of the hall. A Swedish

250   countess asked him, "Did you enjoy the concert? It astonishes me that a human being can possess such natural talent."

To which the odd little man replied, "Talent? Bah! It's courage, dedication, and hard work. Ola couldn't play a note when we began. You've no idea what I went through just to teach him to tune his fiddle!"

EVALUATE

The fosse-grim is a creature of fantasy, but how is the relationship between the fosse-grim and Ola realistic?

_____

_____

_____

_____

_____

_____

_____

_____

_____

_____

EVALUATE

The concluding section of the story in Bergen's concert hall contains a mix of fact and fantasy. What do you think is actually true here?

_____

_____

_____

_____

_____

OWN THE STORY

Credibility   Part of this folk tale is obviously fantasy. The main character, however, is based on an actual person. How credible is the character of Ola as he is portrayed in the story? Consider his feelings and his actions. Think about his decisions to keep on trying. Is this the way a real-life character would behave when he or she wants something very, very much? In a sentence, tell how credible or contrived you found the character of Ola. Give three examples of his actions or feelings to support your evaluation.

Evaluation of the Character Ola

Story detail 1: _____

Story detail 2: _____

Story detail 3: _____

Theme   In a few sentences, sum up what you see as the theme, or message, of this folk tale. Does the message apply only to artists, or does it apply to everyone? Cite specific passages from the story in your answer.

_____

_____

_____

Personal Word List   Astound your friends by using this selection's words in conversation. Of course, write the words in your Personal Word List.

Personal Reading Log   As you enter this folk tale in your Personal Reading Log, note the uses of figurative language that you liked. Give yourself another 4 points on the Reading Meter.

Checklist for Standards Mastery   Use the Checklist for Standards Mastery to see how much you have learned this year.

Ola and the Grim Interactive Reading, page 318

Go Beyond a Literary Text

Biographical Notes   Research the life of your favorite musician. Fill in the following chart with details you find in the library or online. Share your findings with the class.

Musician's Name:

Birth/Death dates: _____

Where born: _____

Parents and family life: _____
_____
_____

Education: _____
_____
_____

Notable accomplishments: _____
_____
_____
_____
_____

Hobbies: _____
_____
_____
_____

Quotation: _____
_____
_____
_____

Personal Word List

Keep track of all the new words you have added to your vocabulary by filling out the following chart. Review these words from time to time to make sure they become part of your permanent vocabulary.

WORD

DEFINITION: _____

_____

_____

WORD

DEFINITION: _____

_____

_____

WORD

DEFINITION: _____

_____

_____

WORD

DEFINITION: _____

_____

_____

WORD

DEFINITION: _____

_____

_____

WORD

DEFINITION: _____

_____

_____

WORD

DEFINITION: _____

_____

_____

WORD

DEFINITION: _____

_____

_____

WORD

DEFINITION: _____

_____

_____

WORD

DEFINITION: _____

_____

_____

WORD

DEFINITION: _____

_____

_____

WORD

DEFINITION: _____

_____

_____

WORD

DEFINITION: _____

_____

_____

WORD

DEFINITION: _____

_____

_____

WORD

DEFINITION: _____

_____

_____

WORD

DEFINITION: _____

_____

_____

WORD

DEFINITION: _____

_____

_____

WORD

DEFINITION: _____

_____

_____

WORD

DEFINITION: _____

_____

_____

WORD

DEFINITION: _____

_____

_____

WORD

DEFINITION: _____

_____

_____

WORD

DEFINITION: _____

_____

_____

WORD

DEFINITION: _____
_____
_____

WORD

DEFINITION: _____
_____
_____

WORD

DEFINITION: _____
_____
_____

WORD

DEFINITION: _____
_____
_____

WORD

DEFINITION: _____
_____
_____

WORD

DEFINITION: _____
_____
_____

WORD

DEFINITION: _____
_____
_____

WORD

DEFINITION: _____
_____
_____

WORD

DEFINITION: _____
_____
_____

WORD

DEFINITION: _____
_____
_____

WORD

DEFINITION: _____
_____
_____

WORD

DEFINITION: _____
_____
_____

WORD

DEFINITION: _____

_____

_____

WORD

DEFINITION: _____

_____

_____

WORD

DEFINITION: _____

_____

_____

WORD

DEFINITION: _____

_____

_____

WORD

DEFINITION: _____

_____

_____

WORD

DEFINITION: _____

_____

_____

WORD

DEFINITION: _____

_____

_____

WORD

DEFINITION: _____

_____

_____

WORD

DEFINITION: _____

_____

_____

WORD

DEFINITION: _____

_____

_____

WORD

DEFINITION: _____

_____

_____

WORD

DEFINITION: _____

_____

_____

WORD

DEFINITION: _____

_____

_____

WORD

DEFINITION: _____

_____

_____

WORD

DEFINITION: _____

_____

_____

WORD

DEFINITION: _____

_____

_____

WORD

DEFINITION: _____

_____

_____

WORD

DEFINITION: _____

_____

_____

WORD

DEFINITION: _____

_____

_____

WORD

DEFINITION: _____

_____

_____

WORD

DEFINITION: _____

_____

_____

WORD

DEFINITION: _____

_____

_____

WORD

DEFINITION: _____

_____

_____

WORD

DEFINITION: _____

_____

_____

WORD

DEFINITION: _____

_____

_____

WORD

DEFINITION: _____

_____

_____

WORD

DEFINITION: _____

_____

_____

WORD

DEFINITION: _____

_____

_____

WORD

DEFINITION: _____

_____

_____

WORD

DEFINITION: _____

_____

_____

WORD

DEFINITION: _____

_____

_____

WORD

DEFINITION: _____

_____

_____

WORD

DEFINITION: _____

_____

_____

WORD

DEFINITION: _____

_____

_____

WORD

DEFINITION: _____

_____

_____

WORD

DEFINITION: _____

_____

_____

WORD

DEFINITION: _____

_____

_____

WORD

DEFINITION: _____

_____

_____

WORD

DEFINITION: _____

_____

_____

WORD

DEFINITION: _____

_____

_____

WORD

DEFINITION: _____

_____

_____

WORD

DEFINITION: _____

_____

_____

WORD

DEFINITION: _____

_____

_____

WORD

DEFINITION: _____

_____

_____

WORD

DEFINITION: _____

_____

_____

WORD

DEFINITION: _____

_____

_____

WORD

DEFINITION: _____

_____

_____

WORD

DEFINITION: _____

_____

_____

WORD

DEFINITION: _____
_____
_____

WORD

DEFINITION: _____
_____
_____

WORD

DEFINITION: _____
_____
_____

WORD

DEFINITION: _____
_____
_____

WORD

DEFINITION: _____
_____
_____

WORD

DEFINITION: _____
_____
_____

WORD

DEFINITION: _____
_____
_____

WORD

DEFINITION: _____
_____
_____

WORD

DEFINITION: _____
_____
_____

WORD

DEFINITION: _____
_____
_____

WORD

DEFINITION: _____
_____
_____

WORD

DEFINITION: _____
_____
_____

WORD

DEFINITION: _____

_____

_____

WORD

DEFINITION: _____

_____

_____

WORD

DEFINITION: _____

_____

_____

WORD

DEFINITION: _____

_____

_____

WORD

DEFINITION: _____

_____

_____

WORD

DEFINITION: _____

_____

_____

WORD

DEFINITION: _____

_____

_____

WORD

DEFINITION: _____

_____

_____

WORD

DEFINITION: _____

_____

_____

WORD

DEFINITION: _____

_____

_____

WORD

DEFINITION: _____

_____

_____

WORD

DEFINITION: _____

_____

_____

WORD

DEFINITION: _____

_____

_____

WORD

DEFINITION: _____

_____

_____

WORD

DEFINITION: _____

_____

_____

WORD

DEFINITION: _____

_____

_____

WORD

DEFINITION: _____

_____

_____

WORD

DEFINITION: _____

_____

_____

WORD

DEFINITION: _____

_____

_____

WORD

DEFINITION: _____

_____

_____

WORD

DEFINITION: _____

_____

_____

WORD

DEFINITION: _____

_____

_____

WORD

DEFINITION: _____

_____

_____

WORD

DEFINITION: _____

_____

_____

WORD

DEFINITION: _____

_____

_____

WORD

DEFINITION: _____

_____

_____

WORD

DEFINITION: _____

_____

_____

WORD

DEFINITION: _____

_____

_____

WORD

DEFINITION: _____

_____

_____

WORD

DEFINITION: _____

_____

_____

WORD

DEFINITION: _____

_____

_____

WORD

DEFINITION: _____

_____

_____

WORD

DEFINITION: _____

_____

_____

WORD

DEFINITION: _____

_____

_____

WORD

DEFINITION: _____

_____

_____

WORD

DEFINITION: _____

_____

_____

WORD

DEFINITION: _____

_____

_____

WORD

DEFINITION: _____

_____

_____

WORD

DEFINITION: _____

_____

_____

WORD

DEFINITION: _____

_____

_____

WORD

DEFINITION: _____

_____

_____

WORD

DEFINITION: _____

_____

_____

WORD

DEFINITION: _____

_____

_____

WORD

DEFINITION: _____

_____

_____

WORD

DEFINITION: _____

_____

_____

WORD

DEFINITION: _____

_____

_____

WORD

DEFINITION: _____

_____

_____

WORD

DEFINITION: _____

_____

_____

WORD

DEFINITION: _____

_____

_____

WORD

DEFINITION: _____

_____

_____

WORD

DEFINITION: _____

_____

_____

WORD

DEFINITION: _____

_____

_____

WORD

DEFINITION: _____

_____

_____

WORD

DEFINITION: _____

_____

_____

WORD

DEFINITION: _____

_____

_____

WORD

DEFINITION: _____

_____

_____

WORD

DEFINITION: _____

_____

_____

WORD

DEFINITION: _____

_____

_____

WORD

DEFINITION: _____

_____

_____

WORD

DEFINITION: _____

_____

_____

WORD

DEFINITION: _____

_____

_____

WORD

DEFINITION: _____

_____

_____

WORD

DEFINITION: _____

_____

_____

WORD

DEFINITION: _____

_____

_____

WORD

DEFINITION: _____

_____

_____

WORD

DEFINITION: _____

_____

_____

WORD

DEFINITION: _____

_____

_____

WORD

DEFINITION: _____

_____

_____

WORD

DEFINITION: _____

_____

_____

WORD

DEFINITION: _____

_____

_____

WORD

DEFINITION: _____

_____

_____

WORD

DEFINITION: _____

_____

_____

WORD

DEFINITION: _____
_____
_____

WORD

DEFINITION: _____
_____
_____

WORD

DEFINITION: _____
_____
_____

WORD

DEFINITION: _____
_____
_____

WORD

DEFINITION: _____
_____
_____

WORD

DEFINITION: _____
_____
_____

WORD

DEFINITION: _____
_____
_____

WORD

DEFINITION: _____
_____
_____

WORD

DEFINITION: _____
_____
_____

WORD

DEFINITION: _____
_____
_____

WORD

DEFINITION: _____
_____
_____

WORD

DEFINITION: _____
_____
_____

WORD

DEFINITION: _____

_____

_____

WORD

DEFINITION: _____

_____

_____

WORD

DEFINITION: _____

_____

_____

WORD

DEFINITION: _____

_____

_____

WORD

DEFINITION: _____

_____

_____

WORD

DEFINITION: _____

_____

_____

WORD

DEFINITION: _____

_____

_____

WORD

DEFINITION: _____

_____

_____

WORD

DEFINITION: _____

_____

_____

WORD

DEFINITION: _____

_____

_____

WORD

DEFINITION: _____

_____

_____

WORD

DEFINITION: _____

_____

_____

Personal Reading Log

The literature you read becomes part of your life, helping you to understand the human condition and unlock the mysteries of life. Take time to fill out a Personal Reading Log entry when you have finished reading a selection.

Reading Meter

Each time you complete a selection in *Interactive Reading,* you move closer to meeting California's goal: that by the end of middle school, students should be able to read one million words on their own.

If you read all the interactive selections in this book, you will read close to 45,000 words and achieve 100 points. After you read each selection, fill in the Reading Meter to show how far you have come.

Number of Words in Selection	Points
About 500 words	1 point
About 1,000 words	2 points
About 1,500 words	3 points
About 2,000 words	4 points
About 2,500 words	5 points
Over 5,000 words	10 points
Bonus for reading every selection	10 points

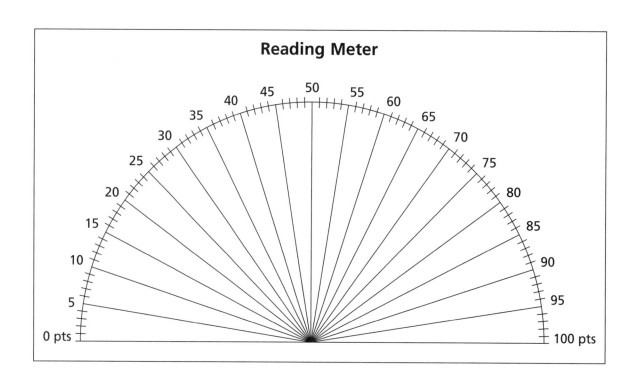

Reading Meter

DATE_____ Selection/Author: _____

Summary: _____

_____

_____

_____

_____

_____

Comments and Evaluation: _____

_____

_____

_____

_____

| READING |
| MeTER |

_____

DATE_____ Selection/Author: _____

Summary: _____

_____

_____

_____

_____

_____

Comments and Evaluation: _____

_____

_____

_____

_____

| READING |
| MeTER |

DATE _____ Selection/Author: _____

Summary: _____

_____

_____

_____

_____

_____

Comments and Evaluation: _____

_____

_____

_____

_____

	READING METER

DATE _____ Selection/Author: _____

Summary: _____

_____

_____

_____

_____

_____

Comments and Evaluation: _____

_____

_____

_____

_____

	READING METER

DATE _____ Selection/Author: _____

Summary: _____

_____

_____

_____

_____

_____

Comments and Evaluation: _____

_____

_____

_____

_____

| READING |
| METER |

_____

DATE _____ Selection/Author: _____

Summary: _____

_____

_____

_____

_____

_____

Comments and Evaluation: _____

_____

_____

_____

_____

| READING |
| METER |

_____

DATE _____ Selection/Author: _____

Summary: _____

_____

_____

_____

_____

_____

Comments and Evaluation: _____

_____

_____

_____

_____

| READING |
| METER |

DATE _____ Selection/Author: _____

Summary: _____

_____

_____

_____

_____

_____

Comments and Evaluation: _____

_____

_____

_____

_____

| READING |
| METER |

DATE _____ **Selection/Author:** _____

Summary: _____

_____

_____

_____

_____

_____

Comments and Evaluation: _____

_____

_____

_____

READING METER

DATE _____ **Selection/Author:** _____

Summary: _____

_____

_____

_____

_____

_____

Comments and Evaluation: _____

_____

_____

_____

READING METER

DATE _____ Selection/Author: _____

Summary: _____

_____

_____

_____

_____

_____

Comments and Evaluation: _____

_____

_____

_____

_____

READING METER

DATE _____ Selection/Author: _____

Summary: _____

_____

_____

_____

_____

_____

Comments and Evaluation: _____

_____

_____

_____

_____

READING METER

DATE _____ Selection/Author: _____

Summary: _____

_____

_____

_____

_____

_____

Comments and Evaluation: _____

_____

_____

_____

	READING METER

_____

DATE _____ Selection/Author: _____

Summary: _____

_____

_____

_____

_____

_____

Comments and Evaluation: _____

_____

_____

_____

	READING METER

_____

DATE _____ Selection/Author: _____

Summary: _____

_____

_____

_____

_____

_____

Comments and Evaluation: _____

_____

_____

_____

_____

	READING METER

DATE _____ Selection/Author: _____

Summary: _____

_____

_____

_____

_____

_____

Comments and Evaluation: _____

_____

_____

_____

_____

	READING METER

DATE _____ Selection/Author: _____

Summary: _____

_____

_____

_____

_____

_____

Comments and Evaluation: _____

_____

_____

_____

	READING METER

DATE _____ Selection/Author: _____

Summary: _____

_____

_____

_____

_____

_____

Comments and Evaluation: _____

_____

_____

_____

	READING METER

DATE _____ Selection/Author: _____

Summary: _____

_____

_____

_____

_____

_____

Comments and Evaluation: _____

_____

_____

_____

_____

	READING METER

DATE _____ Selection/Author: _____

Summary: _____

_____

_____

_____

_____

_____

Comments and Evaluation: _____

_____

_____

_____

_____

	READING METER

DATE _____ Selection/Author: _____

Summary: _____

_____

_____

_____

_____

_____

Comments and Evaluation: _____

_____

_____

_____

_____

	READING METER

DATE _____ Selection/Author: _____

Summary: _____

_____

_____

_____

_____

_____

Comments and Evaluation: _____

_____

_____

_____

_____

	READING METER

DATE _____ Selection/Author: _____

Summary: _____

_____

_____

_____

_____

_____

Comments and Evaluation: _____

_____

_____

_____

_____

	READING METER

DATE _____ Selection/Author: _____

Summary: _____

_____

_____

_____

_____

_____

Comments and Evaluation: _____

_____

_____

_____

_____

	READING METER

DATE _____ Selection/Author: _____

Summary: _____

_____

_____

_____

_____

_____

Comments and Evaluation: _____

_____

_____

_____

_____

	READING METER

DATE _____ Selection/Author: _____

Summary: _____

_____

_____

_____

_____

_____

Comments and Evaluation: _____

_____

_____

_____

_____

	READING METER

Checklist for Standards Mastery

Each time you read, you learn something new. Track your growth as a reader and your progress toward success by checking off skills you have acquired. You may want to use this checklist before you read a selection, to set a purpose for reading.

✓	California Reading Standard (Review)	Selection/Author
☐	**1.4** (Grade 4 Review) Know common affixes, and use this knowledge to analyze the meaning of words.	

	California Grade 6 Reading Standard	Selection/Author
☐	**1.0** Word Analysis, Fluency, and Systematic Vocabulary Development: Students use their knowledge of word origins and word relationships, as well as historical and literary context clues, to determine the meaning of specialized vocabulary and to understand the precise meaning of grade-level-appropriate words.	
☐	**1.1** Read aloud narrative and expository text fluently and accurately and with appropriate pacing, intonation, and expression.	
☐	**1.2** Identify and interpret figurative language and words with multiple meanings.	
☐	**1.3** Recognize the origins and meanings of frequently used foreign words in English, and use these words accurately in speaking and writing.	
☐	**1.4** Monitor expository text for unknown words or words with novel meanings by using word, sentence, and paragraph clues to determine meaning.	
☐	**1.5** Understand and explain "shades of meaning" in related words (for example, *softly* and *quietly*).	

✓	California Grade 6 Reading Standard	Selection/Author
☐	**2.0 Reading Comprehension:** Students read and understand grade-level-appropriate material. They describe and connect the essential ideas, arguments, and perspectives of the text by using their knowledge of text structure, organization, and purpose.	
☐	**2.1** Identify the structural features of popular media (for example, newspapers, magazines, online information) and use the features to obtain information.	
☐	**2.2** Analyze text that uses the compare-and-contrast organizational pattern.	
☐	**2.3** Connect and clarify main ideas by identifying their relationships to other sources and related topics.	
☐	**2.4** Clarify an understanding of texts by creating outlines, logical notes, summaries, or reports.	
☐	**2.5** Follow multiple-step instructions for preparing applications (for example, for a public library card, bank savings account, sports club, league membership).	
☐	**2.6** Determine the adequacy and appropriateness of the evidence for an author's conclusions.	
☐	**2.7** Make reasonable assertions about a text through accurate, supporting citations.	
☐	**2.8** Note instances of unsupported inferences, fallacious reasoning, persuasion, and propaganda in text.	

✓	California Grade 6 Reading Standard	Selection/Author
☐	**3.0 Literary Response and Analysis:** Students read and respond to historically or culturally significant works of literature that reflect and enhance their studies of history and social science. They clarify the ideas and connect them to other literary works.	
☐	**3.1** Identify the forms of fiction, and describe the major characteristics of each form.	
☐	**3.2** Analyze the effect of the qualities of the character (for example, courage or cowardice, ambition or laziness) on the plot and the resolution of the conflict.	
☐	**3.3** Analyze the influence of setting on the problem and its resolution.	
☐	**3.4** Define how tone or meaning is conveyed in poetry through word choice, figurative language, sentence structure, line length, punctuation, rhythm, repetition, and rhyme.	
☐	**3.5** Identify the speaker and recognize the difference between first- and third-person narration (for example, autobiography compared with biography).	
☐	**3.6** Identify and analyze features of themes conveyed through characters, actions, and images.	
☐	**3.7** Explain the effects of common literary devices (for example, symbolism, imagery, metaphor) in a variety of fictional and nonfictional texts.	
☐	**3.8** Critique the credibility of characterization and the degree to which a plot is contrived or realistic (for example, compare use of fact and fantasy in historical fiction).	

Index of Authors and Titles

Vocabulary Development

Pronunciation guides, in parentheses, are provided for the vocabulary words in this book. The following key will help you use those pronunciation guides.

As a practice in using a pronunciation guide, sound out the words used as examples in the list that follows. See if you can hear the way the same vowel might be sounded in different words. For example, say "at" and "ate" aloud. Can you hear the difference in the way "a" sounds?

The symbol ə is called a **schwa.** A schwa is used by many dictionaries to indicate a sort of weak sound like the "a" in "ago." Some people say the schwa sounds like "eh." A vowel sounded like a schwa is never accented.

The vocabulary words in this book are also provided with a part of speech. The parts of speech are *n.* (noun), *v.* (verb), *pro.* (pronoun), *adj.* (adjective), *adv.* (adverb), *prep.* (preposition), *conj.* (conjunction), and *interj.* (interjection). To learn about the parts of speech, consult the *Holt Handbook.*

To learn more about the vocabulary words, consult your dictionary. You will find that many of the words defined here have several other meanings.

---

at, āte, cär; ten, ēve; is, īce; gō, hôrn, look, tōol; oil, out; up, fur; ə *for unstressed vowels, as* a *in* ago, u *in* focus; ' *as in* Latin (lat''n); chin; she; zh *as in* azure (azh'ər); thin, *the;* ŋ *as in* ring (riŋ)

Picture Credits